The
Social Gospel
of
E. Nicholas Comfort

THE
SOCIAL GOSPEL
OF
E. NICHOLAS COMFORT

Founder
of the
Oklahoma
School of
Religion

By Robert C. Cottrell

UNIVERSITY OF OKLAHOMA PRESS
Norman and London

Also by Robert C. Cottrell

Izzy: A Biography of I. F. Stone
(New Brunswick, New Jersey, 1992, 1993)

This book is published
with the generous assistance of
Edith Gaylord Harper.

Library of Congress Cataloging-in-Publication Data

Cottrell, Robert C., 1950–
The social gospel of E. Nicholas Comfort :
founder of the Oklahoma School of Religion /
by Robert C. Cottrell.
p.   cm.
Includes bibliographical references and index.
ISBN 0-8061-2931-X (alk. paper)
1. Comfort, E. Nicholas, 1884–1955.   2. Presbyterian
Church—Oklahoma—Clergy—Biography.
3. Social gospel.   4. Liberalism (Religion)—Presbyterian
Church—History—20th century.
5. Liberalism (Religion)—Oklahoma—History—20th Century.
6. Oklahoma School of Religion.   7. Norman (Okla.)—
Church history—20th century.   I. Title.
BX9225.C73C68   1997
230'.51'092—dc20
[B]
96-36293
CIP

Text design by Cathy Carney Imboden.
The text is set in Bookman Light.

The paper in this book meets the guidelines for permanence
and durability of the Committee on Production Guidelines for
Book Longevity of the Council on Library Resources, Inc.   ∞

1   2   3   4   5   6   7   8   9   10

To my munchkin,
Jordan Alexandra Cottrell

CONTENTS

Contents

ILLUSTRATIONS

ix

x

Illustrations

PREFACE

At one point during the 1930s, members of the Ku Klux Klan, attired in their white robes, ventured near the University of Oklahoma campus in Norman. Directly across from the state's foremost educational institution, they left their infamous brand, a fiery cross. Shortly thereafter, E. Nicholas Comfort, Presbyterian minister and dean of the Oklahoma School of Religion, drove with a friend to Oklahoma City to talk with the state leader, or Grand Dragon, of the KKK. Seated near the Klan chieftain, Comfort simply informed him that the actions of the hooded empire were wrong. Moreover, the Klansman "had no authority to behave the way he did." The entire encounter lasted only ten minutes.[1]

For Nick Comfort, as one close friend later reminisced, "there was a right way and a wrong way to treat human beings." The Klansman represented everything Comfort fought against: small-mindedness, bigotry, and hatred. Possessing a moral antenna that was sharply honed, he was not one to shy away from confrontations. Standing up on matters involving principle came easily to him, whether that resulted in a conflict with rabid racists, hard-line fundamentalists, or political charlatans.

Comfort's strongly held convictions ensured that he remained embroiled in the political, social, and religious affairs affecting the University of Oklahoma and the state of Oklahoma for more than three decades. He continually spoke out on controversial issues involving the liberties of political dissidents, the civil rights of racial minorities, economic inequalities, and U.S. militarism. Due to what he preached at the pulpit, wrote in his newspaper columns, or attempted to put into practice—"He had the courage to be a doer as well as a thinker"—he became one of the most controversial figures in the state. At various points, he was condemned as a "Red," subjected to scurrilous invectives, and investigated by both the House Committee on Un-American Activities and a state legislative inquiry seeking to ferret out Communism in public schools in Oklahoma. At the same time, Nick Comfort was also a much-admired individual, praised by colleagues, friends, and followers in the community of Norman and throughout the state for his "great personal integrity," "moral courage," "great generosity and sympathy," and uncompromising advocacy of deeply held principles.[2]

In another day and age, Comfort might have ended up as the struggling tenant farmer his father had been, or the wearer of the white sheet that certain of his relatives, and many others in the Southwest, were. He might have remained untutored, in the formal sense, acquiring a minimum education by dint of hard-won life experiences. Perhaps above all else, he might have become a narrow-minded sectarian preacher of the gospel, as were so many of his fellow ministers.

Nick Comfort proved to be none of these things. He grew up in poverty, near destitution, amid the political and religious fundamentalism that, during the first half of the twentieth century, dug deep roots into

the soils of eastern Texas and Oklahoma, his twin
native-states. Nonetheless, Comfort, whose love and
affinity for the land made him appear to be a character right out of frontier days, seemingly willed
himself to enroll at some of the finest centers for
theological study in the land. He determinedly made
himself over, becoming a well-respected academician,
acquiring along the way advanced professional degrees as he studied with the likes of John Dewey,
James Howard Tufts, and Shailer Mathews. Not surprisingly, he was a great believer in educational uplift;
after all, it had worked for a poor lad from the northeastern corner of the Lone Star State, hadn't it? He
spoke out on behalf of racial equality, social justice,
and peace, in a period when many Oklahomans
seemed to forget altogether about their state's radically tinged frontier heritage.

Nick Comfort made his greatest mark as long-time
head of the Oklahoma School of Religion (1925–46),
situated in Norman, adjacent to the University of
Oklahoma. Through the School of Religion, Presbyterian minister Comfort became a key figure in the
teaching ministry of the Southwest, continually fighting what he perceived to be the good fight. This came
naturally to him, imbued as he was with his credo:
a dogged belief in the fatherhood of God and the
brotherhood of man.[3] To Comfort, a Christian should
neither look up to nor down upon any other. A Christian necessarily transcended artificial barriers that
divided labor and capital, the rich and the poor, the
ignorant and the learned, the citizen and the alien,
the saint and the sinner. A Christian was compelled
to make God's will his own and strive for justice for
all his brethren.

Comfort's approach was a progressive, ecumenical
one, notwithstanding his own misgivings and even
prejudices about the Roman Catholic Church and the
Methodist Church, the latter of which he had once

been part of. He stood far ahead of his time with his proselytizing on behalf of universalism. Comfort was not lacking biases of his own; after all, he little appreciated the uncaring rich, militarists, or bigots, although he had greater understanding of the latter.

Simply put, Comfort remained imbued with the spirit of the social gospel, in a period when others seemed determined to avoid both its premises and its promises. Indeed, Comfort's sermons, writings, and the work of the Oklahoma School of Religion all demonstrated that the social gospel was yet alive in the newborn Sooner State, no matter the controversies and contentions that swirled all about.

Controversies and contentions abounded, for Comfort clearly condemned Jim Crow practices and thought, decried the transformation of proud Oklahomans into vilified and stereotyped Okies, opposed the drive toward military buildup and the creation of the national security state, and defended the rights of such political pariahs as native communists. Consequently, he and the Oklahoma School of Religion with which he was so closely identified were condemned as "un-Christian," "un-American," and "Communist." At times, political faux pas on his part, such as his condemnation of the U.S. military buildup as the threat of fascism mounted, or his backing of Henry Wallace's Progressive Party as it increasingly became dominated by Communists, seemed to offer easy ammunition to his foes. However, even in such instances, and upon all other occasions, few were inclined to cast aspersions on the principled nature of Comfort's stands. Most seemed to recognize that here was an individual who, in nondogmatic fashion, had declared his intentions to line up with the average Okie, no matter what was implied by the name.

Perhaps most remarkably, the controversies that followed Nick Comfort generally seemed to little faze him. In fact, his equanimity was such that he could put his head down on a table to sleep the sleep of the righteous, while awaiting his turn before would-be inquisitors. He was a man of great character and enormous energy, proud and principled yet altogether unpretentious. He was very much a public man, and love of his family, profession, and state helped to sustain him. That was of no little significance, because despite his considerable store of optimism, he occasionally had real doubts about what he was or was not accomplishing.

As Davis Joyce indicates in his recent book, *"An Oklahoma I had Never Seen Before,"* Nick Comfort was part of that other Oklahoma of rebels and supposed heretics who would not follow the rightward course undertaken by so many others in the state during the post World War I era. As historian Howard Zinn might put it, Nick Comfort's story is part of the lost lore of the American heartland, part of the hidden history of the Southwestern states. Comfort is in the continuum of that dwindling band of progressive thinkers and activists who steadfastly remained true to their own sense of history, though corporatizing trends and scapegoating created a less-than-congenial atmosphere for those with alternative visions.[4]

Along the way, Nick Comfort made a difference in the lives of countless friends, students, parishioners, and readers. He also made a difference, albeit never as grand a one as he aspired to, in the unfolding of his adopted state of Oklahoma. For two decades, his educational ministry helped make the Oklahoma School of Religion a viable concern, a fount of liberal thoughts and action, and a recipient of bitter diatribes. This transplanted Texan championed his school and his state, both of which he believed to be capable of greatness. He blamed himself for the ultimate demise of the Oklahoma School of Religion:

his lack of business acumen and controversial nature undoubtedly proved equally injurious to the cause he heralded. Still, his belief in his own sense of mission was heartfelt and not without merit: to teach the word of God in a progressive fashion to the young people of the American Southwest.

No doubt, Nick Comfort could have done nothing else. Throughout his adulthood, he aspired to further, in whatever small way he could, the tenets in which he believed most profoundly: the fatherhood of God and the brotherhood of man. He sought to do so through education, the vehicle he considered to be the crucial one in a democratic society. He made up his mind to carry out his mission in the region that he made home and that he revered more than any other, the Southwest. Although Comfort retained a fondness for Texas throughout his life, his love for Oklahoma was at least equal. He believed the Sooner State "stood at the last wave of the venturesome, prophetic and revolutionary spirit." Consequently, he reasoned that "to live on these broad prairies with a peanut shell theology is a tragedy."[5]

Nick Comfort, seeking as he did to be a religious pathfinder, nevertheless ended up as little more than a footnote in the history of the State of Oklahoma. This is unfortunate, and Comfort certainly deserves better. This biography focuses upon what made him a noteworthy figure, his involvement at the cutting edge of leading social, economic, and political issues of his times. It does not profess to emphasize the intricacies of the theological doctrine or dogma of the various Protestant churches, but then neither did Comfort. In fact, he deliberately avoided getting enmeshed in such controversies, which can be every bit as convoluted as those involving political sectarianism. Indeed, the very idea of getting ensnared in internecine religious wars was simply alien to him. Furthermore, Comfort was hardly a grand theoretician in any sense; rather, he was a man whose beliefs were basic, but deeply felt, and one who sought to have an impact in the community in which he lived and worked. Almost from the very moment he first came to Norman, that community included the entire State of Oklahoma.

Significantly, Comfort demonstrated that for a good while longer than is often presumed to be the case, there was something of a breathing space—albeit one fraught with perils—for nonconformists in a state that was increasingly dominated by a conservative, even hidebound mind-set. His passing left a vacuum —and not an inconsiderable one—in Oklahoma and the American Southwest that has never quite been filled since.

ACKNOWLEDGMENTS

I first heard about Nick Comfort as a graduate student at the University of Oklahoma. Seeking a research topic for Paul Glad's seminar on the American West, I went to see Jack Haley, the then head of the Western History Collections at OU. After informing Haley that I was interested in working on a subject dealing with reform or radicalism, he immediately brightened up and exclaimed that there was a virtually untouched collection of such papers in the basement of the Western History Collections. The papers were those of a Presbyterian minister by the name of Nicholas Comfort and the Oklahoma School of Religion, which he had directed, Haley informed me. Comfort, Haley continued, had been a highly controversial figure in Norman and throughout the state, had been hauled before investigative committees, and accused of being a Red. Intrigued, I went downstairs and discovered nearly thirty boxes of unchartered and undocumented materials. I spent much of that semester researching and writing a research paper, "The Social Gospel of Nicholas Comfort," which later was reshaped into an article that appeared in *The Chronicles of Oklahoma.*

My dissertation led me onto a different path, as did my eventual employment at California State University, Chico. But in the winter of 1992, I received a letter from Professor Davis D. Joyce of East Central University, asking if I would agree to the inclusion of my *Chronicles* article in the volume that he was putting together, entitled *"An Oklahoma I Had Never Seen Before": Alternative Views of Oklahoma History*. My interest in Reverend Comfort was now piqued once again, and I wrote to John Drayton, editor-in-chief of the University of Oklahoma Press, asking if there might be interest in a book manuscript on that subject. After a short while, a contract was tendered to me and I began delving back into the life and times of E. Nicholas Comfort.

Along the way, I now met and interviewed three of Nick's children, Mrs. Janet Comfort Losey in Dallas, Texas, Dr. Richard O. Comfort in San Antonio, and Dr. Anne Comfort Courtright in Pueblo, Colorado. All three were wonderfully forthcoming, sharing tales of their father, many pleasant and others charged with controversy. They also passed along documents, correspondence, a family history, and photographs, as well as sermons, essays, editorials, and other publications by their father.

Consequently, I am highly indebted to Mr. Haley and other members, both past and present, of the staff of the Western History Collections at the University of Oklahoma. At least equally so, I owe a word of thanks to the Comfort children, all distinguished individuals in their own right. In addition, I appreciate all the assistance I received from the library staff at both the University of Oklahoma and California State University, Chico, especially the interlibrary loan departments.

Other individuals also helped out along the way. My mentor, Paul Glad, shepherded me through the initial revisions, which resulted in the article in *The*

Chronicles of Oklahoma. Bruce Grele and Carl Hein, colleagues of mine at CSU, Chico, read early versions of the manuscript. Bob Miller, an old friend and classmate at the University of Oklahoma, and now a professor of history at Southwest Missouri State University, was tremendously helpful with a series of insightful comments and analyses. My sister and brother-in-law, Sharon and Steve Gerson, both English professors, scoured through the manuscript with editorial skill and grace. A California State University, Chico, Research Award gave me a full-semester leave to craft the manuscript. The Department of History and the College of Humanities and Fine Arts at CSU, Chico, tendered additional grants.

My deepest appreciation goes out to my own family. My wife, Sue, as always, was wonderfully supportive of this project, while my daughter, Jordan, along with the subject, provided the inspiration. A big thanks goes to Adrienne, particulary for her help with Jordan.

I also need to thank John N. Drayton and Sarah Iselin, Editor-in-Chief and Associate Editor, respectively, of the University of Oklahoma Press. John supported this project from its inception, while Sarah helped to ensure that it would appear in the most polished version possible. To that end, I also owe a debt of gratitude to copyeditor Dennis Marshall.

—ROBERT C. COTTRELL

The
Social Gospel
of
E. Nicholas Comfort

CHAPTER ONE

A
PASSION FOR
LEARNING

While still a growing boy, Nick Comfort one day found himself plowing a field with the family mule, alongside black sharecroppers. Suddenly, tears streamed down his face. Nick was reflecting upon how desperately he wanted to obtain an education and how far from reaching that goal he was. When he turned twenty-one, Nick had acquired a fourth-grade education only.[1]

His father, Nicholas William Comfort, was a struggling tenant farmer whose English ancestors had settled in up-state New York in the first quarter of the eighteenth century. Nicholas William's father and Nick's grandfather, James Comfort, was born in Crawford Township in Orange County in the Empire State and served in the War of 1812. James migrated to Russellville, Kentucky, where, in 1820, he married Jane A. Smith, with whom he had thirteen children. The youngest was Nicholas William, who at the age of forty married Eunice Candace Parish, a young widow with two daughters, Maude and Tennie Strong.[2]

Nicholas William's family, in the words of a granddaughter, "was intensely Southern." One brother fought with Morgan's Raiders in the Confederate army; he subsequently died in a federal prison in

Chicago. James Comfort purportedly engaged in such escapades that later progeny should have been like "a young Jesse James." Indeed, despite exhortations to the contrary, Nicholas William refused to discuss his family's history with his son Nick.

Apparently, at some point during the 1880s Nicholas William and his bride traveled to Texas, where they came to reside in Brookston, in west central Lamar County along the Texas and Pacific Railroad line. Once a terminus for railroads shipping grain, Brookston was at the time a little-populated area, a dozen miles from Paris, the county seat. Paris remained a center for railroads coursing through the eastern part of the state of Texas, including the Gulf, Colorado, and Santa Fe line, the Texas Midland, and the St. Louis and San Francisco.[3]

In Brookston, Jacova Candace and Eunice Nicholas Comfort were born. The latter came into the world on May 1, 1884, around three o'clock in the morning. "I arrived sniffling, snortin' and kicking, apparently as mad as a wet hen, because I had been disturbed that early in the morning." It took more than an hour to wash and dress him, as he cried out for milk. Upon finally settling down, the baby slept for a good five hours, having pulled the cover over his head. He quickly took a liking to his father's beard and, within a matter of days, took hold of his neck with both hands and gave off "an odor that made a limburger cheese factory smell like painted yellow perfume."[4]

The condition of his ailing mother contributed to Eunice's being "a very puny baby," and one who nearly died because of bowel troubles. His mother passed away when he was only ten months old and many folks did not believe the baby would survive. Following his mother's death, Eunice might well have starved had it not been for the wet-nursing he received from a woman he later referred to as a kindly old "colored Mammy." By the time Eunice was two, he was becoming plump "and was soon about as wide out as . . . high up."[5]

Eunice early displayed a mischievous side, for which he was later well known; at the same time, he could be extremely sensitive, particularly where family members were concerned. One day, he took his playthings and visited an aunt who lived with her in-laws. They possessed an old cat they doted on, and the little boy placed a long string around its neck and led it about. The cat, becoming annoyed, raced up a tree, all the while still on the string. The boy tried to get the cat down by hurling a stick at it, and when the cat attempted to jump its neck broke. As Comfort later recalled, "the old man was mad as could be and dusted my pants for me." Upset by the whipping, the boy felt unloved and took all his toys, including his wagon, and beat them with axes. He employed two axes, using the bigger to break the smaller, thus ruining both. When his aunt discovered what he had been up to, she sent him on his way.[6]

Perhaps because his mother had died during his infancy, young Eunice could easily be smitten by members of the opposite sex. At five, he had his first love, a young woman with long, curly hair, blue eyes, and ivory skin, packing around 160 pounds on a five-foot-six-inch frame. "Her smile would melt a heart of stone and it set mine in such a flutter I did not know whether I was coming or going." At one point, she put him on her lap, kissed him, and called him sweetheart. Soon, however, some fellow with a mustache came by and "stole her from me."[7]

The boy's father had taken to calling him Eunice in memory of his beloved wife, a schoolteacher who was considered "a kind, intelligent, devoutly religious woman," even by relatives "some of whom were devils on wheels." Nicholas William, devoted as he had been to his wife, never thought of remarrying and now served as "both Pappy and Mammy to us." More than

ever, he tended "to look on the darker side of life."
When chided about why he was so pessimistic,
Nicholas William warned his son "that if things
should unfortunately go with me as they had gone
with him I would be unable to see anything but the
dark side of life."[8]

Maude, the elder half sister, who was considerably
older than Eunice, acted as mother figure for him.
Nicholas William served as an elder in the Cumber-
land Presbyterian Church and, notwithstanding his
poverty and lack of formal education, was a well
respected member of his community. His son remembered him as "the personification of integrity. I have
not met any one who had a higher standard of loyalty
or gave clearer directions to the heart of God." Tenant
farmer that he was, Nicholas William was mired in
debt following his wife's illness. Unfortunately, Nicholas William's own health was fragile, a situation undoubtedly exacerbated by a lung condition brought
on from having worked in a cotton gin and that
ensured the family remained impoverished. Nevertheless, he insisted upon past bills being taken care
of. Shortly before his own death, for instance, Nicholas William asked his son to pay off a $25 debt owed
to the doctor who had delivered him and to send $100
to a friend even though he had struck oil after
heading out West.[9]

Because he had to help his father at home, Eunice
attended school only sporadically. This he regretted
immensely. He and his sister Jacova, affectionately
known as Sukey, walked three miles each morning
to get to class. Cutting across pastureland made the
distance somewhat shorter, but Pappy warned the
two that a spirited bull lay in wait in one of those
pastures. No matter, Eunice chortled to Sukey, "it
makes me sick to think how silly old men are to be
all-fired afraid of bulls. Anyhow we are in school now
and why should we listen to Pappy. I love him but

there is [*sic*] a lot of things he doesn't know." Having convinced his sister, the two headed precisely in the direction their father had told them to avoid. Worried, Sukey turned to Eunice and said, "I wish we had stayed in the road. I'm afraid." But Eunice replied, "Come on, don't be a baby. If that bull shows up I'll grab a club and knock his horns off."[10]

Young Eunice, an adventurous sort, was given to taking risks; however, no sooner had he spoken than a great roar was heard and, seeing the bull thirty yards ahead, the children dropped their lunch pails and began to scream. Luckily, a tree with low limbs stood about ten feet away. Eunice grabbed his sister, cried out, "Up this tree," and pushed her onto it. When they were only ten feet off the ground, the bull charged by. For half an hour, the bull danced around and not until he tired of the game could the children head for the road (pp. 12–13).

When he was four or five years old, Eunice attended "a ten weeks summer subscription affair" held in the home of William Blake Minor. Minor, a stooped and aged Virginian, had ridden into Lamar County in the 1830s atop a sorrel Steel Dust stallion. He had sought permission to pitch camp along a creek. As it was government land, Minor was allowed to do so. With the help of neighbors, Minor constructed a log cabin, which grew in dimensions over the years, until a second story and other rooms were added. One of those rooms served as the chambers in which Minor held court as justice of the peace. Another stood as the classroom where Eunice and other children in the community awaited their instruction, which came their way in the person of Minor's wife; she and Minor had married when she was a young school-teacher. While class was in session, the finest Jersey cows, Berkshire hogs, chickens, turkeys, guinea pigs, and pigeons roamed about; long-eared hounds perched near the kitchen door, waiting for scraps of food; bee stands were situated beneath cedar trees in the back yard. Minor prided himself on the immaculate nature of his garden, with its potatoes, onions, tomatoes, and watermelons (pp. 1–3).

At first, Judge Minor appeared to be a stern taskmaster and Eunice looked upon him with awe. The children who attended Mrs. Minor's classroom longed for the occasions when she or her husband might grant them the privilege of bringing water in from the spring, where Judge Minor had built a basin, a trough, and a springhouse that held milk, butter, and "drafts of cool living water." Close by the creek, he had devised a circular fishpond. Occasionally, Minor would enter his wife's classroom and cry out, "Time to feed the fish. Let's go." The first time he pulled this stunt, pandemonium broke out. A red-faced Judge Minor sternly admonished the youngsters: "Quiet. The next time I invite you to go with me act like ladies and gentlemen and not like a pack of monkeys. Set down the last one of you damn brats! Now get to work before I snatch you baldheaded." As he left, apparently in a state of anger, Mrs. Minor gazed upon her students, broke into a smile, and winked. "Children," she informed them. "Mr. Minor's bark is much worse than his bite. But remember you should behave like ladies and gentlemen. Now let's get back to work" (pp. 3–4).

The following week, the good judge again came into the classroom, now carrying a pan of hot bread under his arm. Quietly he declared, "Ladies and gentlemen, it is time to feed the fish. Will you be so kind as to accompany me in this undertaking? With your permission we will now depart." In orderly procession, they followed the old man, who said "Ladies first, please," as they approached the gate to the yard. Silently, he fed the fish, meanwhile gazing intently upon the gathered youngsters. Apparently deeply moved by the expectant but now well-mannered class, he dabbed his eyes and blew his nose repeatedly. Finally, Mrs. Minor stated, "Now, children, we must get back to our work," and they returned to the classroom, thoroughly delighted (p. 4).

Then there was the time when Minor entered the schoolroom and loudly called out, "School dismissed. Girls follow boys. Boys follow girls. The smallest in each group take the lead." Just ahead were generous portions of ripened watermelon, yellow melon for the girls and red melon for the boys. The snacks having been devoured, the boys carried the rinds to the pigs—any loafers quickly discovering to their dismay that no such treat would be in store for them the next time (pp. 6–7).

One day, while Eunice awaited his turn, Mrs. Minor grabbed one of the pieces of yellow melon, handed it to him, and said, "Run behind the smoke house with it." He obeyed her instructions, and soon buried his face in the melon. Having discovered the theft, Minor roared, denouncing "scalawag boys who would rob hungry girls to fill their own bellies." Terrified but curious, Eunice peeked around the corner until, seeing him, Judge Minor smiled and winked. Never again would Eunice be quite as fearful of the judge (p. 7).

Mrs. Minor's class was held in a large room, built of logs, that was also the family's dining area. The furniture included a sixteen-foot dining table, a dozen chairs, a handful of hard benches, and a great fireplace. A large china basin and a three-gallon water bucket, made of cedar, were perched on a washstand, atop of which was a good-sized square mirror. Next to the mirror was a roller, with a seven-foot towel that was changed daily and beneath the mirror was a leather pouch with a black comb. Beside the washstand was a large, china slop jar. The children, the Minors, and their hired help all used the equipment (p. 9).

The children sat on opposite sides of the table, divided according to sex. The taller students had chairs; the smaller ones had to sit on benches, which left their feet dangling. "As instruments of torture they were superb." All of the pupils were constantly inspected for lice and ticks (p. 10).

Eunice, as the youngest and littlest student of all, became something of "the official rescuer" of wayward pencils. One time, while searching for a fallen pencil, he got caught in the vise-like grip of an obese girl's legs. She seemed determined to squeeze the life out of him. In desperation, Eunice resorted to pulling up her skirt and drawers and burying his teeth into her thigh. "A Comanche war whoop" followed as she bolted to her feet, Eunice still clinging tightly to her skin. His head landed against a table, receiving a good-sized knot as a consequence. Mrs. Minor separated the pair and upon examining them, exclaimed, "I guess you both got what was coming to you (pp. 10–11).

Another member of the opposite sex, one with long legs, caused Eunice additional grief. Seated directly across the table from him, she continually poked him with the tip of her shoe. Initially red-faced about it, Eunice determined to give back as good as he got. The next time she attempted to tease him, he grabbed her feet and yanked: back went her chair, and she slid under the table, flat on her back, much to the delight of the other students. Mrs. Minor "made a face at me and I tittered the rest of the afternoon" (p. 11).

As the youngest child in the school and thanks to the wealth of experiences of Mrs. Minor, twelve times a grandmother, Eunice was basically allowed free rein. Often, he collaborated with the Minor's youngest son, Hugh, who was a teenager, in pulling off pranks that would have made Tom Sawyer proud. One time Hugh asked Eunice if his dog Tiny would kill rats.

The little fellow bragged, "Sure! She is the best rat dog this side of kingdom come." Hugh retorted, "You will have to prove it. Let's go to the barn and we will soon see if she is any good." The two followed Tiny to the barn and in no time the dog had killed ten rodents. Hugh picked them up and took out his knife to skin them, then explained his plan to his little buddy. He had promised to serve squirrels to his friends as a kind of delicacy; instead, he would take them the hind legs of a half-dozen rats. Eunice—who would long be considered by friends and family as something of a prankster—considered this all to be "a tip-top joke." As matters turned out, Hugh indeed fried the rat legs and served them to his friends (pp. 11–14).

Miranda, the Minors' black hired help, did not think well of Hugh. She admonished him at one point, "Mr. Hugh, what you all doin' learnin' Little Man them mean tricks? I's 'shamed of you, I is," she declared and spirited off Eunice back into the schoolroom (p. 16).

Often, Eunice expended a considerable portion of schooldays exploring the old house. By climbing up a tall tree, he was able to get on the roof, where he tossed pebbles down the chimney. One day, he resorted to a good-sized rock, which resulted in soot and ashes flying throughout the schoolroom. Eunice scurried to get down the tree, only to run into Mrs. Minor. He had to clean up and remain in the house for two days. "That jail sentence cut short my roof climbing" (p. 5).

Many of Eunice's most memorable experiences at the Minor homestead involved Miranda. In her own way, she, even more than the Minors, served as a fount of knowledge for him. Her kindly but instructive ways left a lasting impression on him. The troubles that had nearly cost Eunice his life as a baby continued to afflict him as he "never fully regained control of [his] bowel movements." On the afternoon of his third day of school, a sharp pain caused him to double over. He leaned over on the table "and held as tight as possible but to no avail. In a few minutes I filled my pants. A fouler stench would be hard to imagine." Remaining seated with his face covered, Eunice heard his classmates sniffing and complaining, "Phew! Phew!" Soon, Mrs. Minor came over and remarked that the smell of a dead crawfish seemed to be in the air. Immediately, Eunice jumped up "and shot out the door bawling like a bull calf" (p. 5).

Miranda greeted him at the kitchen door. "What's the matter, Little Man?," she asked. Eunice responded, "I have hockied in my pants." "Come here Little Man," she said. "Don't you let that bother you. I has knowed big grown mens to do a lot worse than that. You come with me in the kitchen and we'll fix things up all right" (pp. 5–6).

She took him into the kitchen where she pulled off his pants and drawers and washed him up, before wrapping him in her shawl. As she washed his clothes, she asserted, "Phew! Yo's a mighty little man but you sho can make a big smell." She tossed her head back and roared. The laughter became contagious, with Eunice joining in. As he later recalled, "this good laugh bound us in a common bond" (p. 6).

After he was cleaned up, Miranda declared, "Come on, Little Man, lets go to the barn and git the hen eggs." Together they went off, hand in hand. As they sauntered along, she told him, "Little Man, the next time you gets a pain, scoot to the barn as fast as you can go. But don't you go in dem hoss stalls. Ef you all does, Mr. Minor will skin you all alive. Go out behind de barn. Nobody will see you. Ef dey do, what's the difference? Everybody has to—has to relieve hisself. Now don't you fergit that. Just be sho you does it in time. Dat's all" (p. 6).

In the days that followed, Eunice received additional instruction of a practical variety from Miranda. They counted up the number of eggs available, subtracted those that were potatoes, and played store. In their game, they sold eggs, butter, milk, and honey, and bought coffee, chewing gum, perfume, and a Bible. Eunice finished reading his first book, with its alphabetized picture schema. Together, they washed dishes, made up beds, hoed the garden, fed the chickens, gathered eggs, cooked, and cleaned house, all the while practicing spelling and counting. While showing Eunice how to make soap, Miranda taught him how to spell *tub, pot, lye, pan, ashes, water, fire, meat, worm, full,* and *hair.* When Mrs. Minor came by to check on how he was doing, Miranda reported, "Mrs. Minor, Little Man sho am larnin'. You all listen an' he will spell some for you." After Eunice spewed out all the words that he could now recite, a delighted Mrs. Minor sang both of their praises "until we puffed up like toads." As they walked through the old house, the little boy continued his exploring, searching into every nook and cranny. In the workroom, which piqued his curiosity, Eunice came upon two looms, a spinning wheel, and a stand with loops of leather. He took off his shoes and began driving tacks into them, later proudly displaying the results of his feat to his classmates (pp. 6, 19–20, 22–23).

But it was Minor's courtroom that overwhelmed him. After all, marriages were performed there by the judge, and to little Eunice matrimony was something wonderfully mysterious and sacred. "A man's ability to make two people into one and yet keep them two was beyond my grasp. For a man and a woman to belong to each other for ever and ever and ever was beyond my comprehension." Yet this is what Miranda informed him that marriage was all about. To Eunice, Judge Minor's ability to perform marriage ceremonies made him into something of a magician (p. 21). The law books in the courtroom similarly impressed him. This was to be expected, for Miranda assured him that the law of the land was contained in those volumes. As Miranda indicated, he could not open one up, even if he were paid a thousand dollars to do so, "lest a law jump out, grab me by the nape of the neck and hustle me off either to marriage or jail." All of this made him wonder about the judge, "Is he Adam or is he Moses?" (p. 21).

One afternoon, Miranda took him into the woods to hunt for a missing turkey hen. A nickel reward was in store if he could find the old bird. He spotted it in some underbrush, along with eighteen baby turkeys. When he informed Miranda of his discovery, she grinned and said, "Little Man, if you is tellin' de truth I's gwine to gif you an extra dime." Upon viewing the turkey nest, she exclaimed, "Lord help my soul. Little Man, you sho is learnin' fas'. I's gwine to tell Mrs. Minor soon as I get to the house" (pp. 18–19).

Easily and gracefully, Miranda spun stories that enthralled her young listener. A fair number of them left a lasting mark and served as a counterweight to the kind of rhetoric Eunice must have heard regularly in Brookston. Miranda, who had been born into slavery, spoke of "pore white trash" and admonished Eunice to avoid their ways. As she put it, "It ain't no sin to be po; but it sho a sin to be vulga'. Little Man, don't you ever be vulga'." She was ever ready with apt aphorisms, such as "De color of de skin jist show what's on de outside. It don't say nuthin' 'bout de inside" or "A mean person may be white, but he ain't no man" (p. 18).

The last day of school was filled with spelling, singing, declamations of all kinds, eating, and playing. Eunice was most moved by Miranda's farewell. That morning, after they had made the upstairs beds, she sat in a large rocking chair, humming, and called the lad to come over. She placed him in her lap, hugged him tightly, and kissed his forehead. Then, she sang a lullaby with its plaintive prayer from a mother for her child. A teardrop landed on Eunice's shoulder, and Miranda softly declared, "Little Man, it don't pay to fight back or be sassy. You always be a gentleman specially with women." Then she prayed, "Oh, Lord! Little Man's going away. Please keep him clean and honest! Help him to be a frien' of whites an' blacks. Thank you Lord! Thank you Lord!" (p. 24).

Afterwards, she put him down, dabbed at her eyes with a red handkerchief, and said, "Now Little Man, you run down to the schoolroom and be with the white chilun. Goody, Honey, Goodby!" (p. 24).

The lessons imparted by Miranda and the model provided by his father had a profound influence upon Eunice. Later, to his dismay, his sister Sukey joined the Ku Klux Klan, which had dug deep roots in eastern Texas and Oklahoma. But Eunice somehow remained color-blind. Perhaps he recalled the kindnesses and affection that came his way courtesy of the former slave. Undoubtedly the character of his father—"the personification of integrity"—had enormous impact upon the son. He later was unable to recall anyone who "gave clearer directions to the heart of God."[11]

To his chagrin, Eunice was soon unable to attend school on a regular basis. As the son of a tenant farmer, he had to pick cotton until the middle of November and then plant corn beginning in late February. At most, he was able to acquire three months of schooling a year. Eventually, even that got to be too much and he simply stopped attending altogether.[12]

Before doing so, he had one fleeting moment of early academic glory. That occurred during his last year at a small, dilapidated, one-room country school that catered to the needs of forty students. This ungraded school saw students progress at their own pace, and Eunice's proved to be mixed. He excelled in arithmetic, performed adequately in geography, and was near the bottom of the class in grammar. Nevertheless, he did manage to shine in one area—spelling. On Friday afternoons, the students would participate in spelling contests and declamations, with some inventing their own parables: "Here I stand all ragged and dirty. If you don't come and kiss me, I'll run like a turkey."[13] A pretty, dark-eyed beauty named Molly Owens almost always received top marks in the week's spelling contest and an infatuated Eunice determined to compete with her. Luckily, his Pappy had always required him to study his spelling before bedtime. While making the four-mile ride to school, Eunice often practiced his spelling, thereby becoming far more proficient than the rest of the class.[14]

Eunice now won a succession of spelling contests and Molly told him, "You think you are smart, don't you." Eunice asked what he had done to get her to say that, and she replied, "Now don't act dumb, Old Smarty, you know you are trying to get ahead of me in spelling. But you will never do it. You have turned me down your last time."[15] With only six days remaining before he had to head for the fields, Eunice caught up with her score. At this point, bets flew back and forth throughout the community whether "the city gal or the ticky tenant farm boy" would prevail. On his last day in class, Eunice again earned the highest mark and Molly left the room in tears.[16]

Everyone knew that Molly would end up back on top, because two months of school remained. During that period, Eunice plowed from morning until dark. Then, following the last day of class, he spotted two horses approaching, carrying his teacher and Molly.

He was at a loss for what to do, dressed as he was in an old, torn straw hat and overalls, held up by a single strap. They waved merrily to him and shouted, "Hello, Chick." When they passed by, Molly came up next to Eunice and softly said, "How are you, Old Smarty? I still think you are the nicest man I ever saw." Immediately, Eunice's hat was converted "into a crowned wreath and (his) coat of dust into a knight's armor."[17] The teacher now informed Eunice that Molly had insisted he be awarded the prize as the top speller in the class. Molly had predicted that he would turn down the honor, but the teacher solved this dilemma: two prizes would be granted; Molly received a copy of *The Taming of the Shrew* and Eunice was awarded *Hamlet.* To Eunice, "a large slice of heaven fell down on that Red River Bottom plantation that day."[18]

For some time to come, Eunice glumly watched the other white children in the community setting off to school. It was in the spring that tears filled his eyes, all but blinding him so he could barely make out the tail of the mule pulling his plow. During the fall, as he hauled heavy sacks of cotton down the field, he thought of what friends in his class might be studying in their McGuffey readers. He swore to himself that were his family's economic situation to improve, he would attend school "to his heart's content."[19]

In the meantime, Eunice had other obstacles with which to contend. For the sake of convenience, he had been brought up in the Methodist Episcopal Church. The church in the pocket of eastern Texas where the Comforts resided proved to be "very rigid, very fundamental." His family was "intensely Southern." And poverty, which so afflicted the Comforts, has often been a breeding ground for ungenerous and unprogressive sorts.[20]

The simple need to help sustain the family economically was perhaps the greatest impediment Eunice encountered. His father remained in ill-health and unable to get out of debt. The bills at the plantation store were always several months in arrears. Consequently, Eunice's schooling, which brought him such joy, continued to take a backseat as he headed each morning for the cotton fields. In addition to his work on the plantation, he toiled with the Cotton Belt and Rock Island railroad gangs. When the Lawton branch of the Rock Island Railroad was being built, he skinned mules.[21]

Yet he continued, almost desperately, to desire an education. In mid-June 1898, Eunice, then fourteen years old, took his team of horses to be watered along the Red River in eastern Texas. He heard of a rally that was going to take place a few miles away in Indian Territory. Upon completing his work that evening, he washed his shirt and overalls in preparation for the next day's adventure. He had decided to attend the gathering just across the border in the Chickasaw Nation.[22]

The next morning, he saddled his horse, crossed the river, and headed for the woods. A large crowd had congregated. At the front he saw churchgoing folk and their children, whites and Indians both, dressed in their Sunday finest. Behind them were other members of the community, while on the outer edges were the tougher sorts who refused to take off their hats. Eunice stayed back with this latter group. Soon, whispers could be heard all about, asking, "Is she here?" The answer came back that she had indeed arrived. Then, the following query rang out: "How long has she been back from college?"[23]

After the singing of some songs and a prayer had been delivered, a young Indian woman stood up. Her name was Sue, and her large black eyes sparkled and her raven hair appeared luminous. The crowd was spellbound by her presence. She led the children in scripturally guided verse and song and then gave a short speech regarding a Sunday School program and the need for additional workers to guide the little ones in Christian ways.[24]

When a boring sermon followed, Eunice mounted his horse and headed back to Brookston. Along the way, he informed the animal that they would soon leave behind the Texas river-bottoms. Their destination was uncertain, Eunice knew, but acquiring education was his goal. Now, for the first time, he had encountered someone who had left the area for college and returned, determined to make a difference. If the Indian woman had been able to do so, he reasoned, so could he. Thus, he had come to view education as the means through which someone like the young Indian woman, or even Eunice Comfort, could have opportunities that otherwise would not be available.[25]

Two years later, rumors could be heard in the Red River region that the United States government was about to open an expanse of land in the Oklahoma Territory. Eunice's father decided to pick up stakes and head for Greer County, Oklahoma. Father and son alike saw this as their great opportunity—one they could not afford to let pass. Nicholas William believed this was a chance to start afresh and Eunice hoped that they might at last acquire land of their own. The Opening of 1901 resulted in the southwestern reaches of Oklahoma Territory being made available for white settlers. His sister Sukey, now called Cova, remained in Texas with relatives for a while longer, but Eunice and his father undertook the venture in a Rock Island covered wagon. Their few possessions included a sore-legged mule, an Indian pony, some dirty linen, a well-worn mattress, a gun, a dog, a handful of clothes, a harmonica, a skillet, some dishes and pans, eighty cents, and an ax in need of sharpening.[26]

They staked claim to wooded land on Cache Creek in Comanche County, some half-dozen miles south of Lawton, which at the time was little more than a tent city. In this Comanche-Caddo-and-Kiowa country, Nicholas William "drew lot #82 and filed on #76." At two o'clock one afternoon, they reached the site. It was on high ground, covered by a great vine under two large elm trees and a fifteen-foot thicket. This shielded them from the scorching sun and Oklahoma's north winds and pummeling rains. The boards from the sides of the covered wagon became something of a bedroom, a closet for their meager apparel, and a sitting room in wet and cold times. Logs were gathered to provide a fireplace and a place to sit. Thirty yards away, a spring offered sufficient water.[27]

Before heading for bed that first evening, Nicholas William pulled out his weathered Bible and read several passages by the light of the campfire, including one regarding "every man sitting under his own vine and fig tree." Although normally a man of few words, Nicholas William took time to thank the Lord for this blessed new home. He seemed certain that his beloved wife and his own Mammy were watching over this happy scene, but sought guidance for himself and his son in making the most of their new opportunities.[28]

Worn out by the excitement of that first, long day, Nicholas William soon fell asleep. Not so his son, who now considered the Comforts' immediate future, amid the sound of crickets, locusts, screech owls, hoot owls, and coyotes—"a heavenly choir." Eunice clearly recognized that his father's ill health would prevent him from doing hard work and that supplies were short indeed. There was only enough food for breakfast and dinner, and no feed for the draft animals. There was, however, plenty of grass; timber was abundant, good fishing holes were available, squirrels were all about, and raccoon and possum tracks were to be seen. Fortunately, Nicholas William was something of a sharpshooter, as well as being a fine fisherman, and hooks, lines, and a half-dozen shotgun shells were available. Reflecting upon their situation, Eunice figured that his father could hunt and fish as necessary and could drive wood fuel into Lawton to trade or sell. Eunice would cut wood and posts all day long, thereby both clearing the land and providing a source of revenue.[29]

At first light, he began cutting firewood. By midday, he had loaded the wagon with stove wood. By dinnertime, Nicholas William was on the road with a full load, heading for Lawton. Half the money received in town was to be used to purchase flour, bacon, and potatoes; the other half would buy feed for the horses. By sundown, Nicholas William had returned to the campsite with the groceries and feed he had been able to purchase for $2, the amount he had received for the wood. A short time later, a meal of fried potatoes, baked sourdough bread, and coffee was ready. After dinner, a worn-out Nicholas William went to sleep, while his son washed the dishes, loaded up the wagon with more firewood, and attended to the animals.[30]

With breakfast out of the way by dawn the next morning, the younger Comfort readied for another trip into Lawton, which he had determined to take himself. This time, his bounty included a good ax, axle grease, coffee, and sugar. Back before noon, he discovered his father readying catfish and squirrels for lunch. After a nap, another load was stacked into the wagon. The following day, the team of horses headed into town. Late in the day, Eunice was asked by a fellow if he could have 160 posts ready by morning. As the sun went down, only 50 had been cut. After dinner and with his father fast asleep, Eunice went into the woods again. In the morning, his customer came by to pick up the load, depositing $6.60 with Eunice, giving the Comforts, with the bit of money left over from the last trip into Lawton, a grand total of $8.00. For one of the few times Eunice could remember, he and his father had a certain amount of financial security.[31]

As luck would have it, little rain fell in the fall and the winter was a mild one. Nevertheless, they spent their first Oklahoma winter, with the wind whipping through their bones, without any roof over their heads other than that provided by the covered wagon. Nicholas William's health was the best it had been for some time, and Eunice, already grown to his full height of five feet eleven inches, now weighed a well-proportioned 160 pounds, "with bones of iron and muscles of steel." He could thank his ancestors for the tremendous energy he exhibited and for a mental disposition that left him virtually "free from worry." As a child, he had realized that "worry did not seem to help the cause worried about."[32]

By the following spring, the Comforts had saved enough money to purchase wire to enclose their land and lumber to build a small shack, which lacked a roof and boasted a dirt floor only. They were able to buy a bed, a table, two chairs, a heating stove, a chest of drawers, and more cooking utensils. The stove warmed the little house and a drum oven enabled them to bake. They also obtained the implements needed to clear and cultivate the land.[33]

They were comfortable in their new home, feeling "as snug as a couple of bugs in a rug." Eunice was cheered by the fact that for once they could afford whatever they needed; moreover, he was able to plant what he chose and to sell it when he saw fit to do so. Best of all, "he was his own boss." Due to his father's still weakened condition, Eunice determined how to run the farm. He made plans for cultivating crops for many years to come and had visions of constructing a house, a barn, chicken houses, pig pens, a garden, and an orchard. He was so busy, in fact, that he put aside the notion of ever returning to school. Instead, he now saw himself as becoming a great farmer and, along with his father, looked into the possibility of purchasing an adjacent quarter section of land.[34]

Again, an encounter with a stranger seemed to be a propitious omen. One blustery spring day, with dust swirling all about, Eunice sought to complete his chores somewhat earlier than usual. He had fed the horses, milked a cow that the Comforts had recently purchased, and cut wood before he spotted a man coming over the horizon in a spring wagon. The two met at the gate and the man asked what the chance was for finding a place to stay for the night. Eunice replied that "the chance was the best in the world" and invited him to stay.[35]

Their visitor seemed to be about forty years old, clean-shaven, educated, and a gentleman. As it turned out, he was a Presbyterian Sunday school missionary. Nicholas William had snared three good-sized squirrels for dinner and the missionary said thanks in such a manner as to "set every fiber of the boy's being on a tingle." The natural, heartfelt prayer he delivered seemed to linger in the air for the rest of the evening. After dinner, as Eunice washed the dishes and the guest dried them, the latter spoke of college and his days in a seminary. They talked for hours, with the missionary conversing about literature and ancient civilizations. Around two in the morning, Nicholas William asked the missionary to read from the Bible and deliver a prayer.[36]

The missionary departed the next morning, leaving a pair of books on religion. Eunice returned to his work, but something seemed different. Later, he recalled that he now "knew that his days on the farm were numbered. Instead of new barns and houses he saw halls of learning and knew they were for him." The stranger had helped to rekindle a passion for learning that Eunice thought he had lost along with his youth.[37]

The Comforts continued to eke out a living until his sister Cova and her husband Harry Kahl, a young Indiana farmer, moved to western Oklahoma to take care of Nicholas William. At last, the opportunity had arisen for Eunice to return to school. Because educational institutions were nowhere to be found in the immediate vicinity, Eunice and a neighbor, Harrison Metheney, ventured to Parkville, Missouri, in November 1905, hoping to attend an academy there. Eunice owned "one suit of clothes, one pair of shoes, two shirts, and a change of underclothes, and forty dollars." He immediately went to see the president of the college to inquire into his chances of being admitted. He was informed that his lack of educational background made him an unfit candidate even for the academy's "sub-freshman class."[38]

Discouraged, Eunice headed for Kansas City, where he had been told by a young minister that a new church college had been established. It was autumn 1905. Eunice, now twenty-one years old, had all of twenty-six months of educational training in overcrowded, ill-funded country schools. He prevailed upon the president of Kansas City University to let him enroll in a country high school run by the university, which was offering a review class for rural schoolteachers. After three months of classes, he was called home due to his father's failing health. Eunice remained in western Oklahoma until his father died in July 1906. It was said that his grieving over Nicholas William's death never quite came to an end:

he felt guilty at having left the family home in Oklahoma. Nevertheless, he soon returned to Kansas City to continue his studies at Wilson High School.[39]

Over the next several years, Eunice performed all sorts of chores to pay for his education. He was determined to remain in school, whatever that entailed. He "did plumbing, carpentering, paper-hanging, box car repairing, news butching on passenger trains, farm work, bell hopping, ticket selling, dish washing, house cleaning, ditch digging, construction work, brick making, rock quarrying, library work, YMCA work, and lawn mowing," among other jobs. It was as though he literally willed himself to obtain an education.[40]

Like many other Americans both before and after his time, Comfort viewed education alternately as a means to an end or an end in itself, as a panacea to ignorance and prejudice and as a safeguard against destitution and deprivation. His interest in education was wide and deep. He looked upon it as opening doors, including those of the mind, that would otherwise remain forever shut. Education, he believed, would prevent the animosities that kept people from treating one another like brothers and sisters, and that had led some of his own relatives to join the Klan. He saw education as providing a ladder upon which even a poor lad like himself could escape a life of toil and misery. He now dedicated himself to acquiring the finest and most expansive education possible. Yet even he could not have foreseen how education would become one of the touchstones of his life.

There was something else that he had acquired from east Texas and western Oklahoma. As a good friend of his later acknowledged, Comfort possessed a respect for the common man that was "indigenous." Comfort had himself come out of the agricultural frontier, where one had to toil long and hard simply to eke out a living. On the frontier there seemed to exist a certain degree "of both liberty and equality" and an appreciation for manual labor. Comfort respected men who could work with their hands. He was himself the kind of person who seemed to disdain wearing a coat, feeling "better, freer, more effective in his short sleeves." Also, so-called "aristocrats"—those who worked with their pressed coats on—were viewed with considerable suspicion in the region where he was raised. The Texas of his youth had produced Governor Jim Hogg and populists James H. (Cyclone) Davis and H. S. P. (Stump) Ashby and was favorably disposed to agrarian reform efforts. This was an area where the Populist Party vied for power with the Democrats. This part of the Southwest never left Comfort, who was forever "stamped by this egalitarian philosophy."[41]

CHAPTER TWO

THE MAKING
OF A
SOCIAL GOSPEL
MINISTER

On Thanksgiving Day 1906, Eunice, still three years
shy of being able to attend Kansas City University,
was invited to a gathering held for students who were
away from their homes. While playing table tennis
there, he met and "fell desperately in love" with
Esther Obee, a teacher at the college, who was from
a preacher's family from the Midwest. Esther, who
had compiled the highest grades in the history of the
university, was teaching Greek and Latin classes.
Perceiving that there might be concerns about the
propriety of their relationship, they kept it a secret
from anyone in Kansas City. By the following June,
the two were engaged to be married—an engagement
that would last for four long years. Perhaps because
he had lost his mother at such an early age, Eunice
"really worshipped women in general" and none
would he ever be more enamored of than the young
woman from Whitehouse, Ohio. He "was wildly ro-
mantically in love with Mother, forever, always. It was
a deep love"—one of their children later reflected—
in spite of the fact that she "was a Yankee type" and
he "was always a Texan."[1]

As Esther later wrote, the extended engagement
was not an easy one. In May 1909, Esther returned
to Whitehouse to help tend her ailing mother. Mrs.

Obee passed away in June and Nick went to Ohio for a short visit, his second to Esther's home. After her mother's death, Esther decided to stay on in Whitehouse for a while, despite the implorings of D. W. Stephens, chancellor of Kansas City University, so that she could help to care for her Aunt Libbie, an invalid who had lived in the family home for thirty years.[2]

Nick was actively involved in many student activities, both while at Wilson High School and Kansas City University. He served as captain of the basketball team, manager of the athletic association, editor of the college newspaper, and president of the literary society, among other achievements.[3]

By now, Nick had felt the calling to study for the ministry. This could not have been surprising to anyone who knew him well. Nick appeared to be guided by a strong moral code that had been shaped by his earlier life experiences and by the influence of those, such as his father or the memory of his mother, he most revered. He wanted to find out more about the Methodist Protestant Church, which was a potent force back East. Perhaps Nick was attracted by the recently issued report "The Social Creed of Methodism," which proclaimed that the church stood "for equal rights and complete justice for all men in all stations of life." Whatever the influences, he opted to continue his studies at Western Maryland College in Westminster, Maryland, an established educational institution. After a year away, however, he enrolled at Kansas City University, where he received his bachelor of arts degree; a year later, he was awarded a bachelor of philosophy degree.[4]

Nick's performance at Kansas City University was stellar. He registered for courses on topics ranging from the French Revolution to Sophocles and from *Oedipus* to Christian ethics. He was also evidently given credit for several courses he either had taken at Western Maryland or had placed out of through a special examination, including those on the life of Christ and Old Testament history. The following academic year, as a graduate student, Nick enrolled in another half-dozen classes.[5]

At this point, he decided to discard the name his family continued to refer to him by. Now embarrassed with the moniker Eunice, he began to call himself Nick. This no doubt induced a certain amount of guilt, because, as noted earlier, the name Eunice was given to him by his father in honor of his mother. Years later, Nick would have difficulty convincing officials that he was E. Nicholas Comfort, and younger relatives continued to refer to him as Uncle Eunice.[6]

On June 27, 1911, Nick and Esther were married. It was a double wedding held at the home of Esther's Uncle Henry, with her cousin Isabel Billing and Ernest Oberlitner also taking their nuptial vows. Later that day, the Comforts took the Wabash train to Kansas City, with a brief visit along the way with her sister and brother-in-law, Margaret and Howard Munich, in Lafayette, Indiana. In Kansas City, they made their first home together, a cottage located on Parallel Avenue, close to Kansas City University. In September, due to the illness of another instructor, Esther returned to the university classroom to teach Greek, Latin, and German.[7]

The following summer, on July 31, the Comforts' first child, Janet Candace, was born. While strolling on the college campus one day with the baby in her arms, Esther encountered a student who chortled, "Why Miss Obee! You would look more natural with a book than with a baby!" However, five more children followed, three boys and two girls.[8]

The Comfort clan, as it grew, was about to embark on a journey, orchestrated by the family patriarch, that would take them up north, back East, and then to the Southwest. It would revolve around Comfort's determination to extend his education and to impart to others what he had learned from his studies and from life. Whether or not he was fully cognizant of it at the time, he was about to begin his life's work. Again it was in Kansas City that a seminal part of his odyssey was initiated—the place where Nick had returned to the classroom and met Esther. In Kansas City, Comfort—who received his license to administer the ordinance for the Methodist Protestant Church on September 17, 1910—became more certain than ever that he had received a calling. What that entailed was not ministerial work alone, but rather the transmitting of God's word to the young people of the American heartland.

The God that Comfort considered himself to be a missionary for was a benevolent, generous-spirited higher being, not one breathing fire and brimstone and filled with vengeance and a quest for retribution. The word that Comfort would seek to spread was that of the fatherhood of God and the brotherhood of man. These were the fundamental tenets of what though initially termed social Christianity was increasingly referred to during the Progressive Era as the social gospel.[9]

Comfort's Lord was the God of the social gospel who called for churchmen to fan out into the cities and countryside of the United States to ferret out all types of injustice. Comfort's most profound influence, then, in addition to family and friends, was the religious movement that had appeared in U.S. urban areas in the late nineteenth century and whose proponents had sought to ameliorate the worst aspects of industrial capitalism. Throughout his ministerial career, Comfort remained concerned about social and economic inequities that affected his community, whether that be his local town or rural area or the entirety of the United States. Like other social gospelers, he believed that the church had to become more receptive to the needs of the people, particularly the less fortunate.[10]

Liberal theological doctrines, which highlighted humankind's quest for progress, appealed to him mightily. So, too, did the notion that both the individual and society at large should be judged by the manner in which they treated all in their midst, again especially those who were indigent or persecuted. Thus, it was cooperation that was attractive, rather than the vaunted American individualism of either recent vintage or the frontier variety; although each man and woman seemed less than perfect, humankind was malleable enough that a different kind of social order, one far more gracious and harmonious, could be created.

As Robert H. Craig has suggested, the social gospel at its essence involved "an attempt to Christianize society by reshaping social attitudes and institutions." This goal Nick Comfort was very much in agreement with. Along with fellow practitioners of the social gospel, he desired to awaken his fellow citizens to the plight of others. But in contrast to other religious reformers, Comfort never lost sight of workers and farmers, those whom, in Jeffersonian fashion, he viewed as the backbone of the republic. He never appeared concerned about seeming to favor one class over another. As a consequence, his advocacy of the social gospel was perhaps more radical and consistent than that of most.[11]

While Nick Comfort's far-flung course of studies took him into some of America's greatest metropolitan areas, he always felt most comfortable in the smaller towns and the countryside. Throughout the remainder of his life, even as critics and scholars bemoaned or coldly analyzed the purported death of the social gospel, he engaged in his own brand of humanitarian proselytizing. For Comfort and a small band of other progressive religious activists the vision of the social gospel was constant. It was never far from his thoughts and was a source of his own regeneration. His remaining true to the social gospel gives lie to the notion that such generosity of spirit virtually vanished after the early Progressive Era. He seemed little impressed with either Bible-thumping fundamentalists of a reactionary cast or so-called realist theologians who, in the midst of man's inhumanity to man, insisted upon more hard-headed analysis.

Comfort's vision of Christianity was enmeshed in his belief that it was necessarily "a religion of morals." To Comfort, "love of humanity, love of each other, love for the eternal was important." Undoubtedly, he was pleased that Protestant denominations were increasingly emphasizing the importance of social responsibility. This was in keeping with the zeitgeist of the times and the dominant political philosophy of the period. Since the advent of Teddy Roosevelt's presidency in 1901, Progressivism had dominated the U.S. political landscape. At its heart, the Progressive movement sought to ameliorate the worst aspects of industrial capitalism by addressing problems that involved corporate consolidation, seemingly pervasive corruption, the exploitation of land, resources, and people, and the loss of a sense of community. Comfort sympathized with all such concerns and, in general, the reform efforts to attend to them.[12]

The social gospel, it has been argued, can be viewed "as the religious phase of Progressivism." Application of the principles of the social gospel, Comfort believed, could rectify many contemporary problems. He believed that practicing the Golden Rule, as Jesus had called for, was a step in the right direction. Unlike many religious missionaries he encountered, he did not view Jesus of Nazareth as God, but rather as the son of God. Most importantly, as he saw it, Jesus propounded the ideal of the Golden Rule. Thus, Comfort could best be categorized as a modernistic liberal, who was both an "intelligent modern" and a "serious Christian," to use the apt characterizations of religious historians Ronald C. White Jr. and C. Howard Hopkins. As a modernistic liberal, Comfort was guided by a contemporary perspective and a determination to ground his theological analyses in the sciences, philosophy, psychology, and social thought, rather than standard biblical or Christian interpretations. Like other modernistic liberals, Comfort was "not Christocentric," but he venerated Jesus because he represented the best in humankind and the struggle to attain perfection.[13]

From this point forth, Comfort's belief in the social gospel and his determination to do what he thought was right, no matter the criticism that engendered, resulted in him being a controversial figure. And controversy came early, as exemplified by an episode at the university's Wilson High School, where Comfort had begun teaching and serving as assistant principal. In midsummer 1912, the university chancellor, D. S. Stephens, fired off a heated letter to Comfort, complaining of his part in stoking the fires of student rebellion. Why, Stephens asked, had Comfort insisted on encouraging complaints by students of unsanitary living conditions? Why could Comfort not be more of a "team player"? Stephens referred to "the insurrection" by students that had taken place the preceding winter, and that Comfort had purportedly provided considerable inspiration for. Indeed, charged Stephens, the incident had caused the very existence of the university to become tenuous for a while. Stephens wrote that "the ill-advised criticism" of campus conditions, no matter how "deplorable," by Comfort and those who followed his lead, had little helped matters.[14]

To Stephens, Comfort's actions suggested some kind of character flaw and a lack of loyalty to both the university and himself. Stephens, after all, had helped to make it possible for Comfort to study in the first place. Nick's determined advocacy of what he alone deemed to be important, the university administrator declared, imperiled that which was truly significant. Although he had no doubts that Comfort was well-intentioned, Stephens continued, "I confess that my confidence was shaken in the soundness of your judgment, and in the cautiousness of your prudence." Certain members of the university executive committee, "alarmed by your lack of considerateness," questioned whether he should be reappointed for the next academic year. Stephens reassured Comfort that he, for one, would recommend his retention, provided a promise were made to Dr. Fredenhagen, a key member of the board, that there would be no repeat of the preceding year's experiences.[15]

Comfort refused to talk with Fredenhagen, which suggested a stubbornness on his part and an atypical unwillingness to reach out to those who disagreed with him. Stephens wrote back on August 15, indicating that the failure to do so had confirmed misgivings he had held about his one-time protégé. Despite his belief that Comfort had seriously erred in the past, Stephens still expressed confidence that "you will not be a disturber and a disintegrating influence in our work." Nevertheless, the chancellor was fully aware how important it was that all work together, rather than "at cross-purposes as has too often been the case in the past." Stephens declared that changes would have to be forthcoming.[16]

Other colleagues from Kansas City University saw Nick in a very different light than did Chancellor

Stephens. Mathematics Professor Joseph J. Stotler gave Comfort a glowing reference letter, which spoke of him in the following fashion: "In character, above reproach; in faithfulness, faultless; in ability to grasp scope and details, unexcelled by any other of my many former pupils." Stotler pointedly asserted, "His principles are not for sale." Stotler recognized that Comfort desired "to serve humanity—not for what it yields, but to justify his existence." His friend termed Nick "open, manly, capable," and stated that "he will not mislead, and can be fully trusted." Mrs. Stephens, the wife of his former benefactor, would later write to Comfort, asking if he would be interested in a missionary post in Kalgan, China.[17]

Comfort, who had just graduated from the Dillenbeck's School of Expression in Kansas City, now decided to apply for positions elsewhere. He moved to Adrian, Michigan, never to return to Kansas City University. He helped to make a success of the Community Center Work outside of Adrian, and was seen as having accomplished a great deal with his preaching in the city as well.[18]

In the fall of 1913, the Comforts moved to Chicago, so that Nick could attend McCormick Theological Seminary. The following summer, he also enrolled in classes at the University of Chicago, where at best he received mediocre grades. The Comforts' second child, Hugh Nicholas, was born on October 9, 1914. Nick served as pastor of South Union Church, near Gibson City, Illinois, about a hundred miles south of Chicago. On Saturday afternoons, he would drive down to Gibson City, returning home on Monday mornings.[19]

At McCormick, Comfort's performance was solid, although spottier than at Kansas City University. In April 1915, Comfort graduated from McCormick with his bachelor of divinity degree. The congregation at South Union Church had promised to construct a new church if Nick would come to live in the area. So the Comforts headed south, to reside in the parsonage with its beautiful trees, located close to the church. The people at Union were friendly and supportive and soon implored Comfort to teach in the district school, which he agreed to do. In February 1916, a second son, Lee, was born.[20]

In spite of the seemingly idyllic relationship in Union, Comfort continued to long for still more education, and evidently hoped to study and work in Cambridge, Massachusetts, the home of Harvard University and the Andover Theological Seminary. However, in late December 1916, Comfort was informed by the secretary of the Congregational Board of Pastoral Supply in Boston that a church would not likely be found in the area unless he were to consider entering the Congregational ministry. Comfort possibly contemplated doing so, for a recommendation letter from an old acquaintance and friend, Dr. H. L. Elderdice, the president of Western Maryland College, was sent on to the Congregational Board in January. The note from Elderdice loudly sang Nick's praises, referring to his "quite unusual if not phenomenal" success in Gibson City. "I regard him as a man of ability, vision, tact and energy," declared Elderdice. "His character is gentlemanly and Christian to the highest degree."[21]

Later that month, Comfort received a letter from Arch McClure, of McCormick Theological Seminary, addressed to "Dear Heretic," which over the years would prove to be a familiar salutation. McClure indicated that he had brought up Comfort's name with William P. Shriver, the secretary for Immigrant and City Work of the Presbyterian Board of Home Missions, regarding a position with the Trinity Church in San Francisco. What was needed in that city, McClure indicated, was a ministry of the social gospel variety. An urban, immigrant community would be catered to there, and that involved "everything from preaching to getting employment, running lecture courses, giving picture shows, etc.," as well as toiling alongside foreign pastors. McClure pointedly declared, "It would be a great place for you to face all the social, economic and religious questions that you realize are confronting the church." Whether the California job came through or not, McClure suggested, he felt "it would do your heart good to meet sometime the men in the Presbyterian Church who are facing & solving a lot of these questions now—men who are thinking." McClure noted how inspiring it had been for him to have encountered ministers like Jonathan Day, Norman Thomas, and Kenneth Miller, working in New York City, and Joel Hayden, who was operating in Baltimore. All of these men, McClure affirmed, "are making the Kingdom of God put in its appearance ahead of the time scheduled for it by some of the pre-millenialists."[22]

Soon, however, it was clear that Comfort was not headed for either of the coasts, but had decided to return instead to Chicago. Comfort enrolled at the University of Chicago for the summer quarter in 1917. By the fall quarter, Comfort's performance in the classroom had improved considerably. From this point forth, he took a series of advanced psychology and philosophy courses.[23]

Clearly, Comfort was determined to develop his own empirically based theology, grounded in the social sciences and the natural sciences. This naturalism stood in sharp contrast to the revelation that guided fundamentalists. However, unlike some more radically inclined theologians, Comfort did not seek to discard biblical injunctions altogether or to dismiss the importance of the life of Jesus. He did strive, however, to become more empirical and scientific, while retaining his belief in historic Christian thought. Thus, he was devising the kind of liberal theological viewpoint that was becoming increasingly popular within certain denominations. His philosophy of religion was overtaking his belief in standard theological tenets.[24]

Comfort financed this part of his education first by working as a janitor, then receiving a tuition scholarship, helping out in the Philosophy Library, and serving as pastor of the Methodist Protestant Church in Avalon Park, a suburb several miles south of the university. Once again, the family—with a new addition, Dick, arriving on March 11, 1918—now resided in a comfortable church parsonage.[25]

A virulent influenza epidemic swept the United States and much of Europe during this period, as World War I continued to rage over the continent. In the summer of 1918, Comfort sought entrance into the army as a chaplain. The noted philosopher James Hayden Tufts sent a letter of commendation to the adjutant general of the U.S. Army, declaring that he had "a very high opinion of Mr. Comfort's ability, good judgment and personality." Tufts indicated that he was sure that Comfort "would be an excellent man for this work. He is sincere, a hard worker, a good friend, loyal to his country, and would at all times do his best for the men with whom he might be placed." The president of Adrian College, Michigan, Harlan L. Feeman, also wrote a recommendation letter on Comfort's behalf, deeming him "a young man of natural ability and with thorough training for the work of the Christian ministry." Feeman called Comfort courageous and "a good mixer, thoughtful and ready of speech" who was "devoted to building up the spiritual life of his fellows." E. W. Hart of the Illinois Volunteer Training Corps spoke of Comfort's involvement with the company and wrote that "his loyalty is unquestionable, his disposition and personality, amiable and such that he is a man's man."[26]

On September 12, Comfort had to register with his local draft board in Chicago, and the matter resolved itself with him being turned down for service in the military because of a recent operation for kidney stones. Consequently, he continued with his studies, now working under Professor Tufts, completed all necessary residential work, and passed the requisite French and German exams. He was just about to take his oral exams when an opportunity to return to his native state occurred. Dr. John C. Williams, the husband of Esther's sister Edith and the president of Westminster College in Tehuacana, offered Nick the chance to teach philosophy and religion. Nick was also to serve as minister for the local Methodist church. The salary was set at $150 a month, which must have come as welcome news to Comfort, who continued, as he would throughout his life, to be saddled with bills and debts.[27]

More importantly to Comfort, who never made economic concerns his top priority, the Tehuacana position would enable him to discover whether the fulfillment of a longtime dream was really what he sought: to "put his life into the young people of the South." Unfortunately, this meant that his doctoral studies would never be completed. As Esther later acknowledged, this was "the mistake of our lives." For Comfort never would obtain the degree he so desired. He seemed to recognize almost immediately that "we should have stayed right there until that degree was earned," although he continued to correspond with Professor Tufts for a time about returning to the University of Chicago.[28]

The family stopped off in Oklahoma at Altus and Lawton to see Nick's sisters, Maude and Cova, and their families. Cova and her husband, Harry, still resided in the home Nick had built for the family when they had moved from east Texas into Oklahoma Territory. Lee, then three-and-a-half years old, suffered a close call on Maude's farm, being just rescued by Uncle Hugh from the hooves of a mule he had wandered behind.

On a happier note, Esther was made to feel right at home when she overheard Maude telling a neighbor that Nick's wife was "very highly educated." Such a recognition ensured that respect would be afforded Esther, even though she was little versed in the ways of the South. Maude did her best to help out Esther.[29]

Once back on home soil in the Lone Star State, Comfort seemed to thrive. He "was a different man when he was back home in Texas." The folks in Tehuacana revered him and even took a liking to the Yankee Esther for his sake. She was never treated like an outsider, although there were some early concerns. For example, she often spoke of bags instead of sacks when discussing cotton.[30]

The Comforts, after traveling to Mexia by train, finally reached Tehuacana. The family initially resided in a small but quite comfortable old house, situated just across from the campus of Westminster College. With no kindergarten in the area, Hugh, although but five years of age, entered the first grade, and Janet, too, continued her schooling. In later years, Janet remembered hearing Nick, with his "lovely, mellow speaking voice," deliver an Easter sermon in Tehuacana, which impressed upon her "the concept of the redemptive love of Jesus."[31]

Tragedy befell the Comforts when they had been in Texas for just a short while: Lee was afflicted with falciparum malaria after being bitten by mosquitoes. He died within a week, on October 12, 1919, and was buried in the local cemetery. The death of the little boy, Esther remembered, was "our first great sorrow." As Dick Comfort later reflected, "It is hard on families; you just don't get over it." For Nick, the blow was severe, as Lee seemed like "his kind of kid"—one who "might have been the one to set the world on fire."[32]

Elizabeth was born in Tehuacana on June 12, 1920. There, too, Esther returned to the classroom to teach a freshman Spanish class. Meanwhile, Nick strove to strengthen the church membership in the area. Naturally, he hoped to add members to his own congregation, but he was more concerned about churchgoing practices in general. Characteristically, he indicated that "rigid" denominationalism should be discarded. "We are all trying to get to the same place. We all love the same God. We all want to help our fellows." Consequently, why not pitch in, he asked, to help out the church in the community where one resided? If a Methodist church were available, he acknowledged, then he hoped folks in the community would join it. However, if not, "for the sake of Christ's Kingdom join the nearest church and do all you can to help save your own community."[33]

His steadfast determination to challenge prejudices of all kinds, including those within the Protestant churches, ensured that Comfort was not only a respected figure in the community in which he preached but a controversial one as well. By 1920, general appreciation of both the social gospel and early twentieth-century reform efforts carried out under the Progressive banner had waned. Little helping the cause of liberal theologians was the passing from the scene during the same period of the leading practitioners of the social gospel, including Walter Rauschenbusch, Washington Gladden, Lyman Abbott, and Josiah Strong. And yet, as church historian Donald K. Gorrell contends, the social ministry had become part of mainstream Protestantism.[34]

Comfort's belief in a nonsectarian approach led him to become more conscious of broad social, economic, and political currents. It also resulted in his own name becoming better known among liberal theologians. On April 5, 1920, he was asked by the officers of the World Alliance for International Friendship through the Churches if they could add his name to their roster. The World Alliance, like the Church Peace Union, was striving for a world without war and had determined to back the League of Nations. Comfort was informed that he had been selected as an individual who could well represent his community. William Pierson Merrill, pastor of Brick Presbyterian Church in Manhattan, served as chairman of the World Alliance. Officers included Henry A. Atkinson, of the Church Peace Union, and Frederick Lynch, who edited *Christian Work*. Among the directors were Henry Sloan Coffin, president of Union Theological Seminary and Dean Shailer Mathews, of the University of Chicago Divinity School. On May 22, the International Committee of Young Men's Christian Associations invited Comfort to represent Westminster College at the Race Relationships Conference to be held at Hollister, Missouri, the following month.[35]

On August 26, Comfort received an inquiry from the Better America Lecture Service from New York, asking how his church was assisting the Americanization movement?[36] Comfort, of course, was not about to cast his lot with the unprogressive sorts associated with the Americanization movement. He saw instead more of a need than ever to break the narrow constraints that had afflicted churchmen to date. In fact, in a letter written on September 28, 1920, to a friend in Bellevue, Pennsylvania, the Reverend A. J. Green, Comfort indicated his displeasure with both religious sectarianism and the Methodist Protestant Church in Texas. Denominationalism, he wrote, was all but spent, particularly in the countryside. He had visited a number of rural churches outside of Tehuacana and had not come across a single minister expressing satisfaction with his own denomination's works in the local community. Rather, he saw a religious chasm dividing good rural folk. Baptists, Methodists, and Presbyterians alike seemed incapable of getting beyond simple prejudices directed at another. This did not surprise him: he saw Southern folks as being "more exclusive" and "contentious" than any other. This resulted in revival meetings with tiny numbers of one church group or another. In fact, revivals were held first by one organization, acting alone, then by others. While the ministers complained of the people seeming distant, Comfort saw the churches themselves behaving in an "anti-Christian" manner. "Old-time revivals" would never appear, he reasoned, until entire communities came together.[37]

Sadly, Comfort continued, too many religious leaders evidently felt that the church should seek to save a few only from a world that was doomed. They failed to recognize that Jesus sought "to save the entire world." Consequently, those who spoke of transforming the world "morally, socially, politically, and every other way," had their ideas dismissed as "new fangled."[38]

The bottom line, to Comfort at least, was that the Methodist Protestant Church was simply not accomplishing much in Texas. Comfort had not been back in the state long enough to be certain if the plight of that church were a permanent condition or not. Nevertheless, he was sure that it was "absolutely past redemption as far as any constructive work is concerned." It seemed clear that a good number of people "will die Methodist Protestants; whether they will die Christians or not I am not as sure."[39]

Comfort questioned whether the Methodist Church would ever make real inroads in the American West and Southwest, and suggested that it would do better to concentrate its resources east of the Mississippi River. Such an idea, he recognized, undoubtedly would not be received kindly, but putting it into practice would further the kingdom of God. Admittedly "not good orthodox stuff," he informed his friend, this "is [sic] my deepest convictions."[40]

By this point, Comfort had also come to another important realization. "Unless I change my mind very seriously, I am going to give my life to the building up of the rural work of the churches in the Southwest." What this meant, he feared, was that he likely would not be of much use to any single denomination. In little populated areas, he believed, churches needed to depend upon the goodwill of an entire community and not be divided by denominationalism. Comfort, for his part, was willing to work within a denomination, but if that proved impossible, he was ready "to cut loose" and suffer the consequences.[41]

Comfort was certain about one thing. "I do not any more hear the call of any church but I do hear the call of thousands of boys and girls all through the Southwest" who lacked any opportunity for religious edification, who had not been schooled in the ideals of Jesus, and who had no introduction to the finest literature, science, or much of what "God Almighty has for the human race." Others spoke of the high price of commodities, including labor, but "I hear the cry of the tenant boys and girls whose lives are sad and crushed." Thus, if compelled to choose between a church and such children, there was no question how he would decide. These youngsters, Comfort insisted, simply had to be afforded the kind of opportunity that no denomination in Texas was providing. Indeed, the religious leaders and their churches that ranted about "Holy Ghost revivals" and "Old Time religion," he concluded, appeared to have given little thought to these "white slaves." Comfort closed his letter with the acknowledgment that his friend was undoubtedly "getting tired of this harangue."[42]

No doubt Comfort's attitude was shaped, at least to some extent, by what had transpired at the General Conference of the Methodist Church earlier that year. The passage of a resolution, "For the Settlement of Industrial Unrest," which urged resolving social and economic conflicts according to God's teachings, could hardly have satisfied him; nor would the deletion of a clause that had indicated the church's belief in the "legitimate demands" of organized labor. He must have looked with askance upon the church's call to attend to spiritual concerns rather than present-day problems.[43]

Fed up with the operations of the Methodist Church in Texas and determining that he required still more education, Nick decided once again to go back to school. The family, admittedly with some regrets, left Tehuacana in the summer of 1921, packing their belongings in their "trip car," a Model T Ford that they drove to the southeast coast. Elizabeth, barely a year old, spent a good portion of the travel time in her mother's arms. Dick had turned three; Hugh was seven; Janet was nine. The passage was sometimes arduous. In Louisiana, they traveled along muddy roads that threatened to worsen every few feet. The Comforts hoped to camp at Lake Pontchartrain for the night but were driven away by mosquitoes so thick that they felt compelled to light out for New Orleans. Further down the road, they discovered, much to their chagrin, that their car had to be placed on a steamer to cross Mobile Bay. Other passengers looked well-dressed and affluent, but Nick and the gang were attired in overalls and the like. When asked where his family was heading, Nick replied, "New York," to the questioner's astonishment.[44]

Heading up north, the Comforts spent a lone evening indoors, in High Point, North Carolina, where a Methodist minister and his wife provided lodging for the night. They visited with Aunt Annie and Uncle

Tim in Newark, New Jersey, before leaving for Morsemere, a short distance from the Lee Ferry, which enabled them to cross the Hudson River to get to Columbia University. Later, they occasionally took Janet into the city—a trip she considered her "biggest treat." Esther and her daughter would have lunch in the commons and then browse through a bookstore. They stayed in Morsemere until February, when they moved on to Croton Falls, New York, in Westchester County. Comfort had been named pastor of the Presbyterian church there.[45]

He also served as pastor in Somers, a small village just west of Croton Falls, which boasted a little colonial church building. Among the services Comfort provided in Somers was a memorial service on behalf of a fallen elephant. The passing of Old Bet, considered the first elephant to have been brought into the United States, led the folks in Somers to establish a monument in her honor.[46]

In a manner of speaking, Comfort now decided to return to the fold. His father had once been a leading figure in his local Presbyterian church, after all, and Nick believed that denomination now had more to offer him. The Presbyterians, in his estimation, underscored the sovereignty of God. They reasoned that a divinely ordained plan had been laid for man; within that plan, each individual and mankind as a whole were to be incorporated. It was incumbent upon each individual to discover his place in God's plan so that he could attain the highest level of fulfillment and greatest degree of self-expression. God spoke to man through nature's handiwork. God, although speaking to the conscience of each individual, employed devoted sorts as his "special instruments." But individual judgment was always required. Jesus was "the supreme manifestation of God to man. He is what God wants all men to become."

Thus, "man's salvation here and hereafter depends upon his incarnation of the spirit of Jesus." God revealed himself in a direct manner to those who would listen and respond to his word. Man was best able to conduct his affairs according to God's will through the use of his intelligence.[47]

Particularly appealing to Comfort was the fact that Presbyterians admired order—albeit of a democratic variety—dignity, and education. They were certain that education was God's means of propagating the gospel and believed strongly in a teaching ministry. They emphasized the need to nurture children in the ways of home, church, and school. They felt certain that God desired to save the world "here and now." They stressed the importance of will, both human and divine.[48]

Also attractive to Comfort was the seeming humility with which Presbyterians viewed the world at large and their role in it. They recognized that they possessed no monopoly regarding God's design. Instead, they viewed their church as a mechanism for establishing the kingdom of God on earth. Thus, they gladly cooperated with willing religious and secular groups. The Presbyterians, more than any other sect, in Comfort's eyes, appeared most determined to combine all of these ideals and practices into an "organic whole." Undoubtedly less attractive to Comfort was the raging controversy between modernists and fundamentalists, which also afflicted other Protestant denominations. By the early 1920s, it was particularly virulent in the Presbyterian Church, U.S.A.[49]

Starting in the fall of 1921, Comfort attended classes at the famed Union Theological Seminary in New York City. He also enrolled at Columbia University, studying with John Dewey, among others. Included among Union's well-regarded faculty were

Henry Sloan Coffin and Harry F. Ward. As historian Richard Wightman Fox has noted, interdenominationalism prevailed at Union, which undoubtedly appealed to Comfort. So did the readiness of the Union staff to incorporate psychological and sociological analyses, along with theological ones. The faculty seemed eager to mold ministers into "educators, social workers, and therapists, rather than merely interpreters of the Word of God." Comfort had already adopted a similar perspective. Likewise, the declaration by Union's president, Arthur McGiffert, that religion must remain progressive, could only have heartened Comfort.[50]

Esther, too, now returned to the classroom as a student at Columbia. While Nick remained with the kids on Saturdays, she took classes. She had decided that for her "this was to be 'a lark.'" With no intention of working for a degree, she signed up for Spanish and German classes. Esther, like Nick, took the Harlem Division of the New York North Central Railroad into the city. At one point, she resided in New York for a full summer term, attending classes daily.[51]

The Comforts' three-story home in Croton Falls, edged by a terraced lawn, served as a manse for the church. Among the discoveries found on the property was a carriage house, where Dick, to his delight, came upon a wooden hobbyhorse. The Comforts became close to their neighbors, even taking a trip through New England one summer with the Schworms, Ed, "Mrs. Ed," and their son, Eddie. Nick rigged up a "camp house body" on top of the family car, which the Comforts traveled in. They saw the homes of John Greenleaf Whittier and Louisa May Alcott, visited Boston, with its store of historical sites, and drove up to Maine.[52]

Comfort's academic performance at Union was superior. On May 15, 1923, he received his master's in theology at Union. Esther, too, did well, coming closer than she had anticipated to obtaining a degree from Columbia in German and Spanish. In fact, she, like Nick earlier, completed all of the course work for her doctorate degree and began her dissertation.[53]

Throughout their stay in Croton Falls, Comfort received offers of other ministerial posts. On August 22, 1923, he was asked to become the pastor of the Hawthorne Church, where he had favorably impressed a number of the members of the congregation during a recent talk there. He was also invited to become the minister of a lovely church in White Plains, which would have provided Comfort with a decent salary at long last.[54]

However, Nick by now was more convinced than ever that he was destined to return to the Southwest —specifically to Texas or Oklahoma. In February 1924, the call came in the form of a letter from Theodore H. Aszman, pastor of the First Presbyterian Church in Norman, Oklahoma. Aszman, who had gotten Nick's name from the University of Chicago, inquired whether he might be interested in a position as university pastor for the five hundred or so Presbyterian students at the University of Oklahoma. Whoever would be appointed, Aszman noted, would serve as student pastor and teach classes for the Department of Religious Education at the university.[55]

Campus ministries were not new. Nearly six decades earlier, the Presbyterians had initiated a program at the University of Michigan, spearheaded by the clergyman at a parish church in Ann Arbor. In 1893, a bible chair at the same institution was set up by the Disciples of Christ to enrich public education. Just after the turn of the century, full-time Protestant pastors and Roman Catholic priests worked on university campuses in Michigan, Wisconsin, and Illinois and some time later a rabbi could be found at Illinois. Interdenominational schools of religions, generally of short-term duration, cropped up during this same period.[56]

In 1913, a new, more significant type of campus ministry, the first Wesley Foundation, appeared at the University of Illinois. The foundation's statement of purpose expressed the hope and expectation that it would leave its mark. Traditional church beliefs were to be fostered in small gatherings, but "the scientific atmosphere" that prevailed at many schools had to be appreciated. Most significantly, the Wesley Foundation sought to ensure the presence at major universities of the following: "1. A shrine for worship. 2. A school for religious education. 3. A home away from home. 4. A laboratory for training lay leaders in church activities. 5. A recruiting station for the ministry, for missionary work at home and abroad, and for other specialized Kingdom tasks."[57]

In words that would take on more meaning for Nick Comfort with the passage of time, Aszman reported that the university's facilities for the pastor were somewhat lacking. They would, Aszman reassured Comfort, "improve in time." For now, only a shared office in the Education Building and space at the YMCA, located adjacent to the University of Oklahoma campus, were available. The salary was $3,000, half to be paid by the General Board of Education and half to be voted by the synod.[58]

By the end of the following month, having received a report from a key contact who had been "very favorably impressed" with Comfort, Aszman prepared to tender the offer formally. When it actually arrived, Comfort accepted immediately, and the family took to the road once again. This time, the now forty-year-old social gospel minister, his wife, and their brood of five returned to familiar soil.[59]

Nick Comfort had cast his lot, determined to enter the educational ministry. Now he would be able to fulfill his greatest dream: imparting the word of God to young people in his native Southwest and being allowed to do so in a university setting—fortunately, given his strongly held beliefs and opinionated nature. As Nick headed for Norman, Oklahoma, he continued to be guided by the social gospel and his determined advocacy of the fatherhood of God and the brotherhood of man.

CHAPTER THREE

AT HOME
IN OKLAHOMA

The uneventful trip to Norman during the summer of 1924 ended with the family coming to reside in a small home on Pickard Avenue. Soon, however, the Comforts purchased a bare, ten-acre cotton patch of sandy loam they called 2000 Chautauqua, located about half a mile from the University of Oklahoma (OU) campus and, at the time, beyond the town limits. Nick, who thrived every bit as much working with his hands as he did at the pulpit, in the classroom, or at his writing desk, set to work with a plow. He put in electrical wiring and dug a well, happily discovering the supply of water to be all but inexhaustible. Trees of all kinds—cherry, plum, papershell pecan, peach, and apple—were eventually planted.[1]

Given the continuously precarious nature of the Comforts' finances—"just living hand-to-mouth"—it was fortunate that they were able to garden, cultivate their own crops, and meet their dairy needs. Almost immediately, Nick planted scores of watermelons and muskmelons. He also grew berries, grapes, corn, potatoes, and onions, and kept chickens —although soon after that venture started, a pair of dogs killed forty-seven of his frying chickens. Asparagus readily grew, with the children—once the family had built a house and they were living there—rising early to cut it and bring it inside in bunches before heading off to school. Nick sold the asparagus, along with eggs and milk, at a grocery on trips into town. Later, Nick purchased small chicks by the thousands and the Comforts raised them. When restaurants ordered chickens—with orders in the dozens—the birds would be killed, scalded, plucked and drawn, and packed. Down pillows became available for the family as Nick started raising geese and guineas. In the garden, Esther, too, grew green beans, which she preserved, along with many kinds of fruits, canning and storing them in quart jars in the basement. Striving for self-sufficiency, Nick considered that he did "pretty well for a jack-leg preacher." Word had it among university faculty that the Comforts were "first class farmers," not necessarily the most educated analysis coming from those whose agricultural pursuits were, as Nick admitted, confined "to the back yard." It was Nick's responsibility to do the grocery shopping and other errands, Esther refusing to drive: she had suffered a traumatic experience in Illinois when she was learning to drive, having run over a pig.[2]

The Comforts soon had four acres of cotton, three acres of feed, and a cow to care for. Besides carnivorous animals and worms, they had to contend with Norman's typical dry, brutal summers and the tremendous fluctuations of Oklahoma weather, which can range from dust storms to bitterly cold mornings to humid afternoons to lengthy electrical storms, all within a short span of time.[3]

They also had to deal with the fact that the family "never, never did have any money," and the ten-acre homestead soaked up what little they had. This rarely troubled Nick, who apparently trusted in God's goodwill that everything would work out. He loved entertainment, for example, and was always ready to spend whatever he had to take the kids to the movies. The financial tightrope the Comforts invariably walked was worrisome to Esther, who was far more practically minded.[4]

Shortly after acquiring 2000 Chautauqua, Nick purchased an annex to the Norman High School building that was about to be torn down, taking a team and wagon to load up the lumber and haul it out to the homestead. There he dug a basement and, with the help of Hugh Lawson Minor, the son of his sister Maude, built an eleven-room, two-story house, the dimensions of which initially were forty feet by thirty-four feet. He admitted that he had never worked harder in his life, quite a statement from one who was as driven as he. In addition, he had every family member "about run to death," swinging hammers or running errands of one kind or another. The children would do a little painting, while Nick did carpentry work and plastering. This was to be Nick's dream house, he acknowledged, but for a good while the project was more the source of nightmares. Fruit trees were planted and the entire family went to the city dump to get elm saplings, which could be found there. Eventually, great trees shielded the house from the street. A garage, fourteen feet by twenty-eight feet, with a small apartment above it, was also constructed; nephew Hugh and his wife Dora lived there while they attended the University of Oklahoma.[5]

The close of the Comforts' first academic year in Norman ended dramatically when a cyclone demolished the garage apartment and scattered debris over a half-mile radius. Nick, who was in town at the time, rushed out to the farm to assess the damage. To his dismay, Hugh and Dora could not be found; luckily, they were at a neighbor's home and had escaped with minor injuries.[6] Chastened, Nick opted to rebuild the structure with one story only, eighteen feet by twenty feet.

It took time before the main house was completed, Nick adding on whenever he was able to. The additions were welcomed and necessary as Nick often invited nieces and nephews to live with the Comforts while they were attending the university. As Janet indicated, Nick was not only a firm believer in education, he did whatever he could to make it available to many friends, family members, and acquaintances.[7]

The house, with its patchwork quality, was never completely finished; it remained, rather, "a kind of fluid thing," Nick remodeling as the urge or need arose. One of his children recalled that he undoubtedly had a design in mind regarding the house as a whole, but altered it as materials became available. A large, screened-in porch, covering the east side and much of the south, was positioned across from the living room, which—with windows on the north, east, and south—was, with the porch, where a considerable amount of entertaining took place. This activity included parties and square dancing, one of Nick's great delights. The living room was also where sick family members were placed, so they could be the beneficiaries of a large fireplace and whatever attention they required. The room also held a piano and a number of the children took lessons.[8]

Next to the living room was a spacious dining room, with a closet and a guest bedroom adjacent. The western side of the house boasted a breakfast room and large kitchen, separated by cupboards. At the end was a bathroom, which might or might not have running water, according to the state of the pump located outside the back door on a little porch. A hand pump operated when the larger one was malfunctioning or electricity was not being generated.[9]

The driveway ran down from Chautauqua Street, with a porte cochere making it possible to get out of a car and head over to the porch without getting rained on. On one occasion, one of the children tossed mud pies over the side of a wall, disturbing the generally unflappable Nick.[10]

The upstairs bedrooms, other than the master bedroom of Nick and Esther, continually underwent transformation. A musical-chairs system unfolded, the children moving to the larger rooms, which Nick reconfigured, whenever a sibling left home. The attic was for storage. During World War II, when Norman experienced a housing shortage, the Comforts subdivided parts of 2000 Chautauqua into apartments.[11]

The housekeeping was done by Esther and the children, for the most part. As her daughter Anne remembered, Esther "worked her little tail off" in an attempt to keep the ever-expanding house in order. But Esther was not much of a housekeeper. Nick once commented that it was too bad he had taken a wonderful language instructor and converted her "into a mediocre housekeeper." He meant it as a compliment, but she was deeply offended by her husband's remark. Still, all seemed to recognize that housekeeping "was not her thing," although she did her best. When she ironed Nick's shirts, she inevitably forgot to attend to a sleeve or a collar, much to his mortification. In time, he suggested that one of his daughters should take care of his shirts.[12]

At the far side of the lot, a small house occasionally was rented out or used by family members or a hired hand. A chicken house was located closer to the main house. Across from the kitchen, in the back, was the garage. South of it stood a graveled croquet court with permanent wickets. To the west lay a large field, where baseball was played. In addition, basketball courts and baskets were set up. There was also a big swing, perhaps fifteen feet off the ground, and a smaller one for the smaller children. On the opposite side of the garage was a grand teeter-totter and a merry-go-round. Nick once had a stuffy university faculty member ride it, his coattails flying in the air. On the other side of the well was a spot for a swimming pool, which remained one of Nick's unfinished projects.[13]

Nick devised contraptions of all sorts for the children. A two-wheeled go-cart that he built for Elizabeth, pulled by a horse, did not last long: he failed to place blinders on the horse and it got spooked at one point, raced off, and wrecked the cart, banging up Elizabeth. He also rigged up a slide. This device ran alongside a cable, strung from the roof of the barn to a stake in the orchard, out among the peach trees. After it had been in operation for years, the cable broke, expelling one of Elizabeth's friends, who suffered a broken arm.[14]

The house at 2000 Chautauqua was a beehive of activity, not only for the Comforts—who were augmented on February 6, 1926, by the birth of Anne, soon "old enough to rule the house"—but also for relatives, friends, and university folk, both faculty and students. As a close friend later recalled, the Comforts exuded a terrific hospitality. A Halloween party was held before the house was even finished, with students from the university invited. Soon, social functions were held at the house, with a hundred students or more attending. This was not surprising as Nick loved parties, and the Comforts had them all the time. As Presbyterian university pastor, Nick sought to entertain students, inviting them to the house for parties, where he might do the calling for a square dance or conduct wiener roasts. He also took the lead on hikes. He simply "was so wonderful" dealing with young people, Janet later recalled.[15]

Nick was extroverted and "just loved everybody." He was happiest when visitors came to call. He could make friends with the folks he ran into at the railroad yard as easily as among his colleagues at the university. Esther, in contrast, was very quiet and introverted. But they augmented each other nicely, and she graciously went along with his desire to have people always coming and going. For the parties, she would supervise her children as they squeezed oranges, lemons, and limes for punch, and the playing of the phonograph. Together, Nick and Esther established enduring friendships, both in Norman and elsewhere.[16]

The screened-in front porch, which became a kind of institution in itself, was used for dining on many occasions, for sleeping, by the Comfort girls for sewing, and for countless games of checkers, dominoes, and cards. Friends from the university would visit to play one kind of game or another and have "'a philosophical talk' gathering." Or Nick would play hearts with the kids hour after hour; he was "such a 'game' person." On one occasion, he indicated as much to Janet: "You know, the only thing I ever begrudged the church was that it kept me from dancing and playing cards for so long."[17]

To Anne, this indicated that Nick desired that people "be light and happy." Perhaps he hoped to ensure that his life—like those of his children, at least when they were in his home—was not going to be beset by depression, like his father's had been and his own had threatened to become. Willing to work hard, he loved to play, too. Nick simply loved entertainment. The family had a Croakinol set, its board large and square, with demarcations for any number of games. Croakinols and caroms came along with the board, which was like a miniature billiard setup. With Anne, he played dominoes, night after night; with Elizabeth, he played table tennis in a large game room, downstairs on the porch, that was often used by university students. A net curtain was fitted all around to catch balls and prevent them from flying into someone else in the room. There was also a noisy, frenzied game called box hockey—Nick had evidently ordered it from Tennessee—in which the competitors sought to get the puck away from their end of the box. Then there was plumber's dice, which involved a glass jar with a rubber ring under the lid and curtain hooks with a string attached; whenever someone threw a seven, an eleven, or a pair, the other players would try to pull out before being caught by the plumber.[18]

With his buddies, Nick would play horseshoes, dominoes, checkers, or cards. They would sit on the porch and talk about weighty issues of the day. In the wintertime, they would settle by the fireplace in the living room and converse for hours on end. Among the regulars visiting 2000 Chautauqua were university colleagues J. Rud Nielsen, Cortez A. M. Ewing, Gustave Mueller, Nathan Cort, Tim Kaufman, Antonio de la Torre, and John B. Thompson. Such strong-willed individuals were not always in agreement about the topic at hand, but they invariably enjoyed the discussions.[19] The Comforts rarely had money, but they were involved with "the best circles intellectually." As Janet recalled, "our friends were always cultured people."[20]

Happily for a family that loved books, the porch was also a wonderful place for reading. All types of books could be found in the home, Esther and Nick placing no restrictions upon the reading materials their children devoured. Janet's tastes ranged from Zane Grey to Les Misérables. Esther enjoyed sifting through magazines, such as the Ladies' Home Journal and some lighter works at times. Nick was not so inclined, reading in astronomy, geology, and the like.[21]

The children would study at home, gathered around the table. Esther assisted them with foreign languages and English; Nick tutored them in math, in which he excelled. All of the children seemed to thrive in school, except for Elizabeth, as Nick and

Esther early recognized. Elizabeth seemed to have a "don't care attitude," Nick reported, which upset her mother far more than her father.[22]

Almost as important as the porch in family lore was the fruit cellar, a small room in the southwest corner of the basement. Built by Nick of cement with iron reinforcement, it was as cyclone-proof as was possible in Oklahoma. Shelves on all sides were packed with canned fruit, vegetables, and, on occasion, beef and chicken. Upon viewing the cellar, one friend exclaimed that "it looked like the county fair." Given the often precarious state of the Comforts' finances, the cellar proved a godsend, enabling the family to get by, even during the hardest of times.[23]

Family meals were a delight, with everyone gathered around the table in the kitchen or the dining room, or on the front porch. If someone got up, others would chortle, "You're up, get the pitcher of milk for yourself while you're up! Do this, and while you're up, do that!" After dinner, the Comforts often had ice cream for dessert. They had a five-gallon ice-cream freezer and with all kinds of fruit tree on the premises a grand feast would be had by all.[24]

For a time, Nick would have a glass of wine when he and Esther were invited to dinner at a friend's house. But after being informed that wine contained alcohol, Nick refused to drink anymore, recognizing that some of his relatives had been alcoholics and fearing that he might have a propensity of the same sort. He also would not eat pork, which Esther loved. She and Janet were especially fond of pork and sauerkraut, but Nick reasoned they were not healthy foods. Earlier, he had become sick when eating pork.[25]

Considering himself to be something of a horseman, Nick, not surprisingly, encouraged his children to ride. Esther later recalled that Nick told them how, back in Texas, he used to walk a mile just to get hold of a wild horse so that he could ride a quarter-mile on horseback. Shortly after the Chautauqua property had been purchased, he bought "an old nag" for his children, to go along with his other horses. Next, he planned to get a saddle, because they sometimes fell off the horse. Luckily, the horse was "so good and gentle that she always stops to let them fall off as easily as possible." Soon, the horse had a fine little colt of her own, but Nick sold the colt after she got in a fight with some of his other horses. He ended up with a white-stockinged bay horse, who seemed "nice and gentle for the kiddies." Nick also enjoyed riding this steed, for he would kick up for a spell if the rider stuck his feet in the flanks. This horse required a saddle—he had recently thrown one of Nick's nephews—because Hugh was eager to ride him. As for the horse's feistiness, Nick declared, "I maintain that a boy is not worth his salt until he has been thrown a half dozen times."[26]

Living outside the city as the Comforts did, they had to contend with sandy roads, cockleburs, sandburs, and goat grass, so bicycles could not serve as a means of transportation for the children. Nick worked the horses hard throughout the week, plowing, hauling hay, and so forth. But on Sunday, he did not work in the fields; thus, the children could go horseback riding with their friends. Anne recalled that if she wanted to visit a friend a couple of miles down the road, she would get on one of the horses and ride through the fields or on the road.[27]

Holiday times were often packed with visitors, such as the Christmas season when not only Cousin LeClair Obee and his family, six strong, arrived from Montana but Aunt Cova and a young nephew showed up late in the afternoon. Somehow, the house played host to sixteen people.[28]

Nick wrote to a friend back in Croton Falls about the Comforts' initial Fourth of July in Norman.

Fireworks had been banned that year, he indicated, because of a recent ordinance, which was welcome news due to the fact that he was broke. At least he could run the ordinance excuse by "the kiddies." Snookey, as Nick called the baby, was not pleased, however, and made her daddy "cough up some candy for her. She is growing like a little piggy, and is as sassy as a Billy Goat."[29]

Family and friends visited often, frequently unannounced and in the dark. Occasionally, Uncle Hugh, after whom the Comfort's oldest son was named, and Aunt Maude Minor would stop over from Altus, bringing other members of their family with them. Hugh's unique signal as they approached could be understood only by Nick. Storytelling by Hugh generally followed.[30]

The Comfort boys had some adventures. In the summer of 1926, twelve-year-old Hugh and eight-year-old Dick took a camping trip. Nick helped them get ready, saddling up horses, packing blanket rolls, and giving them money and food. They headed for virgin prairie west of Norman and decided to stay the night there. The next day they went south, ending up in the village of Washington. By nightfall, the folks back home were becoming concerned. Even Nick was a bit worried. He began walking up Chautauqua, hoping to run into his sons. Eventually, he came upon two tired boys, eager to get home.[31]

Invariably, Nick's days were long. He generally got up at four in the morning and completed a host of chores before walking over to the university. He loved the outdoors and thrived upon working outside. He would milk the cows, feed the chickens, and attend to his garden. At some point, he would call out to Hugh and Dick, "Come on, boys! Let's go!" The Comforts invariably got well-cared-for, hand-me-down cars from somewhat more affluent relatives—cars Nick would then proceed to muck up—and when the car was running he'd come home for lunch. After eating, he'd take a nap. In wintertime, the dining-room table would be cleared off and the tablecloth removed for Nick to stretch out on top of it. That room was toasty, thanks to the big coal furnace nearby. In summertime, he'd stretch out on the couch in the living room, where it was cooler, apricot trees and American elms providing shade.[32]

In the evenings, on the days he had gone into town, the Comfort patriarch returned home and labored until after dark. Late at night—or early in the morning, if he was unable to sleep—Nick would go down to his office to read or write. Because his handwriting was all but illegible, he typed almost everything, using a hunt-and-peck method on his old typewriter. He purchased a Dictaphone, a circular recording device made of hard rubber; after recordings were completed, he shaved the disks and used them to rerecord.[33]

Given his workload, it was fortunate that Nick's temperament was so upbeat and positive. He was not without doubts on occasion as to whether he had taken the right road. At times, he was unable to comprehend why some folks behaved as they did, but generally he expressed a rueful acceptance about even that. "They're wrong and I know they're wrong, but they've got their right to be wrong, if that's what they want to do." More often than not, as Janet remembered, Nick was simply a joy to be around. "He was always kidding and joking and laughing, sort of a bubbly personality." On one occasion, he was driving home from town in an old flatbed truck, with Anne in the passenger seat, and they started joking around until they landed in a "bloody ditch." He told her, "Don't bother telling Mom. She thinks I'm crazy enough anyway!"[34]

Nick simply "loved living, loved people." His own family meant everything to him—the wife he revered as "the loveliest, sweetest thing there was," and the children he adored. He considered himself "the luckiest man in the world to have such a great family." He always seemed to be genuinely interested in what the children were doing. He recognized their failings, but "was the most supportive parent you could imagine"; he gave Janet, for example, an uncommon sense of security. As she indicated, "when you have parents who think you are wonderful, you have this security, you have kind of an invulnerability to other things." Nick, for his part, was always affectionate toward both Esther and the children. He readily hugged them and declared "I love you" and "always made us feel that we were perfectly wonderful." Furthermore, he tried to give them everything they wanted. One Christmas, when Janet wanted a ruby ring, he went out and got one for his "Janie."[35]

Nick was not disinclined to mete out punishment as he saw fit. Occasionally, he would resort to a spanking, which made Janet feel as though she had disappointed him somehow. When Janet pilfered something from a candy store at one point, he made her return to the shop to explain what she had done, which proved to be more difficult than a spanking would have been. Esther, quieter, invariably contributed "something worthwhile" when the occasion arose.[36]

Usually, all it took was a knowing look of disapproval from Nick. As Anne recalled, "he was not a person you disobeyed. When he told you to do something you generally did it." At the same time, she was one who "sassed him a lot," which he seemed to enjoy.[37]

In Norman, after all their travels, Nick Comfort had come home, so to speak, and was intent on carrying out what he saw to be his life's work, helping to spread the word of God to young people in the Southwest. The tenets of the social gospel guided him, particularly his belief in the fatherhood of God and the brotherhood of man. What soon became clear was the abiding love he possessed for his adopted state. Comfort had high hopes for Oklahoma, which, in his eyes, "stood at the last wave of the venturesome, prophetic and revolutionary spirit." Thus, what he considered absurd, in the words of a close friend, was "to live on these broad prairies with a peanut shell theology."[38]

Oklahoma indeed boasted a radical heritage, thanks to a once powerful People's Party, a Socialist Party organization that had earlier been the most vibrant in the nation, the prewar militancy of the syndicalist-driven Working Class Union, and insurgent action by the antidraft Green Corn rebels. Imbued with both egalitarian and democratic beliefs, the Oklahoma Populists, as Worth Robert Miller has noted, posed a threat to Gilded Age laissez-faire capitalism, at least for a spell. Oklahoma Populism of the late nineteenth century was guided by democratic ideals and republican principles that were perceived to be endangered by corporate trends. By the second decade of the twentieth century, the Socialist Party in Oklahoma boasted more members, polled more votes, and had elected more officials than it did in any other state. The potency of grassroots Socialism in Oklahoma, as elsewhere in the region, demonstrated that class struggles were real and growing: people heralding the marketplace were standing in opposition to believers in the cooperative commonwealth. The Green Corn Rebellion of 1917 demonstrated the intensity of the class divide, as militant farmers in Oklahoma railed against conscription and envisioned marching on the nation's capital to bring United States participation in World War I to a halt. The Green Corn rebels, James Green

Has argued, possessed a "hazy philosophy of violence" largely adapted from a vigilante-outlaw tradition and from militant Socialist workers.[39]

All those movements ended ingloriously, due to electoral setbacks, internal schisms, or governmental repression. The decision by leading Oklahoma Populists to fuse with the Democratic Party in backing the unsuccessful 1896 presidential campaign of William Jennings Bryan resulted in a splintering of ranks and a loss of identity. As the United States entered the fray in Europe, the Oklahoma Council of Defense, which watched over the state's participation in the war effort, moved to crush the Socialist Party, as well as the anarcho-syndicalist labor organization, the Industrial Workers of the World, and the Working Class Union, whose members believed in direct action. The demise of these radical forces ensured that "political protest virtually disappeared" by the early 1920s, although one last gasp of activism lay just ahead. They nevertheless left a legacy of radicalism of profound significance for Oklahomans.[40]

Although the war period witnessed the quashing of radical forces in the state, socialists had joined with disgruntled farmers and union members in the Farmer-Labor Reconstruction League to elect John Calloway Walton as governor of Oklahoma in 1922. The administration of "Our Jack" Walton, however, proved to be enormously controversial. Many Oklahomans became upset by his unprecedented use of patronage. Others were displeased with his declaring of martial law, a decision undertaken to weaken the Ku Klux Klan, then a powerful presence in the state. Walton was impeached after less than a year in office. The alliance between socialists, farmers, and laborers was torn apart, as historians James R. Scales and Danney Goble have indicated.[41]

All this was happening shortly before Comfort's return, and soon Nick himself was embroiled in controversy. This was hardly surprising, given Nick's determination to preach the gospel as he saw fit, which agitated fundamentalists no end. The 1920s was a period of considerable strife within the Presbyterian Church and other denominations as fundamentalists and modernists did battle. The *Christian Century*, a liberal publication, declared in 1924 that fundamentalism and modernism comprised distinct religions:

> Two worlds have clashed, the world of tradition and the world of modernism. . . . There is a clash here as profound and as grim as that between Christianity and Confucianism. . . . . The God of the fundamentalist is one God; the God of the modernist is another. . . . . That the issue is clear and that the inherent incompatibility of the two worlds has passed the stage of mutual tolerance is a fact concerning which there hardly seems room for any one to doubt.[42]

Champions of a so-called Princeton Theology like J. Gresham Machen of the Princeton Seminary propounded the need for reading the scriptures literally, and they viewed with disdain the possibility of social or political reform. Machen asserted that liberal theological thought was not merely "a different religion from Christianity but belongs in a totally different class of religions." Militant fundamentalists seemed to oppose modern life in all its guises. Such notions belied everything Comfort believed in.[43]

Southern Presbyterians appeared particularly concerned that heresy and "laxity of teaching" be avoided in religious education. Dr. B. B. Warfield, of Princeton, propounded the tenets of "plenary (inerrant) instruction," which called for "destructive higher criticism" of the Scriptures to be avoided. Diehard fundamentalists sounded the alarm: "We have professors in our Seminaries, eloquent preachers in our pulpits and editors of the religious press insisting that a man's doctrine is of little moment, and that his life is everything. They pose as the prophets of peace and good will, and constantly by implication thank God that they are not as other men are, even these rigid fundamentalists."[44]

A number of Presbyterian ministers in the state wanted Comfort to instruct his students in the Westminster Confession of Faith, a creed developed by seventeenth-century English Puritans that had established doctrinal standards for the church. Devised in the second century of the Protestant Reformation, the Westminster Confession shared the emphasis upon analysis and definition of Calvinistic scholasticism. It also served as "the fullest, most 'scientific,' and exhaustive of all the Calvinistic creeds." The Confession's declaration "Of God's Eternal Decree" and "elect infants," conjuring up the notion that some children were less than blessed, was subjected to criticisms by more optimistically inclined theologians during the late nineteenth century. Sharp divisions occurred within the ranks of the church and charges of heresy were leveled against supporters of revision of the Westminster Confession. The General Assembly of 1903 finally enacted some minor modifications to the original confession.[45]

Comfort refused to rely on the Westminster Confession, determined as he was to deal with members of other denominations as well. No sooner had that issue been put to rest than exhortations came his way to state explicitly that Jesus is God. This, too, Comfort would not do, because he believed that there existed one God only, who was "father of all men, including Jesus."[46]

Nevertheless, Nick was encouraged in the early reception he had been accorded, he reported to J. H. "Daddy" Moses, an old friend from Croton Falls. The people in Norman had been gracious toward Esther and the children and had yet to "run me out of town and that is about all I ask." As Comfort indicated, life was very different in Norman than it had been in the sleepy New York village. "Here I am on a constant jump, from one sort of meeting to another."[47]

Thus, as always, Comfort was involved with all kinds of issues, both grand and small. Throughout his early stay in Norman, he attempted to revitalize the role of the Presbyterian student pastor at the University of Oklahoma. He had dinner virtually every Monday evening with President Bizzell, who appeared "to be a bully good chap (who) I think will do good things for the university." Nick was fortunate indeed that Bizzell was long one of his staunchest supporters, and on many occasions the president acted to deflect criticism from his friend. No doubt this was due to the fact that Bizzell, like Comfort himself, believed that the minister was engaged in "unique work" on the campus. Shortly after arriving in Norman, Nick got involved in the drive to construct a student union building on campus. As he indicated in a letter to a leading Oklahoma City businessman, Comfort hoped to carve out spaces for various denominations in the proposed union building. Each denomination would raise $10,000 or so, entitling it to a ninety-nine-year lease on rooms and general use of the facilities. Such a possibility struck Comfort as ideal, for ministers could carry out their work right in the middle of campus. However, as was so often the case with Comfort's grand schemes, at least those involving money, his effort came to naught. So, too, would his notion of eventually sending fifteen or twenty university students to spread the gospel "in the neglected fields of this state."[48]

Although Comfort's vision might have seemed grandiose, his optimism was not necessarily unwarranted. The 1920s was a period when religious education in public institutions of higher learning was experiencing something of a boom. The University of Michigan had reestablished, albeit for only a short period of time, a school of religion, and the

University of Iowa had just set one up. Like Comfort, the individuals involved with those enterprises saw religion and education as inseparable. They sought to provide religious instruction at tax-supported institutions that would be equal to the finest education offered in private universities. The role that religion played in the development of human culture and experience was to be highlighted, but non-Western religions, too, were studied. The expectation was that the instructors at the schools of religion would be as qualified as the rest of the university faculty. An interdenominational approach was adopted, in keeping with the need to ensure that the constitutional mandate of separation of church and state was followed.[49]

Nevertheless, as so often proved to be the case, both Comfort's plans and his ministerial work came up against the harsh, cold reality of finances. In fact, things appeared desperate early during his stay in Norman. In soliciting funds for the Presbyterian Church's Board of Christian Education, he felt compelled to warn that its continuing deficit might result in his position or that of some other university pastor being terminated altogether.[50]

But large ideas, as well as financial matters, continued to hold Comfort's attention. In corresponding with the Reverend Hugh Anderson Moran, of Cornell University, on January 13, 1925, Comfort shared a number of thoughts that had come to mind in reading his friend's new book. Comfort indicated that he proudly considered himself a Modernist, and yet he had been unable to discover any contemporary perspective of evil that sufficed. He found himself asking, how did one separate man from God? Was the divinity of man something to be attained or inevitable? On the one hand, he was inclined to believe it was something God bequeathed to man, who was, after all, made in God's image. On the other hand, it appeared as though divinity had to be attained. The question that came up, Comfort continued, was whether these two matters could easily coexist. In addition, he was perplexed by talk of the infinite. As a result, he had abandoned all efforts to link "the timeless with time, or locate the spaceless in space, or yoke together the finite and infinite." He had determined instead to focus upon "the finite and . . . time and space with the hopes of working thru them to the more vast regions."[51]

Comfort went on to say that undoubtedly Moran would say to himself that

> I am the most obtuse critter that ever came down the line when I tell you that I am not yet sure as to your exact meaning of mysticism. . . . Now I admit, Moran, that I'm thick, but I must confess to you that I have yet to meet the mystic who has ever been able to make it clear to me as to which of the above conceptions is correct. I suspect that my bias against mysticism as a means of vindicating or propagating Christianity is very largely due to the fact that I do not yet understand just what the mystic means.[52]

Comfort saw Quaker scholar Rufus M. Jones as a representative American mystic, who seemed to suggest that mysticism and science were not a good fit. But Comfort was perplexed by this, failing to understand how in an increasingly scientific age, religion could be presented in a nonempirical manner.[53]

During the same period, Comfort wrote to Dean Shailer Mathews at the University of Chicago, a leading force in the Federal Council of Churches, an organization that preached the social gospel. Comfort reminded Mathews of an occasion when the two had shared a ride from Tehuacana to Corsicana, Texas. In addition to counting jack rabbits, they had talked about a speech Mathews was to give to a dozen ministerial students. The encounter had proved to be cathartic for at least three of them, Comfort reported. Thanks to Mathews, Comfort declared, they had abandoned "a narrow, bigoted, Phariseian [sic] point of view toward the broad regions that are open to fellow laborers with Christ."[54]

In February 1925, he also communicated with Kirby Page, a key figure in the Fellowship for a Christian Social Order and a leading U.S. pacifist, and invited him to speak at the University of Oklahoma campus. Thus, Comfort remained in touch with important social gospel advocates. The Fellowship for a Christian Order had been established in 1921, with Sherwood Eddy, international secretary of the YMCA, A. J. Muste, of the Brookwood Labor School, Reinhold Niebuhr, and Page among its most prominent members. Its members envisioned a transformed social order that would do greater justice to Christian ideals. Comfort indicated that he was involved with the founding of a fellowship group in Norman. Although acknowledging that "I am now out on the edge of things," Nick declared that he would welcome any materials that Page cared to send. Despite his basic optimism, Comfort acknowledged, he frequently felt "rather dry, intellectually, spiritually, and otherwise."[55]

The following month, Comfort wrote to Fenton Rote, a friend from his Croton Falls days. In attempting to convince Rote to choose the ministry over engineering, Comfort declared that chaos was all about because of the dearth of strong, principled men who could help to bring order out of chaos. During their lifetimes, Comfort pointed out, religion was being transformed, thus providing a great opportunity. Admittedly, what he was asking of Rote was not easy, Comfort recognized:

> It cost Christ his life, and from the days of Christ down to the present, there has been a long line of martyrs, and the days of martyrdom are not over. If you are to go out into the world as a real follower of Jesus and

proclaim his truth as God gives you to see it, expect
hardships. Misunderstandings will be inevitable, folks
will criticize you, but all of these things are inevitable
for the one who does things, and especially in religion.
It was clear, Comfort pointed out, that the current
generation of young people was cast apart from the
religious heritage of its ancestors, and had, as yet,
discovered nothing to replace it. This sense of drift,
he noted, resulted from the simple fact that ministers
were not speaking of Jesus as "a natural Savior,"
whose life offered a model for others. Should this state
of affairs continue, apocalyptic developments were
likely within the next half-century.[56]

In a letter to the president of the state chapter of
the American Federation of Labor dated July 16,
1925, Comfort indicated that he had orchestrated
Rotary Club meetings for the past few months. He
invited the labor leader to speak at a noon luncheon
for the organization, whose members, he noted, were
the pillars of the community. They included bankers,
lawyers, physicians, attorneys, and businessmen.
Although many of these individuals were originally
farm boys, they seemed to "have forgotten the block
from which they were hewn." Thus, Comfort was desirous of having them hear "Labor's point of view."[57]

The next day, Comfort was corresponding with
another prospective speaker before the club, John A.
Simpson of the Farmers Union. The Farmers Union,
or the Farmers' Educational and Co-operative Union,
had been founded near Point, Texas, some sixty miles
south of Brookston, by disgruntled farmers who
condemned corporate monopolistic practices. Now
Comfort desired to have the plight of the farmers
discussed "without gloves." He urged Simpson to
come talk with those who considered themselves
"the guardians of the country" and to make his
speech "red hot," "the hotter the talk the more worthwhile." Although few of the members were as radical

as Simpson—such as "your correspondent"—the talk might help to rattle "the complacency of some of our Rotarians." Comfort himself was certain that "the whole Rotary program of 'soft soaping' and 'sugar coating' and condescending is wrong." He closed by offering his services at the behest of the Farmers Union.[58]

A little later, Comfort discussed the membership of the Rotary Club with a friend and mentioned that a group of Norman Rotarians was going to an out-of-state meeting; he, for one, simply was not well-heeled enough "to step with that bunch." The Rotarians were going decked out in white and red, the university colors, and that included white shoes and white canes. "It is all I can do to get clothes enough together to wear on ordinary occasions to say nothing about buying a special suit and about paying railroad fare from here to the Rotary Convention."[59]

In 1925, Comfort began a fifteen-year-long association as chaplain at Central State Hospital in Norman, an institution that housed the mentally ill. On Sunday mornings, he delivered a religious service at the hospital. He viewed the operations of Central State as a means "to bind up broken boughs," people whose "thinking apparatus will not sustain them in the work-a-day world." He recognized that some ended up at the hospital due to heredity or disease, but he saw others who were there because of choices they had made, something he later felt compelled to point out to students at the university. Speaking in both scientific and religious terms, he indicated that this was the result of cause and effect, what the Buddhists termed "Karma or the Law of Deed," and what Christians felt was the byproduct of the fact that "A man reaps just what he sows." The proximity of Central State to the university campus—a mile or so away—suggested to him that men failed to recognize this. The existence of the hospital unfortunately demonstrated education's failings.[60]

During Thanksgiving vacation in 1925, Nick visited churches in a host of rural districts throughout the state. From the time he first returned to Oklahoma, Nick adopted the practice of returning to rural Oklahoma whenever he could. This allowed him to keep abreast of what was going on outside the major cities and towns in Oklahoma and to spread the social gospel as he saw it. He found what he saw in the countryside distressing. The churches in Oklahoma, as in Texas, were so divided that not much religious guidance was being provided. Frequently, he encountered no Sunday School programs and no services being offered to youngsters. Unless changes were forthcoming, he feared, rural Oklahomans would soon lack any knowledge of the Bible.[61]

In February 1926, he attended a Ministerial Alliance meeting and left completely disgusted with the refusal of Protestant preachers to invite a pair of Roman Catholic priests to their meetings. In fact, the ministers informed him "where to head in no uncertain terms" when he made such a suggestion. "Your good Methodist brethren [sic]," Nick informed his friend C. A. "Ick" Shaver in Bellevue, Texas, "tooted his horn about the loudest" and ranted about clashes with Catholics. "If that bird is ever lucky enough to get to Heaven," Comfort wrote, "I hope that a priest is on one side of him and a nun on the other and one of the popes sits just in front of him." Once more, he indicated how discouraging sectarianism was. He could understand about "bootleggers and chicken thieves and professional cusses," but he simply could not fathom why men of God were not "big enough to see over their own back yard fence." Unfortunately, as he saw it, not many were able to.[62]

Speaking before the Council of Christian Religion in Oklahoma City in the fall of 1926, Comfort discussed the hopes that the Department of Religion at the University of Oklahoma would soon be converted into a School of Religion. He believed that such an institution could do far more than any mere university department to bring the various denominations throughout the state together to provide spiritual grounding for the students at OU. In early December, he wrote to Ick Shaver in Texas and reported that he had just been named acting head of the Department of Religion. This meant additional responsibilities, but Comfort indicated it was the type of work he thrived on. "I am supremely happy. I would be willing to live a million years at about the same rate."[63] With the Christmas season approaching, he reflected upon the opportunities that lay in store for good Christians. Great opportunities abounded, Nick informed Shaver, to raise children to become "about ten times better than we are." That would make life worthwhile.[64]

CHAPTER FOUR

THE OKLAHOMA SCHOOL OF RELIGION

In the small university town of Norman, Comfort sought to do whatever he could to sustain the best of American traditions and the precepts of Jesus. In the fall of 1926, when he became intimately involved with the founding of the Oklahoma School of Religion, it brought the fulfillment of his lifetime dream closer to fruition. He envisioned the School of Religion, a private religious institution that was indirectly affiliated with the University of Oklahoma, as a means to affording the young people of the region the kind of religious instruction that seemed so desperately lacking.

Comfort had chosen as his life's work to be immersed in the teaching ministry, through which he hoped to spread the gospel as he saw it. He now entered two decades of involvement with the Oklahoma School of Religion, which served as the source of both his greatest professional successes and his largest failures. That involvement would make Comfort a noteworthy figure in the annals of Oklahoma history, a leading Southwestern proponent of the social gospel, and an individual around whom controversy flowed freely.[1]

This was the period when the religious-education movement was more influential than ever before. As

Shailer Mathews, of the University of Chicago, recognized, it seemed to be attracting the kinds of bright, idealistic young people that sociology had appealed to a generation earlier. These religious activists provided impetus for the religious centers that were being established in many university communities around the country.[2] Largely through the devoted efforts of Nick Comfort and a small circle of friends, the Oklahoma School of Religion appealed to such dedicated young men and women.

In the spring semester 1927, Comfort relinquished his teaching load at the university to devote his time to establishing the School of Religion. As he noted in a letter to a minister in Duncan, he saw the School of Religion as helping to ensure the spiritual uplift of students of various denominations. He would never permit, he asserted, "theological discussions to cast a shadow between the warm sunlight of Jesus' love and the crying need of these hundreds of students for whom he lived and died." Consequently, he had determined that the School of Religion was to avoid theological issues.[3]

Now, more than ever, Comfort seemed to be in his element. He was fortunate because many Presbyterians in the Norman church were viewed as "sanely liberals," a good deal more progressive than "the average Princetonian." He lightly characterized himself as "the most harum-scarum rogue of the lot." But most significantly, he viewed his work in Oklahoma as of the utmost importance. "This is a great field," he believed, "the most fascinating field I know of." He recognized that Norman was easily the most congenial place in the state for someone like himself. With the university at hand, he was continually in contact with young, alive souls, who were eager to learn. This appealed to him more than anything he had yet experienced. He was thrilled by the eclectic views that filtered through the university campus.

When days went poorly, he sometimes felt "like committing suicide," but on other occasions he was certain that Heaven had "shed a peculiar bit of beneficence upon our community."[4]

At long last, Nick believed he had found a home for himself, his educational ministry, and his family. After his lengthy odysseys, he looked upon Norman as a city where he would like to dig deep roots. Chance or circumstances might force him to depart at some point, but he could not imagine wishing that to happen. Norman seemed to him to be the best place to raise children. Moreover, "the moral tone is far above the average town." The university provided the intellectual sustenance to encourage young people to obtain an education.[5]

The founding of the Oklahoma School of Religion gave Nick hope that he could provide the young people of the Southwest with the kind of religious instruction that they presently were without. The School of Religion originated in the early work of Rabbi Joseph Blatt, who in 1920 offered a course on the history of the Hebrews for the Department of History. The following year, Mary DeBardeleben, of the Women's Department of the Board of Home Missions of the Methodist Episcopal Church, South, was hired as the first full-time instructor of religion at the University of Oklahoma. That same year, M. J. Neuberg was also chosen to teach religion courses at the university, but departed after one academic year. In 1921, the Department of Religious Education was established in the School of Education, where it remained until 1926, when it was transferred to the College of Arts and Sciences. Meanwhile, H. C. Munro, of the Disciples of Christ, taught during 1922–23 and the following academic year B. N. Lovgren, an Episcopalian, and T. H. Aszman, the Presbyterian minister who hired Nick Comfort, gave courses. Comfort came on board in 1924, as did, the next year, S. Y. Allgood, of the Methodist Episcopal Church, South. Allgood taught from 1925 to 1927. Rabbi Blatt, of the Reformed Jewish Congregations, returned to offer classes during the 1926–27 academic year.[6]

As early as 1926, it was recognized by Comfort and other members of the teaching faculty that the catch-as-catch-can policy of offering religious courses in classes around the university had to be modified. Consequently, plans were drawn up for the establishment of the Oklahoma School of Religion. On February 25, 1927, the initial meeting of a self-perpetuating board of trustees took place. The charter members included the Reverend John A. Rice, the Reverend F. M. Sheldon, Dean Homer L. Dodge, of the Graduate School, and the university's president, W. B. Bizzell, and the Reverend C. C. Weith. Dodge was elected president of the board; Bizzell was vice president, Sheldon secretary, and Comfort director. Eventually, a twenty-one person board came into being, with no more than four members to be drawn from any one denomination. With the passage of time, ten religious groups were represented on the board: Roman Catholic; Church of Christ; Congregational; Episcopal; Jewish; Methodist Episcopal; Methodist Episcopal, South; Presbyterian, U.S.A.; Southern Baptist; and Unitarian.[7]

The faculty was comprised of DeBardeleben, Blatt, Helen Ruth Holbrook from the YWCA, Jesse R. Caffyn, of the Oklahoma Conference of the Methodist Episcopal Church, James W. Workman, of the Oklahoma Conferences of the Methodist Episcopal Church, South, and Comfort. The initial course offerings included introductory classes on the Old Testament and the New Testament and a dozen others: the Social Teachings of Jesus and the Prophets, the Development of Religion, the History of Early Christianity, the Life and Teachings of Jesus and Paul, the History of the Church in the United States, the History of the Jews, the Psychology of Religion, the History of Religious Education, Hymnology, Religious Drama, Teaching the Bible through Drama, and a course on storytelling in religious education. The first semester, Comfort was scheduled to teach the Development of Religion and the Psychology of Religion; later, he taught the Life of Jesus, Comparative Religion, and the Religious Approach to Modern Problems for the Department of Philosophy at the university. The school was to have six departments: Old Testament, New Testament, History, Philosophy, Religious Education, and Music.[8]

The training Nick had received at the McCormick Theological Seminary, the University of Chicago, and Union Theological was clearly apparent in the quality and type of instruction he provided for students of the Oklahoma School of Religion. Also evident was the empirical approach he had acquired from his own studies of the social and natural sciences. By all accounts, he was a provocative instructor who pushed his students to think and to challenge what was being imparted to them, whether in his classroom or that of others. He never tried to convey the notion that he alone possessed the final answer; he did not want students answering like parrots.[9]

The architects behind the establishment of the School of Religion, and especially Comfort, who penned its constitution, believed that such an institution was needed to fill a void increasingly apparent in higher education in Oklahoma. They appreciated the fact that higher education in Oklahoma had passed more and more into the hands of the state: twice the number of students attended the University of Oklahoma as were enrolled in all the denominational colleges. With fewer students attending religious institutions, they reasoned, the School of Religion, provided it avoided sectarianism, could help to shape "the finest type of manhood and womanhood."[10]

The founders of the School of Religion were determined that it remain free from sectarianism, as required under both state and federal constitutional mandates. Religious instruction must discard "its sectarian swaddling clothes" to confront the opportunities and responsibilities before it. That necessitated the devising of "new means of education," such as that afforded by the School of Religion. They expressed their conviction that some good existed in every branch of religion and declared an absolute impartiality regarding different denominations. Rather than any particular denominational dogma, they—and particularly the director—were guided by faith in the fatherhood of God and the brotherhood of man; in other words, by the social gospel, and by the need to put its tenets into practice. Comfort, even more than the other founders, foresaw the School of Religion as reflecting the religious pluralism of the broader U.S. culture. He believed that one of the greatest tragedies of the modern era was the "provincial religious horizon" under which so many individuals operated.[11]

In a note to John Nevin Sayre, Comfort spoke of the efforts to establish the School of Religion. He enclosed a copy of the constitution and asserted that the people he respected seemed to believe "that in a very real way we have scored a signal victory and that the best thing to do now is merely to let the pot boil." That was the approach Comfort was himself following; thus, he was simply waiting "for the right time to come. When that moment arrives I shall strike with all my might in exactly the place where it seems to me striking will do most good."[12]

In November 1927, President Bizzell, Dean Dodge, and Director Comfort obtained a $2,000 loan on a personal note, taken out to cover the first payment on twenty-eight lots of land, adjacent to the western reaches of the university campus. Comfort was particularly fortunate that Bizzell was a good friend and strong supporter of the School of Religion. An eight-room, white-frame residence, stationed on two of the lots, on Elm Avenue, would be remodeled into the building that came to serve as home base for the School of Religion. In December, Claude L. Freeland and Dave Schonwald each put up $1,000 for the down payment on the other twenty-six lots. The total price for the land was $48,500, at annual installments of $8,000.[13]

That month, Comfort wrote to Ick Shaver regarding the school. He indicated how swamped he was in attempting to get the institution off the ground and spoke of plans to obtain a million-dollar endowment and to erect a million-dollar building. Once more, he declared unequivocally, "I am now in my life's work." If this enterprise succeeded, he would feel that he had accomplished "something that is worthy of any man." If it failed, he nevertheless would have been part of "a mighty good cause." At the very least, "I am giving everything I can to this undertaking."[14]

The location of the School of Religion on Elm, near the center of the university campus in an area where most faculty and students lived and where a residential boom appeared to be taking place, was uniquely propitious.[15] The relationship to the University of Oklahoma, directly adjacent to the new School of Religion building and the institution from which it sprang, was to be symbiotic. The secular and the religious were to be melded, even as the constitutional injunction of separation of church and state was to be rigidly adhered to. On February 13, 1928, the two institutions were affiliated by joint action of the school's trustees and the regents of the university. The School of Religion's facilities were to be adjacent to but separate from the larger campus and the courses it offered would continue to receive full university credit. Its instructors were expected to have academic training at least equivalent to that of the university faculty and to avoid denominational bias. The school's open-door policy regarding the state's various denominations asked them only "to agree to differ." This, the charter of the School of Religion deemed to be in keeping with the American tradition of freedom of religion. The school's Magna Carta was to be the first amendment to the United States Constitution and the first two articles of the state constitution, which called for freedom of speech and the press and the right to assemble peaceably.[16]

In the spring of 1928, the School of Religion began to offer courses on its four-and-a-half acre plot of land already developed. The mission of the school, its founders believed, involved "blazing a spiritual trail in Oklahoma." Three watchwords—inspiration, instruction, and cooperation—were viewed as the guiding principles for the school. These touchstones were said to have been "used by man in his climb from the misty vales of uncertainty to the mountain peaks of his greatest accomplishment." Inspiration had enabled man to get through the darkest moments, to prepare for the most difficult task, and to be ready for the noblest of endeavors. Instruction had allowed each succeeding generation to pass on its greatest accomplishments and noblest ideals. Cooperation had made it possible for man to conquer his largest foes, both within and without.[17]

Comfort had spent a lot of time attending conferences or corresponding with other directors of religious programs at state-sponsored institutions of higher learning. As he noted in his weekly radio program on WNAD, he had attempted to devise the ideal scenario whereby a public university and a private religious institution could mutually and beneficially coexist. His radio spot, which helped Comfort to publicize the operations of the School of Religion, served as another venue through which he could convey the social gospel message so dear to his heart. For a time, he was thus a radio preacher, in keeping with the times when a modernist minister like Harry Emerson Fosdick dominated the airwaves, to the displeasure of fundamentalists.[18]

On April 23, 1928, he informed his audience about the purposes and the design of the School of Religion. Its backers, he declared, believed that religion was a necessary component in the life of every individual and nation. They presumed that for people to become religious required religious instruction. To that end, they considered the School of Religion to be providing "an essential element in our personal, community, state, and national life," which could not be delivered by the University of Oklahoma because of its status as a public institution. The sponsors of the School of Religion also saw its mission to involve the training of teachers for Sunday schools, superintendents of religious schools, and other church officers. Ultimately, the trustees of the School of Religion and its director desired that it would "inspire and foster creative, zealous, religious living." They sought to establish a environment where "one naturally desires to live religiously."[19]

As indicated by a detailed set of architectural plans drawn up by Harold Gimeno, of Norman, Comfort hoped that the School of Religion would permit the University of Oklahoma to stand with the likes of Harvard, Yale, Princeton, and Chicago in providing the finest religious instruction in American higher education. A $300,000 chapel was intended to serve as "the heart of the campus." With its simple yet dignified appearance, the chapel was to offer a forum for discussion of vital issues of the present and past and to help bring about "a consciousness of the

Eternal." A $250,000 administration building was to house the offices of school officials and denominational representatives, as well as classrooms, a kitchenette, a small assembly hall, and a substantial lounge area. A proposed $100,000 library would hold the finest religious works and the latest equipment. A $150,000 conference hall would contain a dining hall, private guest rooms, conference rooms, and two dormitories, one for men and the other for women. Thus, as Comfort put it, the receipt of $1 million for the School of Religion would enable him to consider himself ideally situated.[20]

Given the apparently robust nature of Oklahoma's economy, Comfort's optimism did not appear misplaced. Indeed, since 1910, the population of the state had increased by nearly 50 percent. A fair amount of agricultural prosperity followed, which along with the heavy hand of governmental operatives, helped to blunt the radical movements that had once thrived in Oklahoma. A boom induced by oil exploration promised, in the eyes of many, unlimited economic growth. By 1929, Oklahoma would be surpassed only by Pennsylvania in mineral production, mostly oil and gas. Oklahoma crude eventually produced 30 percent of the nation's oil output. Petroleum production reached 277 million barrels a year, connected by 17,000 miles of pipeline.[21]

With the air rife with talk of an economic bonanza, Comfort naturally hoped that the School of Religion would benefit financially. That might well result, Comfort hoped, because of the Oklahoma School of Religion's distinctive interdenominational quality. The School of Religion in Ann Arbor was affiliated with the University of Michigan but had no church connection. The School of Religion in Iowa City was attached to the University of Iowa, with members of various faiths, along with university representatives, comprising the Board of Control. The School of

Religion in Columbia, independent from the University of Missouri, had been established by the Christian Church denomination. Other churches had been invited to cooperate. In Urbana-Champaign, autonomous denominational foundations had been set up around the University of Illinois.[22]

The schools of religion and the religious centers were all intended to provide religious fellowship. Through the nineteenth century, students themselves had bound together in "voluntary associations," united more by "personal, moral, and religious earnestness," than theological beliefs. The students aspired to attain a "wholeness" and "holiness," and sought to have a leavening influence on their campuses. These fellowships, attempting to duplicate the YMCA or the YWCA, at least in part, tended to be nonsectarian and nonclerical. By 1900, clergymen became more actively engaged at a number of universities, and a professionalization of the religious fellowships began to take place, duplicating a phenomenon occurring in other aspects of American life, especially those relating to higher education. Starting in the early 1920s, efforts to usher in interdenominational cooperation and to counter religious prejudices unfolded. In 1924, the Federal Council of the Churches of Christ in America established the Committee on Good Will between Jews and Christians.[23]

The purpose of religious centers had undergone changes. The early societies emphasized "personal piety, missionary recruitment, and service." Later groups attempted to provide recreation and student services, but also to inculcate a sense of civic responsibility. Ultimately, some societies became concerned about theological matters. Historian Glenn Olds perceptively pointed out that religious centers, notwithstanding their differences, had something in common. He noted that *religion,* from the Latin *relegere,* means "to bind together," and that *university,* from the Latin *unus* and *versum,* means "to turn into one." In intent, he said, both terms "bear witness to man's deep need to unify his life and thought around some ultimate principle, object of loyalty, or subject of faith."[24]

The dismissal of his friend Dr. John A. Rice from his ministerial post with the McFarlin Church in November 1928 further convinced Comfort, who had been elected director back in February, of the need for an institution like the School of Religion. In a letter to Rice, he wondered how much time would pass before the Southern Methodist Church was "to get face with the intelligence of this community." The Southern Methodist Church was the church instrumental in the firing of English professor Vernon L. Parrington back in 1908; Parrington had moved on to the University of Washington, where he wrote *Main Currents in American Thought.* Years later, Parrington, having won the Pulitzer Prize for his epic work, was restored to the good graces of the University of Oklahoma when the north oval was named after him.[25]

Comfort personally had viewed Rice's hiring "as the greatest religious event" in Norman since he had arrived in town. Rice's coming, Comfort wrote, enabled broad-minded folk to rejoice. Some felt that finally the McFarlin Church had acquired a soul. Now, "a few pin-headed, thick skinned, bull necked, spiritually blind, shallow brained, miserly ingrates" had acted not merely to endanger their own salvation but to insult the very individual who was making all of that possible. It was almost enough, Comfort continued, to make "me wish that I could forget my Christianity for a short while and turn caveman until vengeance is reeked." All of this had enabled him to comprehend in a manner he had not previously been able to "why Jesus wept when in his Triumphal Entry, he looked over Jerusalem, that was so cursed with blind religious leadership." The "tragedy" involving the McFarlin Church, Comfort asserted, was yet "one more pathetic cry" for the School of Religion, which could help students overcome "blind religious" dogma. Comfort continued to believe, nevertheless, that "there is an eternal cry for light that cannot be hushed by the crooning of bigoted ecclesiasticism. There is an idealism which does and will respond to the heroic call of the man of Galilee."[26]

Despite his concerns over the firing of Rice, Comfort was undoubtedly delighted with the apparent end, by the close of 1928, of a long-standing theological controversy within one of the branches of the Presbyterian Church. Only a short while earlier, the fundamentalist-modernist divide had been quite pronounced, in both the Presbyterian Church in the U.S.A. (the northern church) and the Presbyterian Church in the U.S. (the southern church). Comfort, Southwestern born and bred and concerned about the disputes, was of course educated not only in the region but also in the great metropolitan centers of Chicago and New York City. Concern about the direction the Northern Presbyterian church would take if fundamentalists prevailed in the clash, and worry that splintering of the denomination might follow, resulted in the acceptance of "more moderate, mediating policies."[27]

In the southern branch of the church, by 1928 two conflicts—one regarding evolution and the other concerning modernism in foreign missions—were largely resolved. A declaration was made that no ruling by an assembly could prevail over "the Constitutional Doctrinal basis of our Church." More troubling to Comfort was the decision by Southern Presbyterians in 1929 to instruct their representatives to "bear faithful testimony" to their ideals and advise against involvement in "matters of civil and political nature." The intention was to bring about a severance from the Federal Council of Churches within two years.[28]

During the winter of 1928–29, Nick had to contend with another kind of crisis: a very severe bout of the flu that afflicted his whole family. The Comforts became so ill that members of the Presbyterian church in Norman went out to help at 2000 Chautauqua. Nick suffered a sinus infection and then a mastoid infection—serious indeed in those days before antibiotics. He was taken to a hospital in Oklahoma City and, fearing his death might be impending, he called sixteen-year-old Janet to his hospital room to discuss what to do were he to die. Nick avoided having an operation by keeping his head packed in ice. It was a month before he recovered.[29]

Comfort received a sympathetic letter from Archibald McClure, his old friend who was by then minister of the First Presbyterian Church in South Bend, Indiana. McClure—who had just received word of Nick's illness—declared that although they had not seen one another for some time, he thought of him often and fondly. "I have always honored you for your intellectual courage and your fine, true Christian spirit." McClure indicated his appreciation for "the inspiration of your attitude and your real purpose of service." He was pleased that Comfort had found a place where he could assist college students "to see the greatness of a Christian way of life." He hoped that his friend would be highly influential.[30]

Eight-year-old Elizabeth was hardest hit by the virus. Flu developed into double pneumonia and emphysema and she had to have a piece of a rib removed to facilitate drainage. Confined to bed for nine weeks, she was forced to miss an entire year of school. Janet, who fell three weeks behind in her classes at the university, soon caught up. An excellent student, she carried notes to her professors, explaining why she had been out of class and had to miss her finals. One instructor told her that when she returned, "Your A will be waiting for you!"[31]

By late March, the family had all but recovered physically. Even Elizabeth was now able to get up for two hours or so and move about the house. Her side was still being drained, however, and concern remained for a while about her condition. The illnesses had hit the Comforts hard, precisely where they could least afford it, in the pocketbook. Nick reasoned that it would take a full year to pay off the bills as they became due, but the assistance afforded by the community meant so much. "If I live a thousand years I will be unable to pay the debt of gratitude I owe to this community." One such individual was Dr. W. T. Mayfield, of Norman, who sent the Comforts a bill for the "absurdly small amount" of $50. Nick wrote back to Mayfield, declaring his determination to pay more when the family was in better shape financially.[32]

Soon, Comfort was back that spring attempting to raise funds for the School of Religion, but having difficulty doing so. He had hoped, by this point, to have garnered $200,000 in pledges, but the prospects, he acknowledged, seemed slim at best. Although Comfort was certain that there was a great deal of money in the state, a number of the individuals he had been counting on had come upon hard times themselves. He continued to believe that the School of Religion boasted "an ideal situation" that was in need only of financing. Due to financial constraints, however, it was not possible to match opportunities with accomplishments. Such, Comfort recognized, was the lot of virtually all religious undertakings.[33]

In reality, the prosperity that Oklahoma had experienced during the 1920s, and upon which Comfort so counted, had proved to be remarkably deceptive, for the state as for the nation as a whole. Gluts in wheat and cotton production occurred, helping to drive prices downward. Poor land-management in certain counties led to soil erosion so thorough that many crops could no longer be cultivated. In fact, more than 80 percent of the sixteen million acres under cultivation in 1930 had suffered severe erosion. Many farmers were mired in debt, saddled with mortgages, and trapped by high-interest, short-term loans. More than three out of every five Oklahomans working on farms were tenants, stuck with even higher interest rates than their landowners.[34]

Other sectors of the Oklahoma economy were in an equally precarious predicament. The petroleum industry was severely afflicted by overproduction, which in turn led to enormous waste, lowered prices, quick exhaustion of oil fields, and economic slides in the areas where the big rigs had been planted. Moreover, even in the most profitable times, the capital-intensive oil industry gave work to only some 20,000 workers across the state. The coal-mining industry was already going bust during the 1920s, troubled by labor unrest, poor management, and inadequate technology. Consequently, while more than 8,000 workers toiled in Oklahoma coal mines in 1920, a mere 5,000 were at work a decade later.[35]

By late July 1929, months before the New York Stock Exchange plunged precipitously downward, Comfort complained to Ick Shaver about the deteriorating financial condition of the School of Religion. All was working out as planned, he suggested, but the financial status of the institution seemed to worsen continually. He remained optimistic that things would aright themselves, but for the present felt discouraged.[36] Within two weeks, however, Nick's mood was more characteristically upbeat, as he wrote to another old friend, Martha M. Patten, in New Holland, North Carolina. In discussing his work as director of the School of Religion, he declared it to be "as nearly ideal as one could imagine. There is absolutely no limit to the possibilities for constructive righteousness. We have settled down for a life task."[37]

By the end of the year, Comfort was once more expressing grave concerns about the financial situation of the School of Religion. In corresponding with the Reverend William L. Young, of Philadelphia, Pennsylvania, Nick asserted that an absence of financial support was of greatest concern. He indicated that both the local Presbyterian church and the School of Religion—the two institutions he was working through—were greatly handicapped in that regard. In a typically modest, self-deprecating manner, Comfort explained that "your humble servant is the greatest difficulty. I am a firm believer in the idea that money will naturally accumulate around sufficient personality. I have nobody to blame but myself concerning the financial situation of the School of Religion. To date I have not been big enough to put it over." This was unfortunate, Comfort suggested, because there existed in Norman an unbounded opportunity to do God's work. Other than the shortage of money, the conditions were ideal. The association between the School of Religion and the University of Oklahoma was about all that could be hoped for. The headquartering of the school on land adjacent to the campus was also advantageous, he wrote. The administration of the university was as supportive as anywhere in the nation.[38]

Comfort believed that the School of Religion could be adequately funded. "I am staking my life on it." Little helping matters was the fact that "the local church situation . . . is becoming quite desperate. We are slowly but surely losing ground." Here, Comfort reasoned, the greatest lack involved both personality and vision. The local Presbyterian church, unlike the School of Religion, possessed sufficient funds to do a great deal more than was being accomplished at present. The church also boasted among its parishioners and friends many of Norman's most influential sorts. What was hindering the church was a "spiritual listlessness which is quite demoralizing."[39] As Young also worked within a university community, he could well appreciate, Comfort declared, how difficult it was to discuss the local church situation. Consequently, "my policy has been, and I think shall continue to be, hands off and mouth shut as much as possible." Failure to follow such advice invariably came back to haunt him.[40]

Despite the present difficulties, however, Comfort said he had never met finer people than those at First Presbyterian in Norman. Nor had he before received the kind of cooperation that he did from this church. What was needed was church leadership equal to appreciating "the spiritual needs of university people" and possessing a vision adequate to those needs.[41]

Believing that a firmer financial base simply had to be established for the School of Religion, Comfort and other supporters of the institution began to reach out more and more to well-heeled individuals of whatever political persuasion. On January 15, 1930, the university president, Bizzell, wrote to Lew H. Wentz, a Ponca City oil man, head of the Republican Party in Oklahoma City and bitter antagonist of Governor William "Alfalfa Bill" Murray. Wentz had just mailed the School of Religion a check that enabled its board of trustees to meet a mortgage payment. In his letter of appreciation, Bizzell reported that three factors had operated against the school receiving the financial backing it required. The first involved the novelty of the enterprise, something Bizzell believed would be overcome; after all, he said, he had never encountered anyone in big business who did not consider the school to be "a wonderful idea" that should be given every opportunity to succeed. The second was related to the failure of certain religious denominations to have signed on; this, Bizzell suggested, was the result of the "very conservative" nature of some religious groups. Such groups, he noted, were reluctant to join forces with other denominations or to act in a cooperative spirit, even regarding "the most worthy enterprises." The third resulted from the stock-market crash, which had created a mind-set that made fund-raising still more difficult. When the economy righted itself, Bizzell hoped that this problem would be overcome. That, in turn, would ensure that any investment Wentz made in the School of Religion would be protected.[42]

On February 20, Comfort wrote to A. W. Packard in New York City asking him to contact John D. Rockefeller Jr. about possible funding for the school. Comfort indicated that he had been informed by a number of well-placed individuals that Rockefeller was clearly interested in "what we are trying to do in a religious way at the University of Oklahoma." The trustees of the School of Religion still had to come up with three remaining annual payments of $8,000. Comfort also sought assistance from Raymond S. Rubinow, of the Julius Rosenwald Fund in Chicago. He hoped to meet with Rubinow when he visited Chicago in June. Comfort suggested that a $100,000 pledge from the Rosenwald Fund, contingent upon the School of Religion obtaining the same amount of funds, would surely succeed within three months. "Such a conditional gift from your fund would send a thrill of enthusiasm through this state which would initiate a spiritual rejuvenation that would shake us loose from our sectarianism and give religion in its own right an opportunity to function."[43]

In an effort to drum up greater support, Comfort wrote an article entitled "The School of Religion: A

New Branch of University Training," which appeared in the March 1930 issue of *Sooner Magazine.* A full-page picture of the proposed chapel was included.

Comfort wrote that "all highly civilized peoples" believed character to be shaped by education and a religious perspective, and in his own country "a well rounded culture" cried out for religious training. This was precisely what the School of Religion was striving to provide for the students of the University of Oklahoma. The School of Religion sought to further religious development at the university. It did so by affording all students the opportunity to obtain religious instruction alongside their general academic studies. For those who viewed religion as their life's work, programs and course offerings provided training in their chosen field. The School of Religion allowed denominational groups to link up with university students. Following the eventual erection of a chapel, such as those found at Princeton University and the University of Chicago, Comfort wrote, a forum would be in place for fostering religious leadership and for spearheading "a constructive idealism" for the entire campus.[44]

Two million dollars, Comfort noted, were required to adequately fund the School of Religion, half for construction costs and the other half for the operation of the institution. It was to the people of Oklahoma that the trustees were turning. No major drive was to be undertaken; rather, the plan was to inform Oklahomans of the good work of the school, with the belief that financial support would then be forthcoming. Should Oklahomans respond to the challenge, Comfort concluded, "then Oklahoma will have taken a long stride toward becoming the standard-bearer of the nation in the cooperation of church and state in building the finest type of manhood and womanhood."[45]

In May, J. F. Owens, vice president and general manager of the Oklahoma Gas and Electric Company in Oklahoma City, became an important addition to the school's board of trustees. In a letter to Comfort dated May 12, Owens reminded him that he was extremely busy and would not be able to attend many meetings. Owens also wrote to L. E. Phillips, of the Phillips Petroleum Company in Bartlesville, soliciting support for the school. Owens noted that a movement with great potential had been initiated at the University of Oklahoma. He went on to say that radicalism was having great impact upon the state's institutions of higher learning. Such radicalism, he noted, was rooted "in the various schools of materialistic thought" thriving throughout the country. What those schools envisioned, he declared, was the obliteration of American individualism and its replacement by socialism. To pull this off, he wrote, those who operated such institutions felt compelled to attack all religions.[46]

Owens suggested that for both moral and practical reasons, "men of large property interests" should be concerned about all of this and about the fact that state laws made it difficult to offer religious instruction in public schools. Fortunately, he indicated, the Oklahoma School of Religion was acting to fill the void. Well-regarded individuals served on its board, he pointed out, and the school itself had adopted a nonsectarian, nondenominational approach.[47]

Now a member of the board himself, Owens urged Phillips, too, to join. He admitted having declined such an offer initially, but reported that he had changed his mind after discovering how unique "the movement" was among colleges in the United States.[48]

Perhaps emboldened by support such as Owens's—even though it came from someone with a political stance divergent from his own—Comfort decided in the late spring of 1930 to become full-time director of the school—a job he considered to be "one of the biggest . . . in Oklahoma." For Comfort, that entailed relinquishment of his post as student pastor for Presbyterian students at the university. C. E. Sharpe suggested as Comfort's replacement the Reverend G. K. Rogers, of Heights Presbyterian Church in Houston, Texas. In a letter to Rogers, Comfort listed the requirements as he saw them. Most importantly, he said, whoever would be appointed needed to possess "some underlying moral convictions that nothing on God's earth can shake." Next, he required a broad religious perspective, not one inclined to "tom-tit religion." Third, he must be a tireless worker, but no drone, especially in the spiritual realm. Fourth, he should have "a good store of horse sense." Fifth, he needed formal training at the graduate level. Finally, he should possess an unlimited store of optimism. Comfort added a disclaimer, which acknowledged that he for one would not be capable of fulfilling all these requisites. Whether he recognized it or not, his list of requirements could best be met by someone such as himself.[49]

As matters turned out, Rogers was not offered the job. Following Comfort's official delivery of his resignation as Presbyterian pastor on August 2, 1930, R. B. Henry was hired to replace him.[50]

As full-time director, Comfort had added responsibilities. He now found himself more involved than ever in the everyday workings of the institution, doing still more in the way of fund-raising and trying to convince prominent individuals to stand with the school. One such person he attempted to convince to join the board was Judge H. Standeven, of Tulsa. In a rather elaborate letter, Comfort evidently felt compelled to spell out the mission of the School of Religion. Joining the board placed no obligations on a board member's own church: the school did not seek support from churches directly. Those involved with the school sought to encourage "the best thinking and the most wholesome living" characteristic of religious groups throughout the state. Significantly, the school had no desire "to reduce the creeds of the various groups to a least common denominator"; rather, it wished only to give each religious organization an opportunity to express its viewpoint. It was guided by a belief in "a friendly agreement to differ, to live and let live, and in so far as compatible, help live."[51]

Comfort went on to say that the guiding principle behind the School of Religion was a belief "that truth adequately presented will prevail and that it is the task of all lovers of truth to adequately present it." It relied wholly upon the appeal of its ideals, and possessed "confidence in their therapeutic power over human frailties." Its officials saw education as the means to bring about human advancement. They recognized that the task they faced was a daunting one, but one worthy of the sharpest and most courageous thought. They believed their endeavor to be vitally important for "the very nature of man necessitates religion." They were fortunate indeed, wrote Comfort, to have the enthusiastic support of the administration at the University of Oklahoma.[52]

Unfortunately for both Comfort and the School of Religion, the Great Depression was then wending its way through Oklahoma and the nation. Various communities in the state had experienced an economic collapse even before talk of a depression was heard nationwide, and the economic condition of the state continued to worsen. It was hardly an auspicious time to bring to fruition the kinds of plans Nick Comfort had for the Oklahoma School of Religion. In fact, in the period just ahead, he was going to be waging a never-ending battle simply to keep his own family and the School of Religion afloat.

CHAPTER FIVE

DUST BOWL OKLAHOMA

As Comfort devoted still more of his considerable store of energy and optimism to charting the course for the Oklahoma School of Religion, the Great Depression continued to sweep over the Sooner State. Oklahoma was among the states hardest hit, and the image of suffering Okies in the midst of boll weevils, tumbleweeds, and economic deprivation remains a searing and controversial one even today. Woody Guthrie's sad songs of drought and human pathos and John Steinbeck's anguished tale of dispossessed sharecroppers and tenant farmers, while resonating in American popular culture, infuriated those who believed that the State of Oklahoma was left with dust on its face. It is a matter of fact that the economic calamity that befell the nation starting in late 1929 was a wrenching experience for many Oklahomans, including Nick Comfort.[1]

As W. David Baird and Danney Goble have acknowledged, "Oklahomans could claim to have been hit by depression earlier and harder than the rest of America." During the 1930s, the state suffered a migratory outflow of 60,000 people, with many departing after 1935. With the demise of cotton tenancy, many sharecroppers and owners of small farms paid the price. New Deal programs seemed only to exacerbate the state's economic plight, with landowners eagerly obtaining federal largesse to purchase new equipment or plow crops under, meanwhile pushing tenants off their land. Bank failures abounded in Oklahoma, and factory production was sharply curtailed with a corresponding reduction in employment. The result was a plummeting of the already low level of per capita income in the state. As Douglas Hale indicates, Oklahoma's per capita income stood at two-thirds of the national average in 1929; within three years, at $216, it had receded to barely more than one-half the national average. Forced sales of farms went up fourfold from 1929 to 1933. By the latter year, 42 percent of workers in the state were unemployed.[2]

By 1933, Communist-dominated "unemployed councils" kicked off large and sometimes violent demonstrations in Oklahoma City. In Henryetta, a food riot broke out. The Communists organized some eighty locals, comprised of 30,000 unemployed workers, but the unemployed councils soon were broken up by legal attacks on their leaders. Many of the discontented laborers and farmers then linked up with the Veterans of Industry, which had been established by Ira Finley, a Socialist and one-time head of the State Federation of Labor. Less revolutionary in nature, the Veterans of Industry served as "an effective pressure group for the propertyless" during the Great Depression. It reached a membership of 40,000, including many blacks who had set up their own locals in Muskogee and eastern Oklahoma. Many others supported the Veterans' campaign to boycott the products of those who paid rural workers "slave wages" and to back strikers through pickets and the condemnation of strikebreaking.[3]

Thus, the depressed economic conditions resulted in a resurgence of radicalism in Oklahoma. As James Green has aptly put it, a type of "Indian summer" came over the state, allowing the old Socialists who eagerly awaited each issue of Oscar Ameringer's newspapers (first the *Oklahoma Weekly Leader* and then the *American Guardian*) to dream once more of the cooperative commonwealth. As matters turned out, few of the "pioneer Socialist agitators" remained in Oklahoma and the radical revival first emerged in the Arkansas Delta. Younger activists, determining that the Socialist Party of Norman Thomas was moribund, established the Southern Tenant Farmers Union (STFU), which sought to bring about interracial harmony. Eventually, the STFU headed into Oklahoma, spearheaded by Odis Sweeden's organizing efforts.[4]

During this period of economic distress and high political drama, Nick Comfort sought to transform the Oklahoma School of Religion into a leading spiritual and institutional force in the state. His designs were even more wide-ranging than ever, as he envisioned a day when the School of Religion could stand side by side with other leading U.S. and European institutions as exemplars in the field of religious instruction. However, the times could hardly have been less favorable for such an ambitious undertaking. Indeed, throughout the nation, similar endeavors were confronting the harsh realities of economic constraints and flagging public interest. Many professional religious educators were compelled to leave this part of their ministry behind. The future of the religious-education movement, which had appeared so promising just a short while before, now was increasingly in doubt. So, too, was the continued viability of the social gospel, which was called into question by some of those who had previously been among its strongest advocates. Individuals like Reinhold Niebuhr now believed that far more radical solutions were required to prevent the continued hemorrhaging of the national economy.[5]

The status of the Oklahoma School of Religion was little helped by the fact that its director and leading light increasingly was viewed as a controversial figure, or worse, by many in the state. The growing number of questions and charges that were leveled at Comfort little fazed him or induced him to rein in his beliefs or activities on behalf of hot-button issues, ranging from the local to the international. That only further ensured that neither the School of Religion nor Comfort escaped vilification. The portentous nature of subjects he gravitated to, what with the unfolding of the Great Depression and the rise of right-wing aggression overseas, ensured that Comfort both remained in the public eye and became a figure of some notoriety. In particular, he repeatedly found himself, along with other liberal Protestant ministers, pitted against fundamentalists, who cast aspersions upon his sermons, his public writings, and his activities in general. He also had to contend with the charges of others that the time for the social gospel had long passed, that its invoking of the ideals of the fatherhood of God and the brotherhood of man, in such troubled times, was increasingly quixotic.

Nevertheless, the period began with great expectations for Nick and the Oklahoma School of Religion. To his delight, he soon acquired a new and important forum to spread his version of the gospel to a wider audience. Starting in the spring of 1930, Comfort contributed a weekly column to the *Daily Oklahoman,* Oklahoma City's leading newspaper, run by E. K. Gaylord, a contributing member of the Benefactors' Association of the School of Religion. Thus, in the wake of the radio program he did for WNAD the previous decade, Comfort had now acquired a new vehicle through which to expand his educational ministry. No matter the extra work his column entailed, Comfort was thrilled that he could use it to reach out to those who had never heard his message before. He also fully appreciated that the column would help to keep both his name and that of the Oklahoma School of Religion in the public limelight, a matter of great importance for such a struggling enterprise.

Unfortunately, but not surprisingly, one of his first pieces in the *Daily Oklahoman* resulted in a scathing letter. It came from the Reverend S. B. Williams, of the First Presbyterian Church, Broken Bow, Oklahoma, a minister who would become one of Comfort's earliest and strongest critics in the state. Williams, like many other fundamentalists in Oklahoma, read with trepidation or even horror the pronouncements of Nick Comfort. A running correspondence by mail between the two men ensued, Nick always managing to maintain a degree of civility and a sense of humor about the latest charges hurled his way. At the same time, Nick made it clear that he was in complete disagreement with the narrow-minded perspective of his theological antagonist.

In his first letter to Williams, dated April 17, 1930, Comfort agreed with the notion that "we need honest men in our pulpits." Comfort pointed out, however, that "truth concerning the Bible is neither fundamentalist nor modernist. If it is the truth about the Bible, it is the truth and that is all there is to it. It doesn't make the slightest difference whether it is advocated by a fundamentalist or a modernist." Moreover, he questioned whether the average parishioner or "the humblest minister 'has abundant opportunity to know all that can be known about the origin of the Bible.'" Comfort expressed his delight that Williams had yet to discover any ministers disinclined to search for information themselves. However, "I must confess that I have found several very lazy ones." Comfort went on to say that he had no desire "to slander the ministry"; rather, he was merely attempting to field questions in as forthright a manner as possible. Comfort also noted that the Reverend Williams had failed to acknowledge that his foe "suggested that many ministers are telling the truth, not only about the Bible but concerning all aspects of religion. They are by no means confined to any particular church or school of thought."[6]

The following week, Comfort again responded to a letter from the Rev. Williams. Comfort indicated that should the occasion arise, "I shall surely drop in on you to 'argufy' in a brotherly way concerning many things. I think you are just the kind of man that I should like very much to spend an evening with." In responding to a query from Williams, Comfort declared that the University of Oklahoma paid none of his salary "and has absolutely no control over me other than from a scholastic point of view." Thus, "whatever views I have that may shock you, please do not lay them at the door of the university. I alone am responsible." Comfort went on to say that he had serious doubts about whether any living soul "knows all that can be known about the Bible." The notion that the average minister did, Comfort indicated, worked to endow him "with entirely too much wisdom."[7]

As for himself, Comfort declared, "I am entirely conscious of my own intellectual and spiritual limitations." As was clearly evidenced by his Sunday columns, "I am not a fundamentalist." Not pulling any punches, Comfort asserted his belief that "fundamentalism is robbing many honest and good people of their Christian heritage." He related what happened when a bright young student asked a fundamentalist minister if he had to accept the preacher's teachings "or go to hell." When the minister indicated that he did, the student replied, "Then I shall go to hell gladly."[8]

It was a fact, Comfort declared, that some of his "very best friends" were fundamentalists. He respected and loved them, but believed that they were performing "an irretrievable injustice." Growing older had made him less prone to condemn others to damnation or to characterize them as insincere simply because of differing viewpoints. Rather, he was determined to do everything in his power to bring about the kingdom of heaven Jesus spoke of. Sadly, fundamentalist prejudices seemed to be among the greatest impediments to the coming of that kingdom.[9]

In a brief note to J. G. Puterbaugh, of the McAlester Fuel Company in McAlester, Oklahoma, on April 29, Comfort might have been talking of Williams and those of his ilk. He indicated that "all of our denominational bickerings and theological spleen come from a narrow sectarian religious education." The only answer to ongoing sectarianism, he declared, was through a program of broader religious education such as that which the Oklahoma School of Religion was undertaking.[10]

By early May, Comfort seemed to have won Williams over. In a letter dated May 6, he thanked Williams for his most recent inquiry, and declared, "I forgive you absolutely for being a Fundamentalist and would be glad to give you a good hug as a Christian brother." Comfort asserted that their correspondence only verified something he had long believed to be the case: "that the more you come to know people, the more you are bound to like them." Indeed, the good in human nature coupled with the love of Jesus, he continued, "lifts one into a veritable heaven on earth and makes out of him what through the ages has been called a saint."[11]

As mentioned above, it was Comfort's column in the *Daily Oklahoman* ("Answers to Religious Questions") that had originally drawn fire from the Rev. Williams. This column, which appeared on Sundays, would run for four years and contribute to giving both Comfort and the School of Religion greater notoriety. Comfort fielded questions of both a theological cast and a politically charged nature, and he did so in typical fashion, holding little back. Comfort viewed the column as a means to express his version of social gospel-tinged ideas, as well as to garner some much needed publicity for the School of Religion.

From the outset, he invariably discussed issues that were controversial. During the first few months of the column, he focused, for instance, on the worsening economic condition in the state, discussing the role religion should play in addressing the problem. The church, Comfort believed, was doing a good deal more than many people were aware of. Virtually all congregations, he wrote, had established funds for assisting the poor. Indeed, it seemed clear that they were doing considerably more than both the government and the Red Cross, although both of the latter employed public relations to make it seem otherwise. Comfort indicated that he was chairman of the drought relief commission in Cleveland County, all of whose members were churchgoers. Indeed, it was the churches, he believed, that were furnishing most of the people engaged in relief work.[12]

As was so often the case, Nick was personally in arrears on various accounts, and forced to confess to a creditor that he was one of many who had "been caught in this depression." His salary, Nick indicated, was derived from voluntary contributions to the School of Religion. Recently, those contributions had dried up and he had been unable to draw a salary or pay his bills.[13]

In response to a query on December 28, 1930, Comfort unhesitatingly responded that churches should be concerned about economic matters. Thus, he refused to follow the admonition of the Southern Presbyterian Church to avoid involvement with "matters of civil and political nature." Indeed, for Comfort, who believed that only through such an approach could the fatherhood of God and the brotherhood of man be furthered, there was no question that this was the case. "If God is the father of all men, surely He cares for all of his children, and would have no desire to see a few get practically all of the inheritance while the great majority had a mere pittance. If God is the kind of being implied by the term *Loving Father,* it would seem that He could not be quite satisfied to see a few men surrounded with the great opportunities that a superabundance of wealth offers, while the multitudes are handicapped by the deprivations which accompany poverty." The great religious figures, Comfort pointed out, had spoken of the brotherhood of man. Scientific analyses had apparently justified such an ideal. The progress mankind had experienced compelled acceptance of the notion of the brotherhood of man or a "slipping into retrogression." If the brotherhood of man were a reality, then certain economic implications necessarily followed.[14]

Religion, Comfort insisted, must reinforce these implications. They demanded that the capable do their part to care for the less fortunate. "Say what we will men are not equal," certainly no two of them. The more capable sorts were obliged to lead others toward a more abundant life. Intellectuals, societal bigwigs, economic moguls, and political leaders all required religious prophets courageous enough to make them own up to their responsibilities, as Jesus indicated "in the parable of the talents."[15]

If the brotherhood of man were in place, all should be afforded an opportunity. Equality of opportunity was not possible, but each individual should be provided "a chance for 'life, liberty and the pursuit of happiness.'" Humanity itself was constantly struggling to survive. But religion could never be satisfied with mere survival only. Rather, it sought to cultivate a deeper appreciation of life. To this end, "each one should be a producer." The young, the aged, and the infirm should be taken care of; the able-bodied should be required to work.[16]

One major issue confronting humanity involved the equitable distribution of both natural resources and that which man himself produced. At present, the wealthy became wealthier still, while the less affluent found it more difficult to obtain anything. This resulted in "the rankest injustice." Comfort found it difficult to imagine how Amos, John the Baptist, or James would have stood by silently while such deprivations existed. Workers, he declared, should be allowed to profit from their labor. Religion had to exalt the principles of "justice, righteousness, honesty, and human worth," to allow for social transformation and the just distribution of goods.[17]

If the brotherhood of man were a reality, then "all should be for each and each for all." The present state of world affairs was such that humanity was inextricably linked, "for good or for evil." If only to protect their own self-interest, the healthy should act to vanquish sickness, not only in the medical arena but in the social sphere as well. In fact, the time was ripe to trigger "a comprehensive social engineering program to prevent mental, moral, economic and spiritual ailments." Religion, Comfort wrote, should kick off such a drive. In order for the modern church "to save its soul," it would have to become involved in such an undertaking.[18]

According to Comfort, humanity had progressed through evolution and revolution. Evolution involved the normal pattern of progress, whereas revolution occurred "when those in authority block the path of progress." Although it was little recognized, the United States, Comfort suggested, presently had "the ideal set-up for a revolution. Turn where you will and you can find indications of a storm that is brewing." This was made clear to Comfort when, as he traveled around the state, he picked up hitchhikers. Even some who had always lived honorable lives were "desperate to the breaking point." Their desperation was born of the fact that they were "good men" who loved their families but were unable to provide for them, "to protect their loved ones from suffering," in this land of plenty. "Professional parasites" were heartened by "the possibility of a shake-up"; "the honest unemployed" were "baffled." These latter folk "know something is wrong but why, what, and where they are unable to say." Comfort warned, "Such people furnish good soil for revolutionary ideas."[19]

If wealth continued to be redistributed from the have-nots to the haves, Comfort prophesied, revolution would inevitably result. People needed to recognize that "religion is the only thing that can save the day for social evolution." It could help to bring about greater justice, restore belief in the workings of government, bring to an end public deception and graft, usher in new concerns regarding the suffering of the masses, and consequently "lead us out of our present chaos to a new day." No nation, Comfort believed, "ever offered a greater challenge to religion. The mute pleas for prophets may be seen alike in the worried faces of financiers and the pallid countenances of hungry children."[20]

It was clear that the Great Depression propelled Comfort, like so many other left-of-center Protestant clergymen, to adopt a more radical stance regarding social and economic affairs. Some, like Reinhold Niebuhr, Devere Allen, and Kirby Page, all editors of the World Tomorrow, began to argue that capitalism had been discredited and to champion the Socialist Party. The more militant among these churchmen joined the Fellowship of Socialist Christians. Although Comfort did not directly link up with any explicitly Socialist group, his own analyses were increasingly sharply drawn and highly critical of capitalism as presently constituted. At the same time, he was never attracted to Marxism, which he identified with class conflict, something he believed that men of God should strive to avoid. This was in contrast to a number of other social gospelers, who seemed to accept class-consciousness as a necessary ingredient in the quest for a more humane society. Nevertheless, Comfort, like others influenced by the social gospel, was deeply concerned about the dispossessed and believed that adhering to Christian ethics would help to pave the way for social justice.[21]

His concerns about the impact of the depression upon Oklahoma undoubtedly led Comfort, along with many others, to invest high hopes in the election of William Henry David Murray as governor of the state. During his campaign in 1930, Murray had lambasted the greed of malefactors of wealth and the problems of urban life and promised jobs for the unemployed and a reduction in taxes for farmers and owners of small homes. In reality, as James R. Scales and Danney Goble have pointed out, Murray was a champion of the poor more in style than substance.

On January 12, 1931, the day of Murray's inauguration, however, that was yet to be discovered, at least by Comfort. Nick fired off a brief congratulatory note to the governor. He was doing so, Comfort indicated, to inform Murray how much he supported his program and stood ready to assist the governor in any way he could. For himself, Nick declared, he sought nothing, and offered to assist "the cause which is dear to both of us." That evening, Nick attended the inaugural ball in Oklahoma City.[22]

His early support for Alfalfa Bill Murray was unique for Comfort, who had long ago determined to refrain from commenting on the particular administrations working out of the state capitol in Oklahoma City.

Perhaps he did so because of his recognition that the future of the Oklahoma School of Religion was precarious enough without inciting an attack from the most powerful political figures in the state. Or possibly he had adopted such an approach due to his disinclination to vilify individuals in the manner he was himself so often attacked. After all, at the worst depths of the Great Depression, Comfort never condemned President Hoover as had so many others on the Left. Issues, not personalities, were generally the focal point of Comfort's sermons and editorials, especially the more critical ones.

Unlike Comfort and former Socialist Party stalwarts L. N. Sheldon and Luther Langston, who also backed the candidacy of Alfalfa Bill, most old Socialists in the state refused to support the man who had engaged in Red-baiting in earlier campaigns. So, too, did Oscar Ameringer's *Oklahoma Leader.* The suspicions about Murray appeared borne out when, once in the governor's mansion, he resorted to attacking unions and blacks.[23]

Although Comfort had aligned himself with Governor Murray at the beginning of the new administration, he remained a controversial figure in the eyes of many Oklahomans. Comfort corresponded with Dr. T. A. Williams, of Oklahoma City University in mid-January, after receiving heated letters from Williams—a former colleague at the School of Religion—over a recent book review he had written. Just as he had in responding to S. B. Williams the previous spring, Nick insisted that he always welcomed "protests—the hotter the better. They at least indicate that folks are paying some attention to what I am trying to do." Regarding Dr. Williams's disagreement with his views, Comfort responded, "If we could have no differences of opinion this world would be a pretty tame place. I try to say what I believe and with as little ill will as possible. I assume that other people do the same."[24]

Following a visit by Dean Shailer Mathews to the University of Oklahoma campus, sponsored by the School of Religion, Comfort regretted that Dr. Williams had been unable to meet with the distinguished guest and his hosts. As for the latest fusillades that Williams evidently had hurled his way, he declared:

> Your letter amused me greatly. The thing I don't understand is why you have worked up so much spleen over the matter. Your collection of "Comfortia" seems to me very much akin to a light occupation. You may impugn my motives, collect "Comfortia" and so forth ad libitum but for pity's sake, keep sweet about it. I have been called practically everything in the questionable category but this is the first time anyone has ever indicated to me that I was an opportunist. The greater part of the adverse criticism that has been leveled at me has been just in the other direction, all of which I suppose illustrates Emerson's law of compensation.[25]

In a letter to his cousin Bluford Sturgeon in Paris, Texas, on March 4, Nick indicated that he was experiencing "a very interesting time," thanks to certain ministers in the state. They had taken exception, he acknowledged, to his religious column in the *Daily Oklahoman.* "They are after me hot and heavy," he declared. No doubt referring to critics like T. A. Williams, Comfort insisted that he could easily coexist with them provided they retained the ability to laugh. What he was unable to understand was why a minister was unable to disagree with someone without getting riled "and proceeding to consign him to hell." With the passage of time, he became more certain "that the greatest need of Christendom is for the ministers to have the spirit of Christ." Nick wondered how Pappy would view his reading of issues. "I can imagine he would 'Confound my cats!' and 'By shots!' a good deal before he was through."[26]

That summer, Comfort attended the General Assembly of the Presbyterian Church, U.S.A., in Pittsburgh, Pennsylvania. He was unquestionably pleased to hear the members of his church declare their belief in something akin to the social gospel. The assemblage asserted the need to afford opportunity for work for those who chose to, to ensure that wages were adequate to provide "health and hope" for industrial workers, and to shield those who were unable to protect themselves from the ravages of the marketplace.[27]

The next several sessions of the General Assembly of the northern Presbyterians would hearten Comfort even more. In 1932, the assembly adopted the report of the Committee on Social and Industrial Relations of the Board of National Missions, a document charging that the unfolding of the Great Depression served to indict American capitalism. "Nothing is more obvious than that the present economic order is now on probation and its continued existence and justification must be found not in the wealth produced or the power gained, but in its contribution to social service and social justice." The assembly then called for higher wages, better working conditions, old-age and health benefits, and the right of workers to organize.[28]

In 1933, the General Assembly asserted that "no economic emergency justifies human oppression; that if the right to live interferes with profits, profits must necessarily give way to that right." If the present system failed to take into account social conscience, grounded in Christian beliefs, the assembly declared, it must be replaced by "some more just and righteous social order than will answer our problems." Two ensuing General Assemblies spoke of the need for greater public control over economic resources and institutions and for shielding all citizens against economic insecurity.[29]

———

With the nation beset by the ravages of the Great Depression, which worsened every year until 1933, it is not surprising that many intellectuals, including some in the ministry, shifted leftward during this period. Liberal theological tenets were discarded by many Protestant ministers, who considered them too weak, too rationalistic, too utopian even, in such exigent times, when warring ideologies like Fascism and Communism appeared to be on the rise. A kind of "theology of crisis" emerged, which spoke in dark, pessimistic tones, deeming man a sinner who required God's grace. But, as religious historian Robert Moats Miller has so lucidly pointed out, those same theologians who moved rightward with their religious beliefs, focusing upon salvation by faith and individual redemption, veered to the left politically, headed by Reinhold Niebuhr.[30] The political leftward tilt characterized Nick Comfort's viewing of both domestic and international events during the 1930s; but not so the adoption of neo-orthodoxy, nor the relinquishment of social Christianity, with its more optimistic quality from an earlier day.

Comfort, like Howard Kester and Claude Williams, continued to believe that humankind could transform the world into the kingdom of God. Kester and Williams had both studied under Alva Taylor at Vanderbilt University's School of Religion and became involved with the Southern Tenant Farmers Union later in the decade.[31]

In his column in the *Daily Oklahoman* on July 19, 1931, Comfort examined the relationship between Bolshevism and religion. This piece suggested that Comfort, like so many other U.S. liberals and radicals of that era, was inclined to look upon the Soviet Union sympathetically. Such individuals viewed the events in Soviet Russia as an experiment in social and economic planning, which they hoped was ushering into existence the types of relationships that had previously been considered only utopian. Residing in the world's leading capitalist nation, they compared economic developments in their home country unfavorably with the carrying out of the First Five Year Plan in the Soviet Union. Moreover, these pro-Soviet Westerners were particularly wont to defend the Communist state when it was on the receiving end of right-wing attacks. But unlike many of his fellows on the left side of the political spectrum, Comfort did not look at the Soviets with blinders on.[32]

The suffering inflicted upon the Russian people in Czarist times, suffering abetted by the Russian Orthodox Church, Comfort explained, explained a good deal. The Bolsheviks were not simply waxing theoretical when they declared that religion was the opiate of the masses. They had witnessed religion lined up shoulder to shoulder "with autocracy, superstition, oppression, ignorance and credulity." They had seen millions of their countrymen "cowed by organized religion" until resistance to oppression was not possible. Consequently, they came to associate religion with conservatism and antiquated ways. The Bolsheviks, Comfort declared, sought "a new order and naturally they had to cast out all the forces that kept them from getting it." They considered religion to be the greatest obstacle in their way.[33]

Comfort noted that Bolshevism and the world's greatest religions had a number of points in common, although he did not mean to suggest that the Bolsheviks were adhering to religious tenets. The proponents of both Bolshevism and religion envisioned rising "above race and color lines." This was what Zoroastrians, Taoists, Buddhists, Moslems, Hindus, and Christians had all done at one point or another.

Bolsheviks and these religious brethren sought in their own ways to improve the welfare of the masses. The Bolsheviks declared themselves to be champions of equality of the sexes, something Christians and Jews had done more frequently than any other religionists. Bolsheviks and religious believers insisted upon great loyalty and stirred up fervent devotion. Both stood in opposition to special privilege. In fact, Comfort asserted, "only a degenerate religion can be the tool of special privilege." Unfortunately, that was precisely what often occurred and was something that the Bolsheviks railed against.[34]

Notwithstanding this common ground, large chasms existed, Comfort noted, between men who supported the ideals of Karl Marx and those who championed the tenets of organized religion. The Bolsheviks demanded fealty to such an extent that many saw them as religiously driven in their own right, particularly in their deification of Vladimir Lenin. The Bolsheviks seemed to recognize their movement must be preeminent in the hearts of men or face extinction. What this resulted in, Comfort declared, was "a death struggle" involving religion and Bolshevism. This was inevitable, he suggested, for "the worship of the state cannot go hand in hand with the worship of God."[35]

Additionally, the Bolsheviks appealed to class war, he explained, while the great religions strove to overcome class distinctions. The Bolsheviks used force as a kind of divining rod, and "any organization established by force must be maintained by the same." By contrast, Hindus, Confucians, Taoists, Buddhists, and Christians all unequivocally opposed violence. Their founders preached that those who lived by "brute force" would perish in the same manner. Bolsheviks sought revolution, whereas men of God favored an evolutionary path. Bolsheviks were atheists, unlike those who were devoted to God.[36]

Even while he discussed such monumental issues—
and as the American economy continued to slide—
Comfort somehow managed to maintain a healthy
perspective about what he was attempting to accomplish. Furthermore, in spite of all the hard times,
which coursed their way throughout the state and
caused the Comforts' own economic state to be even
more precarious than normal, Nick retained both his
sense of humor and his self-deprecating manner. On
July 25, 1931, Nick corresponded with Fred Mays in
Los Angeles, seeking to deflect his friend's assertion
"about advancing so far." Nick retorted that "about
the only advance I have made since I saw you is in
number of children and fifteen pounds in avoirdupois.
However, I have lost enough hair to make up for all
the gains." He indicated that nineteen-year-old Janet
would be a senior at the university in the fall,
seventeen-year-old Hugh was about to become a
junior at OU, thirteen-year-old Dick was entering
University High School, eleven-year-old Elizabeth was
in the fifth grade, and five-year-old Anne would
probably be enrolled in the first grade by September.
Both Janet and Hugh would soon be admitted into
Phi Beta Kappa, and Dick was turning up on the high
school honor roll. "Mammy has grown heavier and
gets prettier every day," and was the cause of Nick's
hair falling out. "The older she gets, the harder boiled
she is and you know what she used to be in K.C.U."[37]

Although money was always tight in the Comfort
home, Nick nevertheless continued to strive to provide whatever the children and Esther wanted. When
Janet desired to wear her Phi Beta Kappa key on a
bracelet, Nick said, "If this girl can be a Phi Beta
Kappa, well, she needs to have a bracelet." He loved
style and fine things. One time, while visiting Dallas
on church business, he went into Neiman Marcus and
bought a beautiful dress for Esther, who—though her

tastes were simpler than his—was touched and elated by her husband's thoughtfulness.[38]

Their budget generally couldn't allow for the kinds of purchases he might have liked to make for his family and on occasion even Nick's sunny disposition wore thin. While he was university pastor for Presbyterian students, Nick had enjoyed the sorority and fraternity dinners he'd been invited to. But now, one evening as he and Janet returned home from the School of Religion—she was helping out in his office—they drove past fraternity row and saw students engaged in some type of merriment. Nick sadly declared, "If I were worth my salt, that's where you'd be. I have deprived you of a great deal by not having money to let you enjoy a normal social life." Janet had realized as early as high school, however, that Greek life was not in store for her.[39]

That September, Comfort delivered his director's report to the school's board of trustees. One hundred and thirteen students from the university had enrolled in classes at the School of Religion; that number would soon rise. Nick's religious column in the *Daily Oklahoman* had resulted in no financial remuneration, but it had generated a large number of responses—some admittedly negative, but the vast majority favorable. He also had been called upon regularly to write book reviews for the *Daily Oklahoman*—approximately one hundred of them. In addition, he had led small forums that discussed religious issues on Sunday mornings and had been strongly opposed by certain churches in Norman, because of their meeting times and on grounds of general principles.[40]

What Comfort did not say was that his activities had made him a figure of still greater prominence throughout Oklahoma. That, in fact, had proved a mixed blessing. It afforded him greater access to any number of well-placed individuals; many viewed him as a man of reason and compassion, and found his continued invoking of the social gospel comforting during such trying times; they looked at the School of Religion as a beacon of light in a state suffering through such trying times, including massive unemployment, drought, soil erosion, and dust storms. However, Comfort's greater celebrity ensured that he was a still larger target for those who saw him as a modernist voice poisoning the religious atmosphere in Oklahoma.

Significantly, the School of Religion now sponsored a series of exceptional speakers, including Shailer Mathews, the Reverend Charles Gilkey, of the University of Chicago, the Reverend Ivan Lee Holt, Robert A. Milliken, and Count Carlos Sforza. Well-attended religious conferences for churchmen across the state were held during the visits of Mathews, Holt, and Sforza. Gilkey's visit corresponded with a state convention for YMCA and YWCA officials.[41]

Instructors from the School of Religion had also conducted a pair of teacher-training programs and joined with churches in Norman to orchestrate a teaching-training school. In addition to his full-time load with the School of Religion, Comfort taught three philosophy courses at the University of Oklahoma during the preceding summer, replacing a professor who had suffered a breakdown. The School of Religion came out $600 to the good, as a consequence, when Comfort turned over his paycheck to the institution. He also voluntarily agreed to accept the same 7.5 percent wage cut that university faculty had had to bear. This could not have been easy for Nick or his family, as he remained unable to make full payments on several accounts.[42]

He continued, as always, to believe that the work of the School of Religion would have far-lasting effects upon the people of the state. He recognized more clearly than ever that bringing the plans of the school to fruition would involve "a long struggle." Nevertheless, he remained certain that education was the greatest force for effecting needed change. He appreciated more fully than before that, inevitably, issues had to be faced by "only those who are doing pioneer work."[43]

His belief in the worth of the school's mission and the loving nature of the environment at 2000 Chautauqua enabled Nick to maintain his optimism, despite budgetary cutbacks, brickbats, and insults. The Comforts' home remained humble but was "full of love and good will for the world. We are happy as can be," Nick had written to his cousin Bluford Sturgeon in Paris, Texas. "The children are healthy and good. I am only slightly henpecked. What more could a man ask?"[44]

As the new school year began, Nick and Esther returned from a visit with Maude and Hugh Minor in western Oklahoma. They had discovered that the economic situation in the region had worsened considerably. Another store in the town, a large dry-goods operation, had gone belly-up. The bankruptcy of another store, one that sold hardware, enabled Nick to purchase some sorely needed "bolts, buckles, straps, rope, screw drivers, and such things galore and a couple gallons of mighty good harness oil." The boys and he had to work for about three days just to put all the materials away.[45]

The state of the economy in the region threatened to make the running of the School of Religion still more tenuous. On October 1, Nick wrote to Bishop A. Frank Smith, of the First Methodist Church, South, in Houston, Texas, regarding the possibility of that church's Board of Christian Education temporarily withdrawing assistance from public institutions in Oklahoma. Such an action, Comfort declared, "would greatly weaken the cause of religion here at the University of Oklahoma."[46]

The university administration, Comfort asserted, had been more than supportive in attempting to foster cooperation between the various religious denominations in the state and in favoring "spiritual culture" among both faculty and students. In fact, he knew of none that had been more helpful. Consequently, were the churches to fail, "it would be nothing short of a calamity." Notwithstanding the depression, no deprivation should be allowed to impede the religious progress taking place.[47]

Four days later, Comfort sent a brief note to Dr. R. E. L. Morgan in Ardmore, Oklahoma, regarding the decision by that town's board of education to terminate all funds sustaining religious enterprise in tax-supported schools. Nick appreciated "how hard times are," but he reasoned "that the harder the times, the more firmly should forward-looking, courageous men stand for the great eternal values."[48]

J. F. Owens, now a director of the board of trustees of the School of Religion and one of its strongest financial backers, attempted to elicit support from well-heeled individuals in various communities, such as Muskogee, Oklahoma. In a letter dated November 12, he indicated that Dean Comfort would soon be in that town and would appreciate speaking with them. Owens declared that from a strictly business standpoint, "the stabilizing influence" of religion must not be overlooked. After all, there remained those determined to subvert America's social and economic orders. State universities continued to be afflicted with the teaching of "the grossest kind of materialism." In contrast, he said, Comfort has "a real message for you" that should be received by "some of the other good men in Muskogee."[49]

With funding for religious education more problematic than ever, the controversies that followed Comfort did not help matters. Fundamentalist pastor

C. F. Stealey, editor of the *Oklahoma Baptist Messenger,* attacked Dean Comfort and the School of Religion for "modernistic teaching." The secretary of the school's board of trustees felt compelled to respond, stating that Nick Comfort, "one of the most Christlike men in Oklahoma," required no defense.

On December 1, in the midst of another round of attacks leveled at him, including those from Baptist ministers who cried he was "going to hell," Comfort received a note from Robert A. McCulloch, of Kingfisher, Oklahoma. McCulloch declared that he, for one, didn't give credence to the charge "that you 'belong to the devil.'" McCulloch went on to say, "sometimes he may use any of us as a means of expression, if we are not watchful—even the most dogmatic, as well as the most 'modern.'" McCulloch added that Comfort's response to his accuser, brief and to the point, had been "more wholesome than the tirade of your accuser."[50]

Many defenders of the iconoclastic clergyman cheered his stand as a "liberal Christian" who challenged fundamental ideas. One colleague credited Comfort with having done more than any other minister or educator at the University of Oklahoma to oppose the fundamentalist doctrines that were popular in the state.[51]

The visit to Norman in early December by Socialist Party leader Norman Thomas, sponsored by the Oklahoma School of Religion, undoubtedly did little to endear the institution or its director to his staunchest critics. Comfort invited a number of ministers to attend both a luncheon for the guest of honor at the University of Oklahoma Faculty Club and his public address. The Reverend Percy H. Nickles, of the First Presbyterian Church in Ponca City, thanked Comfort for the invitation. He had been ready every day the past week, Nickles indicated, to write to

Comfort to commend him for his "recent rise to fame and popularity." Hopefully, Nickles continued, such notoriety would also rebound "to the success of the Cause. Don't worry about them riding you, that will put hair on your chest." Nickles pointed out that Harry Emerson Fosdick, another who had attacked fundamentalism in the church, had been on the receiving end of similar assaults.[52] Unfortunately, Nickles wrote, financial considerations made it impossible for him to visit Norman; but he had a question for Thomas: Why had he departed from the church? Speaking for himself, Nickles declared he had to remain in the church as it afforded him a unique means to serve. He closed by leaving Comfort "to the tender care of the Baptist brother. . . . May the fires of hades not envelop you yet."[53]

Within a short while, Comfort again produced the kind of column for the *Daily Oklahoman* that engendered such heated opposition. This time he analyzed the root causes of poverty and the role religion should play in alleviating it. He acknowledged that those who were too lazy to work were consigned to poverty due to "mental weakness." Others were unable to work because of debilitating conditions (he cited hookworm, pellagra, and heart trouble, as examples). Nevertheless, Comfort remarked, some five million people were simply unable to find employment. In addition, many more received wages so low—paid by supposedly legitimate businesses—that they, too, were either relegated to poverty or lived at its edge.[54]

Much of this problem, Comfort argued, was caused by technological advances, which had allowed for great accumulations of wealth. "In the hands of a selfish society," technology worked to further enrich the wealthy and to encumber the poor. However, "a Christian society cannot tolerate simultaneously extreme wealth and extreme poverty." Such disparities challenged the very notion of the brotherhood of man, a core Christian concept. This maldistribution of wealth, Comfort was certain, resulted from the failures of organized Christianity, which had not been courageous enough to declare "we were moving in the wrong direction" and lacked "the vision and power to inspire a new path."[55]

Again Comfort insisted that such conditions could not last. Millions would not quietly "go hungry and cold." Rather, if not afforded the opportunity to provide for themselves, "they will take it by force." Consequently, "enlightened selfishness" and "Christian conscience" both demanded a change of direction. "To redeem its soul," Comfort wrote, the church must inspire its followers to construct a new social order predicated upon the brotherhood of man and the fatherhood of God.[56]

In a January 1932 letter to Maude and Hugh Minor, Nick indicated once again that the Comforts had never been healthier or poorer. That compelled him to keep guessing where money to pay their bills was to come from, but he had always managed to put food on the table. In spite of all this, he was positive he had never been "happier or had as great opportunities for doing good." Ironically, the latest assaults from a succession of Baptist ministers had generated more interest in his work than ever before. "If I had the money I would send each one of these Baptist preachers that has attacked me a quarter."[57]

To help make ends meet, Nick and his boys had gathered old telephone poles and other items from an abandoned golf course near the School of Religion. He had also acquired assorted materials from the university athletic department. Consequently, he had been able to erect the framework for a barn and construct a house, twelve feet by twenty-two feet. He had to purchase the floor and shingles for the latter. A Mr. Tyler, who had been helping the Comforts intermittently over the past three years, was now staying at the little house. Nick had rented the forty-seven acres of land between 2000 Chautauqua and town, and Tyler was going to work it. Esther and the children thought all of this would bankrupt them. Nick was "counting on a young fortune, but I shouldn't be at all surprised if they are right." No matter, he said, at least the enterprise would enable Mr. Tyler to survive.[58]

In early March, Nick discussed Thomas's recent visit in a letter to a friend back East. The venture to Norman by Thomas, himself a former social gospel minister, had resulted in "some of the high power men of the state . . . raising the roof." As Comfort saw it, "I seem to get in bad on every side. If the Baptists don't get me, the millionaires do."[59]

Religious work in the state appeared to be "getting in a bad situation." A number of churches had let their ministers go and many lacked any source of income. Ironically, given the depressed economy and the invectives that continued to come his way, the local Presbyterian church seemed to be thriving more than at any time over the past three years. During the preceding four months, attendance at church gatherings on Wednesday nights had topped one hundred or better. Until recently, Comfort had been in charge of the Norman church's adult division.[60]

Keeping the School of Religion afloat, however, continued to tax all of Comfort's powers. Southern Baptists, he informed Dr. W. L. Young in Philadelphia, "are after my hide hotter and heavier than ever." However, "if it were not for them, life would soon get monotonous." One branch of Southern Baptists was increasingly strident in its condemnation of the social gospel. Its proponents believed in a strict reading of the Bible, decried the belief in the perfectibility of man (which social gospelers subscribed to) and condemned ecumenical approaches.[61]

As events turned out, Nick did not need to trouble about matters becoming too sedate. In a letter dated May 27 to Carl Magee, editor of the *Oklahoma News,* Comfort congratulated him on a recent column that discussed how discouraged and desperate many good folk were and what might result. For having said the same kinds of things to leading businessmen in the state, Comfort had been labeled a Red. Name-calling of that kind, he said, "makes very little difference to me however."[62]

Several weeks later, Comfort discussed the same issue. For Nick and other proponents of the social gospel, the economic calamity that had engulfed the nation called into question existing social and economic relationships in the United States. The depression led them to wonder about the moral probity of American capitalism, which had resulted in millions of their countrymen being thrown out of work and millions being displaced from home and family. Such a system, Comfort wrote, at the very least appeared to be inherently immoral, and maybe was worse.[63]

In his column for the *Daily Oklahoman,* Comfort analyzed whether revolution could be avoided in the United States. Such a scenario was possible, he thought, if an evolutionary path were followed. But should business-as-usual practices continue in industry, education, and religion, revolution might well be in the offing. This was something any rational individual should be able to recognize. Little helping matters had been the idealization of the man-on-the-make. Art had been reduced to pandering for business enterprises; education had been transformed into something geared to the pragmatic; the political system had been corrupted by the power of money; and the laws of the land had been so perverted as to facilitate the pilfering of hard-working people's earnings.[64]

Comfort added a warning: "When any society gets to the place where the chief distinction between the conduct of a business and highway robbery is one of method, then that society is on the verge of an explosion. In some instances we are dangerously near that situation." Millions of "honest, industrious, intelligent people" were in dire straits and denied the opportunity to provide for themselves and their families. A desperation point was being reached, Comfort again warned, that "cannot be brooked much longer." The best of these indigent folk were the ones most apt to take matters into their own hands.[65]

A status quo approach at present, Comfort predicted, was "suicidal and can only end in revolution." Religious prophets through the ages, he suggested, had the answer. Honest men should be placed in power. Justice in all areas of life should come about. Each man should be treated as one's brother. God should be revered and all should seek to do his will. Intelligence should reign supreme. Concern for the greater community should be fostered. The weak and helpless should be cared for. New ideas should not lightly be discarded. Actions should be based on rationality. Should such ideals be put into practice, Comfort concluded, no revolution would be required or desired in the United States.[66]

The year 1932 witnessed the continued collapse of the economy and record numbers of foreclosures, bread lines, soup kitchens, and the unemployed. Unrest threatened the social and political order in both urban and rural America and talk was heard as seldom before of the need for radical change. Many worried that both workers and farmers, as at no time since the 1890s—another period of grave economic dislocation—were on the verge of revolt. Individuals as disparate as novelist John Dos Passos, the poet Langston Hughes, and philosopher Sidney Hook went so far as to back the presidential candidacy of William Foster of the Communist Party.[67]

By year's end, Comfort felt compelled to reprint in his column in the *Daily Oklahoman* a letter from a friend asking whether the might of the church and Christianity could "be mobilized for the cause of humanity." Given what was expressed in the letter, much of it could easily have been written by Comfort himself. It acknowledged the feeling held by many that the church invariably represented the interests of the ruling class. Men of the clergy, it declared, should be made aware of the injustice afforded the less fortunate and the peril facing American society in general, if needed reforms were not effectuated.[68]

It simply would not do to maintain a system in which a small number of wealthy individuals controlled most of the nation's wealth and millions were reduced to the condition "of paupers and near paupers." All of this had resulted, not from any Malthusian occurrence—nature, famine, pestilence, or war—but from "man's work." And such was the case in affluent America, with all of its bounty.[69]

"The power of God and the aroused conscience of the church," the letter suggested, could rectify the situation, preventing the use of the whole educational system, for instance, to sanctify capitalism. Man's conscience was "the greatest force in human life," and the Golden Rule the most fundamental criterion for any necessary social transformation. The church simply had to become involved in the plight of the dispossessed or its appeals to common folk would dissipate. Declaring that God was concerned about man's soul but not about his lot in life was simply not good enough. Men of God should lead the fight to right wrongs and the church "become a living body instead of a hollow shell of formula and barren faith."[70]

The continued pain and suffering inflicted by the depression upon the American people seemed to revitalize the social gospel movement, although some observers then and later deemed it inadequate to confront the economic collapse at home and the totalitarian threat abroad. Discussions about the church's relation to social ills, Christian socialism, and Christian sociology abounded in leading publications of the era. At the very least, this demonstrated something Comfort had hoped for: a greater sensitivity by religious groups to the plight of the less-fortunate and a stronger recognition that reform was needed.[71]

The Great Depression once again compelled a number of Protestant ministers to expand their horizons beyond personal redemption. Even churchmen who had long sought to avoid commentary on social or political issues now saw fit to speak out. Circumstances and their congregations seemed to demand as much.[72]

In April 1933, Comfort discussed whether Christianity had any practical solutions for the problems confronting the U.S. nation. He reiterated yet again that the fundamental precepts of Christianity involved the fatherhood of God and the brotherhood of man. The brotherhood of man called for the placing of humanity's welfare above selfish concerns. It required fundamental honesty to avoid the loss of faith that had characterized the economic collapse. At all levels, from Wall Street down, he asserted, dishonesty was soiling American business. Dishonesty was, of course, wholly antithetical to Christianity.[73]

Like so many of his countrymen, however, Nick continued to hope and believe that the economic woes of the era would bottom out. He witnessed its effect on his own family, when, in the early summer of 1933, eldest daughter Janet, complete with her Phi Beta Kappa bracelet and a master's degree in English, could not find work. And there were hundreds of other graduates from the University of Oklahoma, he informed a friend, with similar stories to tell. Some, in fact, were two or even three years removed from their studies and still without jobs. Most strikingly, it did not appear to matter what discipline one was in. A while back, OU engineering graduates had been eagerly sought by employers; now, even the sharpest of them lacked employment prospects. Nevertheless, Comfort retained a certain confidence that such individuals would eventually succeed. The best ones, he indicated, would make their way to the top, in spite of whatever competition existed. Perhaps he felt this way, not due to his belief in anything remotely approximating social Darwinistic thought—so recently discredited once again—but because of his own, hard-fought life-experiences.[74]

Dust Bowl
Oklahoma

CHAPTER SIX

TURNING SWORDS INTO PLOWSHARES

At the beginning of the 1920s, Nick Comfort, like so many other social gospel ministers, became involved in the peace movement. As historian Charles Chatfield has indicated, key liberal pacifists like Kirby Page and Norman Thomas not only were determined to condemn war altogether but believed there existed rational, nonviolent alternatives to mass bloodletting. They felt certain that aggression on a national scale could be reined in by nonmilitary approaches if undertaken soon enough and collectively. They also argued that the root causes of international strife must be dealt with, including the dividing of the world's peoples between haves and have-nots. Page, Thomas, and others like them believed too that disparities of wealth within nations produced oppressive competition across national borders. What was needed, then, in their eyes, was social change resulting in much "greater equity, democracy, and stability."[1]

Comfort was increasingly drawn to the ideas of the liberal pacifists. Yes, he had attempted to enter the U.S. armed forces as a chaplain during World War I. However, the aftermath of that conflict evidently left him, as it did numerous of his countrymen—religiously inclined or not—with a deep distrust of involvement by the United States in the affairs of other nations. Furthermore, mid-America was the most isolationist section of the nation during the interwar period. Comfort was approached by the World Alliance for International Friendship, which championed the League of Nations, as early as 1920, and corresponded with such well-known U.S. pacifists as Page and John Nevin Sayre. Many U.S. Protestant leaders, ranging from Harry Emerson Fosdick to Shailer Mathews and Graham Taylor, urged entrance by the United States into the League. Comfort also helped to start a local chapter of the Fellowship of Reconciliation, which along with the American Friends Service Committee led the campaign to devise humanitarian alternatives to war.

As the decade wound to a close, Comfort's concerns about U.S. militarism heightened. He was no doubt appalled when officials at the University of Oklahoma prevented Sayre from speaking on campus after an army officer described him as "more dangerous than an open communist." On January 3, 1927, Comfort, in a note addressed to "My dear Sayre," thanked him for sending copies of a charged letter from a Colonel Lewis directed at the Norman branch of the YMCA. "That is just the kind of stuff," Comfort declared, "that I want my hands on," as did "our bunch here at the university." It seemed to Comfort that "we have a hold of dear Colonel Lewis where the wool is cut short." What Comfort found most intriguing was the U.S. War Department's determination to shift responsibility.[2]

Comfort went on to indicate that a local chapter of the pacifist organization had been formed in Norman. For his part, Comfort declared that he had been deeply honored to have met Sayre, and hoped "to prove worthy of your association." In spite of his own failings, Comfort wrote, "I feel sure that my heart is in the right place, and I shall count it a privilege to do everything I can to foster the finest of American traditions and establish as the real power of the earth the ideals of Jesus."[3]

On April 4, 1927, he informed Sayre that presidents of public universities were caught "between Scylla and Charybdis," or at least believed themselves to be. He, too, remained perplexed about how to alleviate the pressures experienced by the secretary of the local chapter of the YMCA. Some people, Comfort declared, were naturally fearless; others required someone to stand up for them.[4]

The National Defense Acts of 1916 and 1920 had encouraged military training in public schools and the War Department was authorized to set up Reserve Officers' Training Corps (ROTCs) in colleges and universities. By 1927, some eighty-six institutions of higher learning required male students to enroll in ROTC, forty-four made ROTC elective, and high schools in fifty-three municipalities offered such programs. In 1925, the Fellowship of Reconciliation, following Sayre's lead, had produced a pamphlet condemning ROTC for popularizing military training and the War Department's perspective. That same year, the fellowship spawned the Committee on Militarism in Education (CME), which, over the course of the next decade and a half, led the campaign against compulsory military training. After 1926, the CME agitated for congressional legislation to prohibit compulsory military education.[5]

Like others involved with the Fellowship of Reconciliation, Comfort opposed compulsory military training in educational institutions. He, too, believed that the ROTC bred militarism, authoritarianism, and dogmatism. As a consequence, Comfort, like Page, Sayre, and others, was viewed as suspect by self-proclaimed patriots.[6]

As he became more involved with the peace movement, Comfort likened its goals and precepts to those of Jesus. Increasingly, he thought that his teaching ministry required participation in the campaign against militarism at the University of Oklahoma. Thus, his belief in the social gospel, especially the doctrines of the fatherhood of God and the brotherhood of man, demanded that he work to ensure that his own nation would war no more. His involvement with groups like the Fellow of Reconciliation eventually engendered some of the sharpest attacks upon both him and the Oklahoma School of Religion.

On May 23, 1929, Comfort informed Sayre that "militarism seems to be in the saddle with us just now." There was room for optimism, nevertheless, because on the campus of the University of Oklahoma several individuals desired to promote "creative peace." Sayre responded four days later, indicating that the Committee on Militarism in Education was progressing nicely. Sayre informed his "dear friend" that he was sending a copy of a recent speech delivered by Ross A. Collins, chairman of the House Subcommittee on Army Appropriations. Congressman Collins had turned to CME documents to criticize waste in ROTC programs.[7]

On February 27, 1930, Comfort wrote once more to Kirby Page, editor of *The World Tomorrow*, enclosing a $2 subscription fee for that leading journal of the religious pacifist Left. He had just read Page's "Jesus or Christianity," which was "positively the best thing I have seen along that line." Comfort had endorsed it in the literary section of the *Daily Oklahoman* and was handing out copies to faculty members at OU. Comfort closed with the observation that he hoped Page would learn a great deal during his impending worldwide trip, which might assist "those of us who are tethered out in the woods."[8]

Comfort was referring to the fact that, in spite of a few kindred souls, not much in the way of an antiwar movement existed in Oklahoma at the time. Moreover, a pacifist viewpoint was little appreciated in the state. Thus, it was not surprising that he took advantage of every opportunity to reach out to pacifist forces nationwide. Communicating with figures such as Page and Sayre enabled him to feel connected, in some small way, to a much larger movement. It allowed him a sense of fellowship with pacifist leaders whose ideas he fully shared.

Later that year, he apprised Tucker P. Smith, another leading figure in the Fellowship of Reconciliation, that the Oklahoma Synod of the Presbyterian Church, U.S.A., was opposing compulsory military training in state schools. Furthermore, the synod was asking OU's board of regents and the State Board of Agriculture of Oklahoma A&M College to make military training optional. Additionally, the synod was requesting that other denominations follow suit. Such action, Comfort believed, would affect "the military situation" in the state.[9]

A month later, Comfort wrote to Oklahoma senators Elmer Thomas and W. B. Pine asking them to do whatever possible to ensure congressional approval of the World Court Protocols. The Permanent Court of International Justice, or World Court, had emerged out of the ashes of World War I. Pacifists like Kirby Page hoped that support for the World Court would prove complimentary to the move in the 1920s to outlaw war altogether.[10]

In a pair of his "Answers to Religious Questions" columns in the *Daily Oklahoman*, Comfort discussed the practicality of nonresistance as propounded by Jesus and Mahatma Gandhi, the pacifist who at that time was deeply involved in the struggle to drive the British out of his native India. Gandhi was a larger-than-life figure for many U.S. pacifists, including Richard Gregg, author of *The Power of Non-Violence*, who seemed to require just such a role model. As

Charles Chatfield has suggested, Gandhi was physically distant enough that his apotheosis could occur without a recognition that the Indian pacifist's methods might be best suited to particular circumstances only. At this point, Gandhi's American supporters, including Nick Comfort, viewed him as the embodiment of selfless love.[11]

On April 6, 1930, Comfort declared that the "100 percent" patriots and the backers of a big army and navy viewed pacifism as the height "of folly and perversity"; in Comfort's eyes, the more heated the opposition to pacifism, the more potent a force it became. This suggested to him that the nonresistant philosophy of Jesus, which he deemed pacifism, was imminently "practicable."[12] Moreover, Comfort explained, its roots, ingrained over the centuries, were the cornerstone of a number of the most sophisticated religions. Most significantly, the question of whether pacifism was "practicable" was the key question confronting mankind at present. In the economic realm, Comfort pointed out, workers worldwide would either be fairly compensated or violence would result. If financial moguls had any sense, he declared, they would never compel the masses to turn to the barricades. The unrest that was already brewing, Comfort insisted, could be attributed to greater education and a resulting determination to avoid exploitation. Such unrest could be dealt with in one of two ways, he noted: "Remove the cause" or "kill the restless."[13]

In the political sphere, the fundamental issue in Comfort's eyes was whether an arms race or arbitration would prevail. A campaign on behalf of disarmament had been one of the first waged by the postwar peace movement. The "big army and navy" crowd insisted that a strengthened military was the nation's best defense. This was the philosophy that the U.S. had subscribed to, as evidenced by the expenditure of 80 percent of the national budget on wars, past, present, and future. If nothing else, Comfort asserted, this suggested how tenuous operating in such a manner had become. Such an approach had resulted in "misery, poverty, disease, and sorrow."[14]

There now appeared signs, however, that change might be in the works. International efforts to resolve disputes peacefully promised "to displace force." In India, the world's greatest nonresistance movement was seeking to throw off British imperial rule. The success of this endeavor, Comfort predicted, would demonstrate the efficacy of Jesus's nonresistant philosophy.[15]

The leader of the Indian nonresistance movement, Gandhi, was viewed by Comfort as one of the world's greatest leaders. Indeed, "it is quite likely that he is making more history than any living man." Gandhi was grappling with a triad of problems that the modern era simply had to contend with: relationships between East and West, a people's right to self-determination, and the use of force. Gandhi was striving for peaceful coexistence between East and West. He refused to accept the notion that western culture was inherently superior to that of the Orient and reasoned that the champions of each could find something of value in the other. Nevertheless, Gandhi was committed to expelling the British from his homeland and thus could be considered "the Washington of India." Although these two founding fathers had opted for different approaches to ensure national autonomy, Comfort declared, their objectives were similar. What Comfort found incomprehensible was how his countrymen could exalt the Founding Fathers of the United States while denigrating Gandhi and his nonresistance campaign.[16]

Gandhi would succeed in his quest, Comfort hoped, which would result in a freedom every bit as meaningful to the Indian people as liberty had been to the American colonists. If he failed in his endeavor, blood would flow, Comfort believed, and "folly and horror" would surely follow. Should Gandhi prove successful, on the other hand, the Indian pacifist would have demonstrated the power of ideas.[17]

On January 8, 1931, Comfort congratulated Kirby Page, whom he now addressed simply as "Page," on having managed to keep *The World Tomorrow* afloat. Nick wrote that, had he been able, he might have helped Page out, but the precarious financial state of the Oklahoma School of Religion prevented him from making any kind of donation. The institution's budget had been pared "to the bone," but things remained so tight that he almost felt ready to give up.[18]

Nevertheless, Comfort expressed a desire to become more involved with those who were striving to "fight for right, freedom of thought, and so forth." There were, in Norman, a few like himself who were doing what they could and believed they were accomplishing something. Still, they frequently felt isolated and longed "for a good visit with people like you."[19]

At the same time, Oklahomans and Texans, Comfort recognized, considered themselves capable of handling their own affairs, and possessed an aversion, more than might be suspected, to "outside pressure." Writing to Tucker P. Smith on March 2, he indicated as much in referring to a letter the Fellowship of Reconciliation had sent to an Oklahoma minister involved in the anti-ROTC campaign.[20]

In his religious column in the *Daily Oklahoman* on April 3, Comfort analyzed precisely who made up the opposition to compulsory military training in state schools, and the source of their opposition. This opposition counted Comfort among its ranks. The antimilitarists included the Ministers Convocation, sponsored by the Oklahoma Council of Churches; the Synod of Oklahoma, Presbyterian Church, U.S.A.;

and several hundred students enrolled at A&M College in Stillwater. The reasons for their opposition were multifold. They viewed compulsory military training as antagonistic to American ideals and believed that compelling students to take such training amounted to class discrimination. Fearing that "the military regime fosters class and caste ideals," they reasoned that "the war spirit" violated the very spirit of Jesus' teachings. War, they wanted all to recognize, "means dirt, blood . . . hate, cruelty, sorrow, hospitals, death."[21]

In late May and early June, Comfort attended the General Assembly of the Presbyterian Church, U.S.A. in Pittsburgh, Pennsylvania. His church, Comfort noted, had long been troubled by the spread of militarism in the United States. The southern branch of the church, when it gathered in 1929, had declared that "the Church should never again bless a war or be used as an instrument in the promotion of war." The assemblage in Pittsburgh now condemned— Comfort was undoubtedly heartened to discover— compulsory military training and overblown propaganda. This conclave of leading Presbyterians opposed militarism of any kind. Instead, the churchmen favored the cultivating of peace sentiments and cooperation. Such a pronouncement was designed, the assemblage reported, to demonstrate "our devotion to the Prince of Peace." Not surprisingly, then, they stated their support for Presbyterian conscientious objectors, insisting they be treated like Quaker pacifists. The assembly also affirmed support for U.S. entrance into the world courts, which it viewed as permanent instruments for international peace.[22]

Pacifist sentiment garnered widespread support among Protestant ministers during this period. Indeed, peace groups, including the Fellowship of Reconciliation and the Federal Council of Churches' Commission of International Justice and Goodwill, tended to be dominated by liberal church positions. A poll undertaken by *World Tomorrow*, the publication of the Fellowship of Reconciliation, indicated that more than 60 percent of the respondents believed the church should not sanction war anymore. The Reverend Harry Emerson Fosdick spoke of the disillusioning aftermath of World War I, its horrors and violations of the spirit of Christianity, and declared his intention never again to give his blessing to war.[23] On July 21, Comfort sent Tucker P. Smith a list of ministers around the state whom he believed would be interested in the efforts of the Fellowship of Reconciliation. Two weeks later, he recommended the Reverend F. M. Sheldon, of the Pilgrim Congregation Church in Oklahoma City; the Reverend Don Schooler, of the Methodist Episcopal Church, South, in Stillwater; and the Reverend W. Ward Davis, Director of Religious Education at the First Presbyterian Church in Oklahoma City, to serve on a statewide branch of the pacifist organization.[24]

Pacifism was the subject of one of Comfort's religious columns in the *Daily Oklahoman* in September. He wrote of the Essenes, a Jewish sect that flourished in the early Christian era, dwelled in isolated communities close by the Dead Sea, and displayed "distinctly communistic and pacifist principles." Celibates, Sabbatarians, and vegetarians, the Essenes sought a mystical communion with the Lord. Comfort's discussion of the Essenes led to others regarding biblical commands to kill and pacifism in general. Comfort acknowledged that Moses and Samuel delivered such orders—orders "diametrically opposed to the sixth commandment, the teachings of the prophets and the teachings of the New Testament."[25]

Pacifism, Comfort explained, relied wholly upon goodwill and rational discourse and taught that force resolves nothing. Great weapons of war did not "blaze the way to truth." Justice was not achieved through poison gas. Grand armies did not make for a contented and happy populace. "The mailed fist has not yet and never can produce peace." In a more positive vein, pacifism spoke for the notion "that right, truth, justice, good will, faith" enabled a civilization to endure. A fundamental tenet of pacifism, Comfort continued, was the notion that man, if afforded the chance, would deal with his fellows in an amiable fashion; man was no predatory creature instinctually. Regardless of what had transpired in the past, Comfort asserted, man had progressed to the point where mutual goodwill had to prevail or the human race would self-destruct.[26]

Great armies and navies were not only financially debilitating, Comfort insisted, but bred the rankest "suspicion, fear, hatred and desire for vengeance." The pacifist reasoned that, when the costs of past, present, and future wars were so burdensome, "our whole perspective of life was wrong." Other nation-states could only view the United States as "a militaristic nation." Moreover, such a program, Comfort was convinced, was "basically unchristian." It was "sheer hypocrisy" to chart such a course, all the while signing pacts with other countries. Even more bluntly, Comfort declared such an approach to be "insane."[27]

Not militarism and imperialism but missionary work, Comfort believed, should receive church blessing. In a biting column in the *Daily Oklahoman*, he assailed "American vested interest in foreign lands, our political corruption and imperialism . . . our selfish attitude in world affairs, our disregard for law . . . our high handed insolence and unbearable egotism when dealing with foreigners." He deemed it hypocritical to seek God's blessing for U.S. military forces that subjugated the Filipinos while expressing horror at Japanese aggression in Manchuria. He pointed out that it was the "so-called Christian nations," including the United States, that had schooled Japan in the very tactics that it was employing in the Far East.[28]

Oklahoma's own senior senator, Elmer Thomas, had charged that at present "the United States is the most disrespected and hated nation in the world." There were valid reasons for just such a perspective, Comfort wrote, although many happily were of recent vintage and could be rectified. Religious sanction for such practices, followed by the sending of missionaries, he declared, amounted to the greatest hypocrisy. What individual ministers had to do was "to come clean on these vital Christian issues." This was no academic matter but rather "an issue of life and death. We are at a crisis point in history."[29]

Christianity appeared to have two roads before it. One way led to degeneration "into a priestly cult whose sole function is to say grace at the feasts of Mammon and perform funeral rites at the carnage of pagan states." The other way would enable the church to represent progress and lead men toward the ushering in of the kingdom of God. It was time, he repeated, to stop being hypocritical. The United States had to become "Christian in spirit." That required making the U.S. flag "the symbol of freedom, the token of love, the ensign of truth, the synonym of justice, the sign of service, or else withdraw our far-flung missionary forces and admit that Jesus was wrong and that we have been duped." Should the U.S. be made Christian, he was certain, other peoples would "follow us in hot haste."[30]

In his religious column for the *Daily Oklahoman* on April 9, 1933, Comfort insisted that the fatherhood of God and the brotherhood of man demanded an end to war. These fundamental Christian tenets, he reasoned, could not easily coexist with martial pursuits. Indeed, nations could not be Christian and wage war. Every Christian should oppose war with all of his might, avoiding the equivocations that had devitalized the church. Again, he wrote, "One can't worship Mars and his Loving Heavenly Father who looks upon all men as his children."[31]

On January 21, 1934, Comfort's column in "Answers to Religious Questions" focused on the issue of whether Christians should ever wage war against one another. He felt compelled to rely on the New Testament alone, which he saw as "the only purely Christian scripture." Moreover, there was little doubt in his mind that approval of war could be found in the Old Testament, although in the noblest of the Jewish scriptures a strong disapproval of war could be uncovered. However, it was clear to Comfort that nary a teaching in the New Testament gave sanction to war. Any such notion, he declared, was so ludicrous as to be absurd. Only in a lone passage, in Matthew 10:34, Comfort indicated, could there be uncovered any evidence suggesting Jesus' approval of war. There, Jesus warned: "Think not that I came to send peace on earth. I came not to send peace but a sword." Comfort pointed out that Jesus was referring to personal relationships only. To use such scripture as an invocation for war required a "meaningless" misinterpretation.[32]

The Jesus that Comfort recognized took the Old Testament admonition "Thou shalt not kill" and strengthened it, teaching that one should not express anger toward one's fellows. His Jesus also taught the need for forgiveness, to love one's enemies, even to "pray for those who persecuted them and despitefully used them." The Jesus in whom Comfort believed taught his followers to live peacefully with others and refused to allow the sword to be used in his own self-defense. For Comfort, the teachings and life of Jesus provided many lessons. War was simply murder on a mass scale and stood in opposition to everything the Son of man represented. "Peace was the theme of his life to such an extent as to make war unthinkable."[33]

Christianity was held together, Comfort again indicated, by the fatherhood of God and the brotherhood of man. For him, it was impossible for martial conflict and brotherhood to exist side by side. Thus, Christians had to confront the question of which side would triumph. The warfare that had broken out in distant corners of the globe was "the world's supreme blasphemy. By the side of this faith-destroying and soul-crushing giant, atheism and infidelity are mere babes in the woods."[34]

Christians, Comfort declared, must strive to be like their Maker. "The Christian God is the God of love, peace, forgiveness, mercy, gentleness, intelligence, purity." To attempt to invoke God's name on behalf of war-lust, he explained, was "the supreme heresy, the absolute denial of the faith, the complete stifling of the spirit."[35]

From the end of World War I through the midpoint of the 1930s, Protestant churches in the United States continued to believe that peace could result from international cooperation. By and large, they opposed both an isolationist stance and jingoism. Thus, they favored U.S. entrance into the League of Nations and U.S. adherence to decrees by the World Court. They also favored a cooperative approach regarding disarmament.[36]

Antiwar sentiment was fueled most of all by lingering disillusionment regarding the U.S. involvement in World War I, the model of Jesus, and Gandhi's example. To explain their antiwar stances, ministers frequently referred to the war, and the Treaty of Versailles following it, that had failed to bring about the liberal, democratic world order envisioned by Woodrow Wilson. American clergymen, like their countrymen in general, were highly influenced by the hearings and subsequent disclosures of the Nye Committee in the United States Senate. This committee in 1934 began examining the purported causes for U.S. entrance into the war in Europe. The committee, headed by Gerald P. Nye, of North Dakota, and influenced by the Women's International League for Peace and Freedom, claimed that private munitions makers had taken the United States into war, thereby violating U.S. neutrality and, in the process, obtaining excessive profits. The Nye Committee called for war profits to be taxed, for war industries to be regulated, and for legislation insisting on U.S. neutrality involving commerce and travel by private individuals during periods of belligerency.[37]

For many ministers—including Nick Comfort—the model provided by Gandhi was an equally important fact in sharpening their antiwar perspectives. Thus, when questioned about the viability of nonviolent resistance they responded, as Comfort did, that Gandhi's use of such a weapon had proven remarkably successful. Little surprising were the results of a poll of ministers conducted in 1934 for *World Tomorrow* by Kirby Page. It indicated that more than two-thirds of those queried believed their churches should refuse to sanction future war.[38]

However, around the middle of the decade, the Protestant churches began to divide sharply on issues of foreign policy. The Italian invasion of Ethiopia in 1935 and the outbreak of the Spanish Civil War the following year caused some to adopt a position that seemingly aligned them with the isolationists. Other former pacifists now determined that a triumph by right-wing aggressor states— militarist Japan, Fascist Italy, and Nazi Germany— would prove a fate worse than war even. Consequently, they called for collective security, urging the use of economic sanctions against those nations that violated the territorial integrity of other states. Another group of peacemakers continued to champion a pacifist approach, renouncing war as a solution to conflicts between nations. Nearly 2,000 ministers eventually signed the Covenant of Peace Group, which affirmed that the signatories would not "participate in, sanction, or support war."[39]

Throughout the remainder of the 1930s, as the guns of war flared in Asia, North Africa, and central Europe, Nick Comfort was one of those who continued to adhere to a pacifist point of view. By the middle of the decade, he was gladdened by the emergence of a student peace movement on many of the nation's college and university campuses, including the University of Oklahoma. Public hearings by the Nye Committee regarding the purported economic origins of U.S. involvement in World War I seemingly lent support to pacifist arguments. Pacifists like John Nevin Sayre and Dorothy Detzer passed along materials to Senator Nye and then helped to publicize his committee's findings. The hand of the isolationists was undoubtedly strengthened by the U.S. Senate hearings, with neutrality legislation soon to follow, which the great majority of churchmen supported. Not surprisingly, one of the most influential figures in cultivating antiwar sentiment in Norman was Nick Comfort, who was disturbed by the disclosures of the committee.[40]

Beginning in 1934, 25,000 students in New York City alone, led by the Student League for Industrial Democracy, which was affiliated with the Socialist Party, and the National Student League, dominated by Communists, participated in an antiwar strike. They also took the equivalent of the Oxford Pledge, which had first been employed by undergraduates at Oxford University, who refused to "fight for King and country in any war." In 1935, approximately 175,000 students participated in a second nationwide strike, which also had the backing of the National Council of Methodist Youth, the Inter-Seminary Movement, and the American Youth Congress and Youth Section of the American League Against War and Fascism, both largely Communist-driven. Although the following spring's student strike would be larger still, the peace movement soon experienced divisions between proponents of collective security, isolationists, and hard-core pacifists. Particularly was this so as the threat of Fascist aggression loomed larger and as the Soviet Union became the most determined advocate of an anti-fascist alliance.[41]

Leading Protestant ministers, especially those who believed in the need to help usher in the so-called City of Man, were among those most favorably disposed to the student activists. In Norman, no one demonstrated greater support for the student movement than Nick Comfort, who saw his involvement in the peace campaign as an extension of his teaching ministry and a means to ensure that the seminal ideals of the social gospel, the fatherhood of God and the brotherhood of man, were not lost sight of, notwithstanding mounting examples of inhumanity across the global expanse. Comfort was pleased that students from the Oklahoma School of Religion were among those in the state most steadfast in their opposition to war and military training.[42]

During the 1935 Christmas break, Nick felt privileged to spend some time with Toyohiko Kagawa, the Japanese pacifist who had condemned the rape of China by his nation. Kagawa, who was afflicted with trachoma, was viewed as a pariah by some, but the Comforts welcomed him into their home. What impressed Nick most was his guest's fearlessness and apparent ability to confront Japanese militarists with graciousness and goodwill. This man, Comfort indicated, was involved in a great cause and was striving to build the kingdom of God.[43]

The visit by Kagawa passed largely without public incident, but greater controversy loomed ahead in the springtime. A furor developed over the showing at the University of Oklahoma of a pair of plays by Clifford Odets, *Waiting for Lefty* and *Till the Day I Die,* and the formation of a student chapter of the Veterans of Future Wars, an antiwar organization. The two plays spoke to the political and economic dilemmas the nation was confronting.[44]

The Veterans of Future Wars had been founded by students at Princeton University. By the use of satire, they sought to highlight the cries by World War I veterans for bonuses and regarding war in general. The Veterans of Future Wars called for "an adjusted service compensation" amounting to $1,000 for each American male aged eighteen to thirty-five, with the bonus to come due on June 1, 1965. The student organization insisted upon immediate payment of the bonuses, with 3 percent annual interest added, in order that those Americans maimed or killed in the next war sponsored by the United States could reap their nation's full gratitude before their time of service. The students claimed to have set up nearly four hundred branches nationwide, with thirty thousand members. Ladies' auxiliaries were established, seeking pensions now "for future war widows and a trip to Europe in 'holy pilgrimage' for all mothers of future soldiers."[45]

Regarding calls for outside influences to be excised from the university, Comfort pointed out that such an approach would result in the termination of ROTC programs. But not only that: it would also end federal projects that provided employment for students. Similarly, it would mean that professional and religious organizations would no longer be welcomed; that members of the American Legion would be diverted from campus; and that groups ranging from the Young Democrats and Young Republicans to Phi Beta Kappa would have to close shop.[46]

None of this made any sense to Comfort, who argued that a public institution of higher learning must deal with issues of statewide and national importance. For example, the question whether the United States should enter a war needed to be considered. Political and economic questions likewise affected the well-being of the state, and students needed to field such queries. Furthermore, the right to hold any beliefs or to sponsor any political party or program, provided no legislative enactment was violated, involved fundamental democratic principles.[47]

The appearance of the Veterans of Future Wars on the University of Oklahoma campus pleased Comfort. So, too, did the decision of the university administration to allow a thirty-minute "strike for peace." This undoubtedly delighted Nick, who remained good friends with University of Oklahoma President William Bennett Bizzell. Thus, the spring of 1936 at OU witnessed the ushering in of the 1930s student peace movement. With more than one-third of the nation's one million college students participating, the antiwar message seemed more appealing than ever. The student actions had the backing of the Emergency Peace Campaign (EPC), which aligned itself with the American Student Union that had adopted the Oxford Pledge. Harry Emerson Fosdick was chairman of the EPC; Kirby Page and Albert W. Palmer, head of the Chicago Theological Seminary, were members. Comfort was one of some 3,500 ministers throughout the nation who agreed to give peace talks that summer.[48]

In the fall, just prior to Armistice Day, Comfort insisted that a new brand of patriotism was required. It simply wouldn't do, he suggested, to call lustily for more arms, to exalt the military spirit, to view force as the last resort for domestic and international differences, and to engage in "an orgy of flag-waving and emotional super patriotic prejudice." Rather, what was required was the construction of a nation that demanded no defense. Such a nation, the justice of which would surely be universally recognized, would neither be feared nor threatened by any other. Such a nation would aspire toward "opportunity for all, and license for none." If Americans truly sought to honor those who had fallen in World War I, Comfort declared, they would seek to make war "as obsolete as the cave man's civilization." If Americans desired to respect those who had been "led to slaughter" in that earlier crusade to make the world safe for democracy, they would pledge anew to uphold the nation's democratic precepts.[49]

Comfort had a series of more specific proposals for how Armistice Day 1936 might prove to be truly enlightening. One-third of the money used for the military would be expended on peace propaganda. At the University of Oklahoma, for example, that portion of the ROTC budget would be employed to teach peace classes and the hopelessness of war as a means for resolving national or international disputes. All students who were physically able would be required to play peace music; pacifists would be viewed as heroes; "queens of peace" would be selected, and peace societies would be established. With such a changed atmosphere, "mankind's natural love of peace might blossom as a rose instead of being smothered as it now is."[50]

He also suggested that $1 out of every $3 presently expended on the U.S. Navy be applied toward erecting peace institutions around the world. Major disasters would meet with a show of American beneficence. An international university would be erected outside of the United States to enable students from across the globe to engage in cordial dialogue.[51]

Equally important, those who declared war would be required to man the war front. They would be stationed there until the conflict terminated or they fell in battle. The elderly would be conscripted first. No profits would be allowed from the war effort and all would be required to toil for the good of the nation during the period of hostilities. Military pensions would be abolished and all the money previously so targeted would be used for the oldest and neediest of Americans. Finally, "all tinsel" would be removed from the professional warriors; when not drilling or practicing they would perform such essential tasks as street cleaning, garbage removal, and road construction. When soldiers died, they would be buried without "pomp or glory," just as other useful citizens were.[52]

Comfort's analyses appeared remarkably naive and altogether simplistic, to say the least. Perhaps this was due to the fact, as John Gordon Bennett of the Union Theological Seminary has suggested, that the social gospel inadequately prepared its followers to confront the horrors of the 1930s and thereafter. Appalled by the death and destruction that had accompanied the World War I, advocates of the social gospel were determined that their nation not revisit those terrors. However, in the 1930s the threat posed by the right-wing aggressor states was of a far graver nature than that presented by the imperial forces of World War I. Increasingly, a pacifistic stance in the face of Fascist aggression made less and less sense.[53]

A few weeks later, Comfort again analyzed the foundations of "the new patriotism" that he advocated. First, the democratic nature of the U.S. nation was of paramount importance in his estimation. Americans needed to bring democratic ideals to fruition. The opportunities to be afforded to the American people were to be not only political but also economic, social, and intellectual. Second, freedom of expression had to be maintained. Those who sought to rein in public discussion and to prevent the masses from fully participating in the political process must not be heeded. Third, equality before the law was of great significance. Each citizen had to possess the protective shield of the law against acts of violence, such as that delivered by superpatriots. If the law were invoked to violate fundamental liberties, then democracy in the United States was doomed and violence certain to result. Fourth, "adequate national defense" was required. What that called for was recognition that "all men are very much alike" and that the American people were no less aggressive than others. It involved acknowledgment that the amassing of great armaments fostered fear, and fear invariably led to trouble. Rather than building up arms, patriots should strive to make their nation the kind that others "will like, trust, and want to live." Fifth, patriotism could not be forced upon people. Fear produced not loyalty but a cowed people. Thus, the better approach would involve the eradication of external force as a means to ensure loyalty. Finally, it had to be appreciated that patriots were those who continually devoted themselves to the good of the commonweal. "They are strong and brave enough to live for their country as well as to die for it. It takes a great deal more courage to live a long life on the side of right than it does under emotional stress to give one's life in a few short moments to a cause. The new patriotism asks the citizens to live for their country so that no one will have to die for it."[54]

In his column on December 6, Comfort called attention to a recently published article in the *National Legionnaire* by the American Legion's national commander, Harry W. Colmary. As Colmary put it, "TRUE Americanism" involved belief in America's democratic system of government and the ideas it represented. It did not involve an effort to quash those whose ideas one disagreed with or disliked. "That is the very essence of UN-AMERICANISM," wrote

Colmary. Comfort was heartened by the acknowledgment of the American Legion's "own unpatriotic activities"; he was pleased that the head of the organization did not pull any punches concerning those in the legion's ranks who supported a coup d'état, thereby disgracing fellow veterans. He was gladdened that Colmary seemed to be informing his compatriots that vigilante activities, like those carried out in the past, would make the American Legion "a stench in the nostrils of decent people and a thing to be purged from the national life."[55]

Actual practices, not high-sounding phrases, Comfort declared, determined the quality of any particular action. Recent moves to storm meetings by American Communists, he stated, had demonstrated that it was "the self-styled patriots" who "were the real enemies" of the United States, because they set out to destroy "the very things that have made our nation possible." Comfort urged the commander to repeat such admonitions until lawbreakers recognized "just how despicable a lot of their doings have been." Comfort hoped that Colmary's display of "awakened conscience" might lead other military men "to look within and see just how far they have wandered from the truly American spirit." Not only the military needed to engage in such self-examination; so too did businessmen, educators, politicians, and religious leaders.[56]

To Comfort, the danger that the American people confronted did not reside with Japan, Russia, or Germany but "within ourselves." He explained why this was the case: "The soul of America was born out of the travail of men and women who loved liberty more than life, who suffered for freedom's sake, and who ventured all in the effort to strike the shackles from the human conscience, mind, tongue, and pen. All hail to any person and every person in any group anywhere who has the courage to take a stand with those who have given us our ideals of liberty, freedom, responsibility, and democracy."[57]

The following April, another antiwar gathering took place at OU; hundreds more were unfolding across the land. Many seemed less inclined to pacifism; a call for collective security and support for the Spanish Loyalists was heard time after time. In Norman, however, a half-hour "strike for peace" took place with the administration's approval and Comfort's blessing. He admitted in the *Oklahoma Daily*, the campus newspaper, that the student efforts would "be mere gestures toward peace," which would in no way change the course of national policy; however, he reasoned that if several thousand such rallies were held, the U.S. military program would be greatly affected. For now at least, "it's a gesture; and again, it's in the right direction." He asked his readers to rejoice in such gestures and in the attempt to follow the antimilitarists' lead.[58]

The congregating of some two thousand students at a peace rally and the signing by two hundred of a petition requiring the American people to vote on a declaration of war represented the pinnacle of the antiwar effort at the University of Oklahoma. Encouraged by the Nye Committee report in Congress, Comfort declared that the advocates of war did not dare to speak the truth to the American people. If fully apprised of the situation, he told the crowd, his countrymen would refuse to fight. Comfort decried munitions makers as "dollar-chasers." He proposed that $3 out of every $10 allocated for military expenditures be used to promote peace and postulated that the remainder of the money would not then be needed for long.[59]

As the new academic year began, Comfort warned that international tensions were setting the stage for a great deal of "foolishness, insanity, and sheer madness" in the United States. The appearance of those who "will try to out-muscle Mussolini," might soon result. Consequently, courageous people had to "clip the wings of such self appointed embryonic dictators." Already, "a flock of vultures," in the name of U.S. interests, were insisting that their commercial interests be safeguarded everywhere. For material gain, Comfort cried, they would drive the United States into war.[60]

Comfort warned that, to avoid entrapment in martial conflicts, Americans had to keep their possessions and countrymen out of harm's way. Americans had to be evacuated from war zones or warned that should they remain there the risk was their own. Comfort said he could not understand "what dishonor, either national or personal" surpassed that of reaping financial gain "from the butchery of men."[61]

As Christmas approached, Comfort noted that once more "the birth of the Prince of Peace" was being celebrated as warfare unfolded. It was tough to hear Yuletide caroling or Santa's sleigh bells, he declared, while Mars was ascendant. War was raging in Asia, as others frenetically readied "for an impending holocaust of slaughter." It seemed as though "all that is good and sane in us turns in utter nauseation, horror, and disgust." How long, Comfort wondered, would the world's masses allow "the thousands of maniacal militarists to lead them to slaughter and death?" When would the former learn that military might resolved nothing and failed to produce needed foodstuffs, a brighter world, or human liberty?[62]

Consequently, Comfort explored the dilemma of why, in the midst of overwhelming opposition, war still took place. Nations resorted to war with both expansion and self-defense in mind. Few seemed to recognize the blatant contradiction between the teachings of Jesus Christ and Mars. "The last orgy of sacrifice" to the latter had weakened Christianity's hold upon millions. Now, false worship of Jesus should cease, along with the shepherding of "his little brothers and sisters" into armed camps.[63]

Comfort's reading of international events during the 1920s and 1930s was guided by his moral precepts and his Christian ethics. It was shaped in considerable part by his analysis of U.S. involvement in World War I—an analysis shared by many peace activists. Horrified by the pain and suffering unleashed in that conflict and appalled by the lessons they drew from the Nye Committee hearings, they were determined that war be avoided at all costs. What many failed to recognize, however, was the immensity of the challenge posed by right-wing totalitarians to Western-style democracy and civilization itself. Furthermore, they lacked the foresight to envision the sweep through Europe, the Middle East, and Asia, that the right-wing aggressor states were engaging in. Consequently, as the thirties neared an end, such pacifists began to appear—even in the most favorable light—like Jeremiahs prophesying only to the already committed.[64]

Others, more comfortably situated in the isolationist camp, delivered their own warnings as the guns of war sounded once again; many of these warnings Comfort and a number of pacifists also delivered. Isolationists challenged the need for and desirability of large military expenditures, particularly involving the U.S. Navy. Believing that Germany, Italy, and Japan posed no threat to the United States, isolationists reasoned that a military buildup invariably resulted in armament races, strife between nations, and war. Fearing that great military appropriations only enriched shipbuilders and arms manufacturers, they similarly distrusted military men who so eagerly sought new weapons of mass destruction.[65]

On December 28, Comfort heard Ralph Bates speak in Oklahoma City of his experiences in the Spanish

Civil War. Bates discussed how the rebels had been guided by General Francisco Franco and Spanish aristocrats. He indicated how the upper class in Spain had long oppressed the masses, relying on superstition to keep them grounded in poverty. A "liberal" Spanish government had sought to enact measures akin to Roosevelt's New Deal programs. Franco's rebellion would have been thwarted early were it not for outside help from Mussolini and Hitler. Comfort remarked that it would be hard to find "a more barefaced example" of other governments attempting to subvert a legitimately constituted one. As Bates made clear, this was the same thing Mussolini and Hitler were attempting to do elsewhere in Europe. To that end, they were being assisted by the Roman Catholic Church, which was both backing the Spanish army and serving as a fifth column. This was the case even though diverse elements, including Communists, other radicals, and conservatives, in Popular Front fashion, stood behind the Loyalist government. Thus, Franco's alleged striving to obliterate Communism was only a pretense. What Franco actually sought, Comfort declared, was to construct a dictatorship to Mussolini's and Hitler's liking.[66]

Comfort seemed to accept Bates's argument—which proved to be sorely wrongheaded—that Russia was not sending emissaries to Spain, only ammunition. Comfort erred in viewing Russian aid as altruistic only. He fell into the same trap as many leftists regarding the perceived good intentions of the Soviet Union in meeting the Fascist threat. These Sovietphiles also failed to highlight the repression meted out by Communists to anarchists, the POUM (a dissident Marxist group), and left-wing Socialists.[67]

Instead, Comfort wrote that guns were not "labeled 'please be a Communist'"; they involved financial considerations alone. What Bates found reprehensible about all of this was the failure of the democracies to sell arms to the duly constituted Spanish government. Nevertheless, the people of Spain refused to be cowed, despite the bombing of civilians, which only made the masses more determined to assist the Loyalists. Nick—demonstrating he was not an absolute pacifist—asserted that he could not help but be encouraged that "women and children were helping build fortifications, feed the fighters, and sometimes doing the actual fighting." Comfort reported that Bates remained confident that the Loyalists would prevail. Their army was now well-organized and somewhat better equipped. To Comfort, Bates's talk should have caused thoughtful listeners to reflect on the Spanish situation and to view with skepticism the commonly held refrain in the United States that "It can't happen here."[68]

Peace Day in April 1938 proved to be quiet in Norman. No public rallies were held. Around the country, a new oath was taken by 750,000 high-school and college students. As members of the American Student Union (ASU), they pledged to battle Fascism. The local chapter of the ASU had splintered in the fall, as did peace groups nationwide, over choosing between an isolationist and noninterventionist stance and a quarantine against aggressor nations.[69]

By this point, the threat posed by the Axis powers—Germany, Italy, and Japan—loomed ever larger, causing further splintering in the antiwar ranks. Germany had repudiated the Versailles Treaty, rearmed, moved into the Rhineland, and effectively taken over Austria. The Italians had occupied Haile Selassie's Ethiopia. In Spain, Franco's Falangist rebels were continuing to draw succor from the Italian Fascists and German Nazis. Japan had initiated the Second Sino-Japanese War, attacking Peking. In the fall of 1938, the Munich Pact was carved out, resulting in the dismemberment of part of Czechoslovakia. For many, like Reinhold Niebuhr, Munich served as a "point of no return." Peace in Europe no longer appeared possible. "There will be either war or a capitulation to barbarism," he insisted. His analysis was now shared by many who had so recently been aligned with the American antiwar movement.[70]

Others, like Nick Comfort, remained determined to keep the United States out of war. This determinedly pacifist stance was one held by many, both inside and outside the ministry. However, it would soon make both Comfort and the Oklahoma School of Religion still more controversial as the mobilization toward war preparedness went forward.

Young
Eunice
Comfort
circa 1900.
*(All
illustrations
are courtesy
of Janet
Comfort
Losey and
Anne
Comfort
Courtright.)*

Graduation
day for
Eunice
Comfort,
Kansas City
University,
1911.

Nick
Comfort
with his
firstborn,
two-year-old
Janet, 1914.

Nick and
Esther
Comfort,
circa 1920.

Father-and-son outing at 2000 Chautauqua Place, Norman, Oklahoma, the home of Nick and Ester Comfort, April 1928.

Nick Comfort at work, circa 1930.

The Oklahoma School of Religion, adjacent to the University of Oklahoma campus, Norman, Oklahoma, circa 1933.

The
Reverend E.
Nicholas
Comfort,
circa 1934.

Dick Comfort; Tom and Janet Losey; Anne, Nick, Esther, and Elizabeth Comfort, on the front porch at 2000 Chautauqua, 1936.

Grandpa Comfort and Nick Losey at Comfort Hills, 1950.

Nick Comfort, circa 1953.

Nick Comfort at the banquet in his honor held at Norman's First Presbyterian Church, February 21, 1956, shortly before his death.

CHAPTER SEVEN

SO
THIS IS
LIFE

We remember his concern for intellectual honesty,
for fair play, and for social justice, and his ceaseless
efforts to arouse his fellow citizens to seek solutions
to the problems of the day in the spirit of common
sense and Christian love. He never lacked courage
to point out what he thought was wrong nor to stand
up for his convictions.[1]

Whether through his newspaper columns, at the
pulpit, in the classroom, or on his front porch at 2000
Chautauqua, Comfort "was constantly challenging
men to think." As Cortez A. M. Ewing recognized,
"he was, by nature, a gadfly, the best I have ever
known." Ewing was one of a group of close friends,
including John B. Thompson, Nathan Court, J. Rud
Nielsen, and Antonio M. de la Torre, who regularly
joined Nick at his home for an evening of discussion
of the great issues of the day. Thompson was Nick's
colleague at the School of Religion; the others taught
at the university, in disciplines ranging from mathematics to theoretical physics to modern languages.
Differences of opinion were more than welcomed;
they were expected. "Ideas—bold, unadorned, dis-
tressingly embarrassing ideas" greatly appealed to
Nick. While not opposed to small talk altogether,

Nick, another friend remembered, "would invariably bring up some important question for discussion or some plan for action." Nick always had an open mind about whatever topic was being bandied about, as well as the intellectual ability to grapple with the heart of the matter. To his friends, "he was a man who was always searching for truth rather than one who had found Truth (with a capital *T*) once and for all." That openness, one recollected, kept him intellectually stimulated as well as those who engaged him in conversation of this sort.[2]

Nick's honesty and openness, however, were not appreciated by all those who were aware of his political, social, or economic perspective. Controversy of one kind of another was never far removed from either Nick or the Oklahoma School of Religion. Undoubtedly, at times at least, the topic of discussion at 2000 Chautauqua was something controversial Nick had said or done or written that had caused a new political storm to roll over Norman and the state. Thus Nick must have shared with whatever guests were present the news that his contributions to the *Daily Oklahoman* were about to come to an end.

By late 1934, Nick's notoriety, which stemmed from his determined advocacy of Christian pacifism, along with his views regarding the still troubled U.S. economy, racial relations, and a host of other issues, had come to trouble the powerful and highly conservative editor of the *Daily Oklahoman,* E. K. Gaylord. Gaylord's newspaper, like most of Oklahoma at the time, was declared by its publisher to be in the Democratic Party camp. As James R. Scales and Danney Goble have noted, however, the *Daily Oklahoman* soon boasted a rabid anti–New Deal line. Nick Comfort's passionate entreaties on behalf of peace, like those condemning the uncaring rich, or Jim Crow practices, must have been disturbing to Gaylord and his editors.[3]

168

So
This Is
Life

No matter how radical Comfort's columns were viewed by the likes of E. K. Gaylord and fundamentalist preachers in Oklahoma, his calls for righting the economic ship of state appeared relatively mild in comparison with those delivered by many others who had entered the ministry. Socialist Party leader Norman Thomas, who had been ordained at Union Theological, shifted leftward for a spell during the so-called Red Decade. A. J. Muste, who had trained for the Dutch Reformed ministry, flirted with Trotskyism before returned to the pacifist fold in the mid-1930s. The Reverend Harry F. Ward, who taught at Union, chaired the American Civil Liberties Union for nearly two decades and was considered a radical social gospeler or fellow traveler, depending on the listener's perspective.

Comfort was perhaps closest philosophically to Kirby Page, who had toiled with the overseas ministry of the YMCA and served as director of the speakers' bureau of the Emergency Peace Campaign, which promoted nonmartial solutions to international conflict and sought to keep the United States out of another world war. It was Page who, in 1934, had indicated that "among all the trades, occupations, and professions in this country, few can produce as high a percentage of Socialists as can the ministry." The managing editor of the *Christian Century*, Paul Hutchinson, declared that numerous church bodies were calling for "a society purged of the profit motive." Reinhold Niebuhr, then in the process of leaving his pacifist, social gospel ideals behind for a more radical perspective, however temporary, asserted in 1934 that in the United States more left-wing thought could be found in churches than anywhere else.[4]

As many churchmen veered left during the early and mid-1930s, Comfort did, too, although his political perspective was remarkably close to what it had been ever since he had first become an advocate of the social gospel. He continued to speak of furthering the fatherhood of God and the brotherhood of man, not about Socialism, Communism, or any Marxist variant, let alone Leninism, whose authoritarian emphasis was simply alien to his core democratic ethos. Perhaps this can be explained by the fact that Comfort was never a rigorous theoretician. He was not one to pour over sacred texts, other than the Bible. But perhaps his stance is best explained by his fundamental belief in American democracy, no matter its failings. In the manner of Franklin Delano Roosevelt, whom he looked upon favorably, Comfort undoubtedly would have proclaimed himself, even during this charged period, as an American, a Christian, a Protestant, and a democrat, albeit not necessarily in that order. He was not an ideologue of any kind, other than a true believer in those fundamental tenets of the social gospel.

Though Comfort, in no longer writing for the *Daily Oklahoman,* had lost one vehicle from which he could espouse his strongly held beliefs, he garnered two more—ones undoubtedly even more dear to his heart. On March 24, 1935, Nick began writing a Sunday column, "So This Is Life," for the *Oklahoma Daily,* the campus newspaper at the University of Oklahoma. He saw this as a means to expand his teaching ministry and broaden the influence of the Oklahoma School of Religion. Now, he could attend to the entire flock of students at Oklahoma's leading public university, not simply the 150 to 200 students a year who enrolled in classes at the School of Religion. For one devoted to bringing the word of God to the young people in his native region, this opportunity must have been welcome indeed. Using "So This Is Life" as an extension of his educational ministry, Nick propounded the ideals of the social gospel, once more underscoring the need for all to celebrate the fatherhood of God and the brotherhood of man.

As he noted in his yearly report to the trustees of the School of Religion, Nick believed that his columns each week brought "new friends, and new foes." Characteristically, he considered it a delight to be on the receiving end of high praise one week and unrestrained invectives immediately thereafter. As he saw it, such ambivalence flowed from individuals as disparate as members of the university board of regents and school janitors. He also heard from nearly all the churches in Norman and a host of individuals across the state.[5]

The university's president, William Bennett Bizzell, and John B. Thompson, pastor of the First Presbyterian Church in Norman, indicated that the first thing they turned to on Sunday mornings was "So This Is Life." As Esther Comfort humorously suggested, Dr. Bizzell looked for it with some trepidation: What might Nick have written about now, he mused to himself, that would set off some important backer of the university? By contrast, Thompson searched for the column with "an anticipatory twinkle in his eye." His office was located just above Nick's in the School of Religion building, and occasionally Thompson got an early look at the column, before Esther or the school's secretary had edited it.[6]

In 1936, Nick, determined to bring stimulating, even controversial speakers to the community, helped to establish the Norman Forum. During the forum's formative period, he and others met with President Bizzell. Nick spoke of the need for public discussion, whereas Bizzell expressed concerns about the reprobation the university might receive. When Bizzell suggested the formation of a dinner club as an alternative, Comfort bristled that there already existed too many programs geared for academics alone; all of this had resulted in the very real danger that the university was "dying on the vine because it over-nurtured the innocuous." Nick's arguments prevailed and the Norman Forum, with Comfort as its president, served as "an oasis for more than a decade in the wasteland of inertia," his friend Cortez Ewing asserted.[7]

The program offerings of the Norman Forum were highly diverse. Edwin Elliot spoke on "The Work of the National Labor Relations Board"; Sir Ronald Storrs talked about "The Problem of Palestine"; Upton Close analyzed "The Far Eastern Situation"; German Consul Herbert Diehl discussed "Germany Today"; Maurice Hindus, known as a fellow traveler, led a discussion entitled "Asia Aflame" and Texas Congressman Maury Maverick kicked off one on "The State of The Union."

After the first year's offerings, Comfort declared that the speakers the Norman Forum had brought to campus were at the cutting edge of American idealism. Many, either directly or by inference, had informed attentive audiences "that our only hope lies in the type of civilization advocated by liberal Christianity." Even Harry Barnes, who had not so long ago discussed the waning of Christianity, asserted that it was not science, education, and economics that held the keys to the future but liberal Christianity.[8]

In response to a letter requesting information about the forum, Nick explained that it was designed to uphold the fundamental traditions of the United States. Comfort saw a great need to educate the American people regarding both the worth and the tenuousness of democratic institutions, which had to be sustained. He proclaimed himself "a Democrat in the etymological sense of the term," while "politically I am anything that seems to meet the situation." No greater contributions could be made, he felt, than to ensure that democratic ideals were embedded "more deeply into our social, economic and religious life." Comfort—referring to the forum—asserted that he was "not half so inclined as some of my good friends to look upon my american [sic] experiment in democracy as a mistake." Rather, he was certain that, without democracy, "all that is dearest to us" would be lost. Thus, he was interested in vehicles like the Norman Forum that encouraged self-expression and an awakening "to the benefits of our American ideals."[9]

As Bizzell feared, and Nick no doubt expected, controversy soon developed concerning the Norman Forum, whose guest speakers included locally and nationally prominent pacifists and Socialists, among others. Sending an invitation letter to E. P. Ledbetter, of Oklahoma City, Nick noted that a member of the OU board of regents with whom he had recently spoken was "grossly misinformed" regarding the intentions and design of the Norman Forum. In his letter to Ledbetter, Nick enclosed a copy of the Forum's constitution, which clearly demonstrated that the speakers' group sought to sustain such basic American traditions as freedom of speech and assembly. Unfortunately, as Nick pointed out, movements existed in the United States and in Oklahoma that were determined to subvert those ideals, which made up "the very life blood of our country I think all informed people will admit." Furthermore, the sponsors of the forum believed that democratic ideals did not simply exist; they had to be carefully and perpetually cultivated. Consequently, the forum had been established as a means to enable students, faculty, members of the community, and others throughout the state to obtain firsthand information regarding vital issues.[10]

The forum, Nick noted, did not represent any particular political, economic, social, or religious tenets. During the political campaigns in 1936 it welcomed speakers from across the ideological spectrum, including Communists, Socialists, Republicans, and Democrats. Similarly, it provided a means for a discussion about social security by delegates from Congress, the White House, and the Public Welfare Commission. The forum members themselves—who included some two hundred members of the OU faculty—were from all across the political landscape. They were, however, of like mind regarding one fundamental belief: "That the only possible way to a satisfactory solution of any problem is to have all sides fairly and accurately presented."[11]

Should the American traditions of free speech and assembly be deemed radical, Nick admitted, "then the Forum is as radical as it knows how to be." Anyone with an appreciation of the spirit of the American nation, he insisted, would recognize that the forum was "neither radical nor conservative but essential and truly American." For such "Americanism," its members would deliver no apology whatever. The members of the forum also believed, Nick wrote, that its modus operandi was of a piece "with not only the finest educational traditions of America but of all the world." Indeed, "the very term University implies a universal search for truth in all realms of life."[12]

The sensationalistic press coverage the forum sometimes received, Nick explained, was the inevitable byproduct of the inexperience of reporters and their ignorance regarding fundamental American precepts. Knowing journalists as he did, Nick declared, he had long ago determined that most of their misstatements were the product of ignorance, not malice.[13]

All of the forum speakers who were black, and any other distinguished black visitor to campus, stayed at 2000 Chautauqua, due to Norman's unwritten code regarding segregation. Norman was known as a sundown town, where blacks were required to leave by nightfall. This meant that Anne Comfort, growing up in her parents' home, was able to meet "fantastically intelligent, talented" blacks, far different from some of the "scroungy white people" she encountered in the area.[14]

In 1936, the General Assembly of the Presbyterian Church, U.S.A.—undoubtedly to Comfort's delight—spoke out forthrightly on the continued destitution and deprivation facing so many in the United States. Its Permanent Committee on Moral and Social Welfare declared human rights to be supreme to property rights and called for improved working conditions, higher wages, shorter hours, security against illness, unemployment, and old age, and the extension of democracy into the economic sphere. Within a short while, the committee urged relief for the unemployed; in particular, it condemned sharecropping, arguing that in certain cases this practice effectively resulted in debt peonage. The northern branch's assembly, which had earlier backed labor's right to bargain collectively, now expressed larger dissatisfaction with an industrial system that afforded no security for children, widows, the elderly, and those injured in industrial accidents.[15]

His Sunday columns in the *Oklahoma Daily* and his involvement with the Norman Forum ensured that Nick Comfort and the School of Religion remained highly controversial throughout the depression decade. Comfort's concerns about the plight of the dispossessed and his advocacy of changes in the existing socioeconomic structure were voiced repeatedly as the number of landless and jobless Oklahomans lengthened. Although never expressly declaring himself to be a supporter of Franklin Delano Roosevelt, Nick on occasion praised New Deal–type programs. He considered the opposition to government regulation of business to be wrongheaded and simpleminded. "Some sort of social control of business operations," he noted, had been employed by "practically all highly civilized people." He worried that each day appeared to bring the United States closer to "class and national strife."[16]

In a series of columns in the *Oklahoma Daily* starting in the winter of 1936, he analyzed the various paths down which the American people could travel. One was the revolutionary road, which was increasingly attractive—in Comfort's estimation—to many who failed to understand the reasons for mass suffering in a world of plenty. This "was a revolt of despair and anguish, founded on an all consuming emotion and guided by ignorance and prejudice." Knowing not where they were heading, the long-suffering masses who opted for a violent upheaval dealt with their foes in the manner the latter well appreciated: through "brutality, rapine, murder." Comfort noted that the Russian and Mexican revolutions sprang to mind and that similar upheavals threatened in China and India.[17]

Until recently, such revolutionary stirrings had been little heard in the United States. Possessing great natural bounty and lacking the problems of overpopulation faced by other countries, "a few coins of charity" had generally sufficed to placate the needy. With the advent of the Great Depression, however, the phenomenon of mass poverty in a land of abundance had made its appearance. Little helping matters was the deliberate policy of destroying material resources that might have helped to feed, clothe, and house the long lines of the unfortunate. As a result, greed and selfishness had produced the same potential for class unrest in the United States that existed throughout the globe: "The depression like a hypo put the causes of mass uprisings into the blood stream of our underprivileged classes." Blaming such discontent on foreign propaganda, Nick pointed out, was simply wrongheaded. What was actually taking place was that the American poor, several million strong, were finally becoming class-conscious.[18]

The Roosevelt administration, Nick declared, sought to right the economic ship of state through the greatest infusion of government spending the world had seen to date. However, all recognized that "this is only a temporary expedient and is doomed to ultimate failure." When palliatives such as soldiers' pensions and work relief proved unavailing, the plight of the American underclass would appear starker still. At that point, even the most ignorant would recognize the imminence of revolution.[19]

Then, it might become clearer that economic moguls and military men alike were determined to take the nation down another path. Already unprecedented moves were afoot to curtail basic American liberties. Teachers, clergymen, and politicians were pressured to subscribe to "the ideology of the wealthy."[20]

Either of these routes, Nick believed, would result in class war, something that many considered to be all but inevitable. Although mankind's past history certainly suggested such a possibility, a third way, Nick argued, still might come about. This way, he declared, was "democratic in the etymological meaning of that word." It called for dealing "with man as man," and not as a member of a class. It insisted upon rising above racial, religious, and economic differences. "The best in American life," he felt certain, had resulted from such an approach.[21]

What had to be remembered, Nick wrote, was that the United States was "the world's first large scale experiment in democracy." Democracy and class war were "contradictions in terms." Those who supported American democracy, consequently, must do what they could to avoid class war. The surest way to prevent such a possibility was "actually to build a democracy" by allowing the people to participate more fully in the affairs that affected them and to choose whatever means of government they desired.[22]

Still, Nick indicated, political democracy alone was not enough. Without "intellectual, social, economic, and religious democracy it withers and dies." Public education, the printing press, and the radio had ushered in a large degree of intellectual democracy. A look at Old World Europe demonstrated how far the United States had progressed in the social sphere. The presence of great numbers of religious sects indicated that democratic influences were at work in that realm, too.[23]

Nevertheless, "American economic autocracy and political democracy," Comfort insisted, were presently involved "in a struggle to the death." Economic democracy—which Nick considered to be essential—was far from a reality and would require championing by the American people. To bring about economic democracy on a large scale would be an unprecedented undertaking, he believed—one that would require perseverance and determine the fate of political democracy.[24]

Unlike certain of his countrymen, Nick refused to view democracy as antiquated or reactionary. He was unwilling to accept their pronouncements that either a dictatorship or Communism lay in store for the United States. He acknowledged there were problems, even evils, in the present system; however, he did not view them as intrinsic to the American political or economic system. Instead, the actions of "unprincipled men" now were to be blamed.[25]

Clearly, Comfort backed the so-called third way, or what could best be described as democratic reform. At this point, during the mid-1930s, many American liberals and radicals were thinking along the same lines—a process encouraged by both Fascist aggression abroad and by the calls for a Popular Front, bringing together the forces on the left of the political spectrum. Fascist terrors made some view democracy less dismissively than any number of leftists previously had, while the Soviet Union, considered to be at the forefront of societal change, had championed the idea of anti-fascist alliances.[26]

As Comfort saw it, an evolutionary approach would avoid the pain, suffering, and bloodshed necessarily engendered by revolutionary transformation. The democratic course was also the only one that would ensure the retention of fundamental American traditions, including those freedoms encompassed in the Bill of Rights. "The democratic way is the essentially Christian way of procedure," he declared. Authoritarian rule directly contradicted the ideal of the brotherhood of man. For Comfort, "greed, stupidity, force, superstition" were warring with "brotherliness, intelligence, good will, honesty." He posed the question, "On which side are you casting your lot?"[27]

Due to his concerns about the plight of the dispossessed, Nick, along with a number of preachers, both white and black, including Howard Kester and Claude Williams, became involved with the biracial Southern Tenant Farmers Union (STFU). He received an invitation from H. L. Mitchell, executive secretary of the STFU, to attend its third annual convention in Muskogee, Oklahoma, in mid-January 1937. The Socialist-driven STFU strove to improve living and working conditions for sharecroppers and tenant farmers by unionizing and through governmental assistance.[28]

Comfort possessed great empathy for the downtrodden. He had himself been a member of that underclass, compelled, as a tenant farmer's son, to leave the classroom to work in the fields. He had managed to do what so many with similar backgrounds had been unable to do: after striving mightily to acquire an education, he improved his lot in life; then, having attended some of the finest institutions of higher learning in the land, he had

returned to his native Southwest to minister to the needs of its young people. Yet, even after a full decade and more as a leading religious figure in the region, he and his family remained mired in tough economic circumstances. Repeatedly, he was compelled to inform one creditor after another that he was simply unable to meet obligations on time.[29]

It could have been no surprise to those who knew Comfort well to read his column of May 9, 1937, in the *Oklahoma Daily*, an account of a small shack near the university golf course in Norman. In the shack, each piece of aged carpet suggested squalor. Torn canvas shreds were visible. Squares of tin bespoke deprivation. This shack, wrote Comfort, "cries out, yes screams the message of neglect, lost opportunity, illiteracy, misery, exposure, shiftlessness, thwarted hopes, crushed spirits. This shack is a symbol of the condition of an ever increasing number of people in this land."[30]

A short distance away was the publicly financed golf course, paid for and maintained by taxes placed on the people of Oklahoma. What must the children dwelling in the shack think, Comfort asked, when they witnessed university students knocking golf balls around on the lush sporting grounds. He asked his readers if they had ever dwelled in a place like the shack. Had they had ever gone hungry while plenty appeared all about? Had they had ever toiled until they were ready to collapse? Had they ever been compelled to wear the same clothes for months on end? Had they ever been degraded by those who considered themselves superior? Had they ever felt their pride trampled "in dust" by poverty and their hopes quashed? For Nick himself, the answer was clear. "I know how these children feel," he declared. "Such experiences have so seared my soul that it will require an eternity to heal the wounds."[31]

It made little sense to Comfort for state-financed "luxuries" and "magnificent, endowed churches" to exist amid "shacks of rage and refuse." Moreover, "armories constitute a scene which a Christ would die to obliterate and a Devil would give all to propagate." Such realities appeared to Comfort to be "cancerous" and dangerous to the well-being of the republic.[32]

As Comfort saw it, the continued deterioration of the economy in Oklahoma could be explained by selfish, exploitative practices that reduced many to a life of near subjugation. W. David Baird and Danney Goble have pointed out that economic conditions in Oklahoma actually worsened toward the end of the decade. As director of the Oklahoma School of Religion—one of a mere two hundred full-time workers nationwide now employed by churches to engage in campus work—Comfort felt obliged to carry out itinerant work around the state. There, he confronted firsthand the ravaging effects of the Dust Bowl and the Great Depression. His travels taught him a great deal and made him fully cognizant of the deteriorating conditions.[33]

Early in 1938, in an eastern Oklahoma county, Nick encountered a Joad-like family with "three generations of tenant farmers" herded into a wagon. Altogether, they were "a droopy, malarial, hookwormy lot." The fair-haired children were covered with dirt and mucous. It was clear to Nick that such folk "never have had and never will have anything except children." To him, they were starkly representative of "our basic social ignorance and indifference." They clearly demonstrated that "tenantry, soil erosion, commissary supplies, debts, malnutrition, and listlessness are in their blood stream so thoroughly that it will take long and patient study and protection to tell whether new environment or sterilization has the final answer."[34] The statement—which may sound startling, coming from Comfort—suggests the Darwinistic bent he was occasionally prone to.

In contrast, Nick saw another tenant family—a thirty-year-old man, six feet tall and wearing a corduroy suit and a smile, and his young wife, with baby in hand, both happily responding to pranks played by the man upon his mule team. Their wagon was used but painted; their harness was well-cared for; their mules were freshly shorn, and their appetites were obviously sated by fresh foods, clearly displayed. Although Nick could not tell where this trio was coming from, it was "perfectly clear where they are going." They were renters now, he said, but wouldn't be for long. "They will get along in good shape, depression or no depression."[35]

One day in late April, Nick preached at opposite ends of Oklahoma City, in the morning on the north side and in the evening across town. During the time in between, he visited city parks and the railroad district, which was viewed as the toughest spot in the urban area. Thousands of people were congregated in the parks, while in a four-square block region could be discovered "flop-houses, 10 cent meals, gambling dens, houses of prostitution, pawn shops, Negroes, whites, Chinese, Indians, and what-have-you in a hodge-podge." Poverty could be found everywhere, along with "dirt and degeneracy." Virtually, the only bright spot was the presence of the Salvation Army, with a clean building located in the middle of the district. At best, Nick declared, "it is a rescue mission." What was required was "a good dose of prevention."[36]

Nick came away from his visit with two main impressions. He appreciated anew the work the churches were doing in providing something of "a respite in better things." He was more convinced than ever that there was little sense in expending precious resources to send church missions abroad when the home front itself was in such need. Saving one's own community, he felt, should have the highest priority so that "cancerous spots" could be eradicated.[37]

In the summer of 1938, Nick, who believed that more must be done for those who could not do for themselves, got involved with an organization that would make him more controversial still. Earlier, he had expressed his support for the Southern Policy Committee, a liberal forum that examined the region's economic problems. He had hoped that a like-minded group could be founded in Oklahoma to deliver "the unvarnished facts about our state" and make needed recommendations for change. The organization Nick now became drawn to was the Southern Conference for Human Welfare (SCHW), a by-product in part of President's Roosevelt efforts to carry the banner of the New Deal in the American South. As historian Harvey Klehr has noted, the president, the previous spring, had urged Southern liberals to focus more particularly on problems of the region. An administration report soon followed that highlighted the area's economic deficiencies. Liberals called for a convention that would respond to the administration findings. At the same time, Joseph Gelders, once a professor of physics at the University of Alabama and, by most accounts, a member of the Communist Party, sought to hold a civil liberties conference that would underscore incidents of repression in the region. A decision was made to fuse the two concerns: the Southern Conference for Human Welfare was the result.[38]

On August 31, Nick received an invitation from Alabama Congressman Luther Patrick to serve as a sponsor and member of the arrangements committee for the conference. Five days later, Nick responded that he would "do all that I can to help forward the Southern Conference for Human Welfare." He indicated that he had long believed there existed "the need for just such a conference." Nick declared that he would contact others in Oklahoma City and throughout the state to elicit support for the gathering. On September 28, Judge Louise O. Charlton, the general chairman of the Southern Conference for Human Welfare, asked Nick to indicate which committees he would like to serve on.[39]

In his column in the *Oklahoma Daily*, Nick indicated why he was drawn to such an organization. He discussed the deplorable conditions that could be found in the black district of Shawnee, where more than one thousand people dwelled in huts and shacks, some constructed of boxes. The average weekly income of the black families was less than $2. Unconstitutional and "inhumane segregation laws," he wrote, doomed those who dwelt in such dilapidated living conditions.[40]

If Jesus were present, Comfort wrote, he would be aiding his "suffering and dying" flock. Comfort indicated that interracial cooperation was essential and did his best to publicize the efforts of the Reverend Donald Hyde, pastor of the First Presbyterian Church in Shawnee, and others, who had recently formed an interracial committee to provide more educational and recreational opportunities for black youth. Other self-proclaimed religious people, Nick suggested, could do equally good work if they were of a mind to; indeed, he felt certain that it would be difficult to find an Oklahoma town that was not desperately in need of "Christian love and intelligence." It was particularly incumbent upon educated folk, he wrote, to "shake ourselves out of our benumbing complacence, throw off our air of superiority, confess that we are damned sinners, and yield ourselves without reserve in the guidance of the Man of Galilee."[41]

The record of Presbyterians on racial relations had been decidedly mixed. Even the response of social gospel ministers to the race problem was uneven. In 1919, the General Assembly of the Presbyterian Church, U.S.A., denounced mob violence. The following year, its Standing Committee on Freedom called for "a brotherly hand" to be extended to blacks. A resolution passed in 1922 urged members of the church to help blacks obtain everything that a Christian community required. The 1928 General Assembly delivered a forthright condemnation of racial intolerance and during the 1930s the assembly highlighted the issue of civil rights repeatedly. The 1937 gathering declared, "We accept completely the ideal of the brotherhood of all races, as all are the children of God."[42]

The southern branch, after a call by its General Assembly in 1921 for justice and righteousness to prevail in racial relations, had largely avoided the issue for the next decade and a half. Then in 1936 and 1937, the Committee on Moral and Social Welfare clearly focused on the grievances of black Americans.[43]

With his church having adopted a bolder stance in condemning racial injustice, Nick Comfort looked forward to the convening of the initial Southern Conference for Human Welfare to be held in Birmingham, Alabama, from November 20 to 23. The conference pamphlet asserted that there existed "many liberal thinkers and leaders in the South," whose number was mounting. "Progressive ideas and the desire for progressive action," it was declared, had greater and greater appeal. Isolated liberal leaders required "a meeting ground" that would "promote mutual trust and cooperation between them for greater service to the South."[44]

The Norman contingent, headed by Nick Comfort, included President Bizzell and OU professors C. M. Perry and Maurice Halperin. Also at the conference were Senator Lister Hill and Governor Bibb Graves of Alabama, Frank Porter Graham, president of the University of North Carolina, Eleanor Roosevelt, Aubrey Williams, second-in-command of the WPA, Supreme Court Justice Hugo Black and some 1,200 delegates. The conference opposed allowing wage and freight differentials in the various regions of the nation, backed the Farm Security Administration, championed Senator Robert La Follette Jr.'s committee that was investigating attacks on civil liberties, condemned Congressman Martin Dies's House Committee on Un-American Activities, and called for federal money to be expended on "housing, slum clearance, and parks and recreation."[45]

To the chagrin of some delegates, efforts were made at the conference to hold desegregated meetings, in clear violation of Jim Crow ordinances. Nick orchestrated an unsuccessful battle against racial segregation within the organization. He also encouraged an alliance among various groups that desired change. "Labor, farm, civil liberties and government, housing, race relations and suffrage," he stated, were related concerns. However, Birmingham City Commissioner Eugene "Bull" Connor and a group of policemen appeared. The delegates shied away from confrontation, opting instead for a resolution that attacked Birmingham's segregation ordinances.[46]

Comfort's involvement with the Southern Conference for Human Welfare—altogether in keeping with his belief in the social gospel—made him and the Oklahoma School of Religion still more controversial in the eyes of many Oklahomans. They seemed particularly put off by his efforts to orchestrate a challenge to Jim Crow practices in Birmingham, and by implication in Oklahoma. Perhaps the greater visibility the gathering afforded Nick is what especially infuriated them. What he fought for in Alabama was no different than the battles he had long waged at home.[47]

On December 4, Nick wrote about the conference in his column in the *Oklahoma Daily*. The gathering—with its amalgam of "all types, colors, and creeds"—had shaken up "old Birmingham, that smoky citadel of southern prejudice and ideals." To Nick, those who showed up in Birmingham were among the South's finest. The long-suffering delegates, he believed, were "hardheaded realists," scarred by "the fight for right and justice," who nevertheless believed that only through reason, justice, and fair dealing could the "Beloved Community" come about. Nick felt heartened by the "humble courage" and "grim determination" of his fellow conferees. The conference itself, he believed, held "great promise for all lovers of Dixie." So, too, did the election of such noteworthy figures as Frank Graham (president), Mollie Black (secretary), and Clark Foreman (treasurer). Nick's friend and colleague at the University of Oklahoma, Cortez Ewing, had been named vice chairman for Oklahoma.[48]

President Roosevelt sent a message of support, declaring that "the long struggle by liberal leaders of the South for human welfare" had received "unprecedented" assistance from the federal government during his tenure in office. Others saw the SCHW in a far different light. The Alabama Council of Women's Democrats Clubs dismissed it as Communist-inspired. The Dies Committee sought to uncover evidence that money from the Communist Party had helped to finance the gathering. Even Howard Kester and H. L. Mitchell, leaders of the Southern Tenant Farmers Union, charged that Communists had taken charge of the conference. Others were more concerned about the biracial makeup of the SCHW. One leading Birmingham businessman wrote to Graham, the SCHW president, declaring his unflinching support for the doctrine of white supremacy and disdain for an organization in which whites did "mingle and associate with negroes."[49]

The political heat resulted in several key individuals quickly disassociating themselves from the SCHW. Alabama senators Lister Hill and John Bankhead, Congressman Luther Patrick, and Democratic national committeeman Brooks Hays were among those who refused to have any further involvement with the organization.[50]

With the depression continuing to wreak havoc in Oklahoma, Nick staunchly supported what he perceived to be the aims of the SCHW, which increasingly appeared to be one of the few organizations he could identify with. As the 1930s wound to a close, the Indian summer of radical resurgence in Oklahoma ended, too, as Okies migrated westward en masse. The great trek removed the very folk who had peopled the state's radical rural movements for half a century. In addition, Ameringer's *American Guardian* began to experience financial problems as it became something of an antiwar weekly.[51]

Comfort attended the second gathering of the SCHW, held in Chattanooga in April 1940. He came away from the old Southern city afflicted with "a mysterious apprehension and an inexplicable sadness." What troubled him most was the sense of futility he felt in witnessing the continued vitality of the issues that had helped to usher in the American Civil War. The black section of Chattanooga was "as bad as any I have ever seen. Hatred, superstition, ignorance, poverty, disease, crime, and death lurked on every hand." The miserable plight of the black masses vividly demonstrated that Christians were too little interested in the world at hand. So, too, did the dearth of religious figures at the conference itself. In the halls of the conference rang out tales "of the dastardly and cowardly beatings and crimes of the Klan." Clearly heard were accounts of brutalities meted out by "thugs retained by the industrialists." Racial discord and class conflict seemed ever present. Among the delegates themselves, the vast majority of whom were concerned about the underclass, a clash between Socialists and Communists threatened to bring matters to a halt.[52]

Repeatedly, speakers expressed fears of how religion could be employed as "a weapon of class struggle." The "painfully conservative" religious workers whom Comfort encountered were deeply distressed that their religion might thereby be compromised. Only John B. Thompson, of the Norman contingent, and Mordecai Johnson, president of Howard University, expressed the view that Christianity could be a dynamic force to attack social ailments. Comfort believed that educated Christians were missing a wonderful opportunity to construct a new South.[53]

All of this was unfortunate indeed, Comfort declared, because the SCHW was "the greatest potential force for sane reconstruction in the South that is now on the horizon." It seemed more representative of the whole region than anything else he could recall. It involved an attempt by the people to cooperate with the Southern elite. Consequently, a failure to respond graciously to this effort would demonstrate that Southern leaders were "either indifferent or dumb." Individuals like Frank Graham, Aubrey Williams, Myles Horton, Maury Maverick, and John Thompson were attempting to accomplish what he believed to be necessary: "to weld the people of the South into a cooperative and understanding unit that will agree upon a step by step solution of the living issues facing all the people."[54] Such an approach Comfort considered to be essential, and in keeping with the social gospel he believed in. Any other solution he felt certain would result in a pall descending on the American South for some time to come.

So
This Is
Life

CHAPTER EIGHT

A DEATH
IN THE
FAMILY

Public issues were not all that held Nick Comfort's attention during the 1930s. As always, he was a family man first and foremost, enamored as ever with Esther and a doting father to his children. Generally, he was "always happy, upbeat, positive in his dealing with things." By all accounts, his marriage to Esther was a highly fruitful one, and rarely a cross word passed between the two. At the same time, they were very different personalities: Nick was far more buoyant and easygoing; Esther, more careful and determined—as befitted her straitlaced, Methodist background—to do what was proper.[1]

Esther was, at the same time, not without strongly held beliefs of her own. She was an "adamant teetotaler" and a member of the Women's Christian Temperance Union. On one occasion, she took beer that one of the boys had brought home, opened it, and poured it down the kitchen sink. She seemed in basic agreement with Nick's stands on political and social issues, but was "much more conservative and more party-line" than her husband in theological matters.[2]

The only time the children could recall their parents fighting was one occasion when Nick wanted Esther to decide what they were going to do for entertainment. Were they going to the show? Which show did she want to see? Esther was so little used to making such decisions that she became upset as Nick continued to press her. He wanted her to choose—because she was always doing "his thing"— but the discussion continued to deteriorate until tears flowed down her face. Generally, as Anne recollected, Esther was "just a very quiet, compliant kind of person as far as Dad was concerned."[3]

At the same time, Nick obviously respected her views and appreciated the fact that she recognized his faults and foibles . She was sometimes put off by his less-refined ways. For example, she hated his old, ton-and-a-half flatbed truck, with its unpainted sideboards. She did not care for the way Nick treated their other vehicles: he would take the cars given to him by his daughter Janet and her husband Tom Losey and trash them. He hauled whatever he needed to in both the truck and the cars, until they were dirty, torn, and dusty. If the truck had to be used for transportation to church, Esther would park it— which she viewed as "not a very respectable looking vehicle"—some distance away and indicate to the children, "We can walk!"[4]

On more than one occasion, a sheepish Nick would softly indicate to his children not to let their mother know what had just transpired. There was the time when Elizabeth went into town with him to get some hay. The load was a good-sized one and he had her ride on top on the way home, to help keep things balanced. At some point, the top section of hay, Elizabeth, and a pitchfork flew off the truck, while Nick continued tootling merrily on home. On arrival, he spoke to his daughter and discovered that she was nowhere to be found. He was "petrified and horrified." Saying nothing to Esther, he went back along the path he had just taken, finding Elizabeth, hay, and pitchfork awaiting his return. As they rode back to

2000 Chautauqua, with Elizabeth now in the cab, he said, "Let's don't bother telling Mammy about this! We would only worry her." As far as Elizabeth knew, Esther never learned of the incident.[5]

Esther seemed to tolerate her husband's idiosyncratic ways. While Nick "was always doing something crazy like that," the two were all but inseparable throughout their long years together. Friends and family members alike continually reflected on the fact that Nick could not have accomplished what he did without Esther's support. One example involved her editing of his writings. He was filled with all kinds of ideas and sought to get them down on paper, but his grammar was somewhat deficient, unlike his wife's. She would pour over his manuscripts, making many suggestions as to grammar and syntax.[6]

Both of them believed in public service. Thus, not only Nick made his mark as a public figure in Oklahoma, but Esther did, too. Their son Dick, in fact, believed that his mother "could get things done, while Dad would froth at the mouth; he left blood lying all over the place. Mother probably made more progress in what they were trying to do. They both had a common commitment. They were as different, in some ways, as they could be, but they had a common commitment to these things, which I think is the thing that kept them going." For many years, she was president of the Oklahoma district of the YWCA. The district organization served all of the state, other than the large urban areas that could sustain a city association. Statewide meetings were held every year, with teachers congregating at the YWCA building in Oklahoma City, along with their students, who might be white, red, or black. This took place throughout the time Jim Crow laws remained in effect.[7]

The Oklahoma YWCA broke new ground. When a weekend retreat was held at a rural site, the girls all slept in a large room, with no consideration given to race. Teachers from one town felt compelled to inform the parents in their community of the situation and the girls were ordered home. The rest stayed and, as Esther reported, a new experience was had for the other girls. Later, a black schoolteacher informed others in the organization that the Oklahoma's district YWCA "had much to do in building race relations in Oklahoma."[8]

No doubt Nick was proud of his wife's determined stand, so much like his own. It was yet another reason why he continued to view her as his soul mate: he was not the only member of the Comfort household willing to act in a manner likely to engender controversy.

Though he was a loving father, who thought his offspring "were all just wonderful," he was not blind to their faults. He did not seem to worry about his eldest, Janet, figuring she would simply "get married and make some fellow a good wife." He did have concerns about Elizabeth, however, for she seemed to have "an artistic temperament, moody and whatnot." Nick had reservations about Hugh, too, considering his son to be inflexible; he was not sure Hugh would make a good husband.[9]

During the 1930s, the makeup of the Comfort household changed, as children completed their education or got married and left home. Janet had graduated from the University of Oklahoma in 1932 and received her M.A. degree in English the following year. She married Tom Losey, an engineer, on November 4, 1933, at 2000 Chautauqua, with Comfort delivering his blessings. Tom had already been warmly welcomed into the home, with Janet bringing him for dinner whenever she desired. When a friend held a wedding shower for Janet, Esther informed her daughter that Nick had bought her a present. Sarcastically, Janet tossed out, "Probably a rolling pin." "Well," her mother informed her, "he had gotten a rolling pin." Nick was so wounded by Janet's reaction that he took the pin and hurled it into the furnace and bought her something altogether different. Janet, in turn, was terribly upset that her father had been angered by her offhand comment. However, the episode did nothing to alter the fact that his firstborn remained his favorite—a "Daddy's girl" without question.[10]

Hugh and Esther received their master's degrees during the summer commencement in 1935, Hugh having studied English, his mother classical languages. Not surprisingly. Hugh, like Janet, had been a Phi Beta Kappa.[11]

Hugh briefly taught English at Central State Teachers' College in Edmond, a dozen or so miles north of Oklahoma City. In the summer of 1938, he offered English classes at the University of Oklahoma. That fall, Hugh and his fiancée, Lucille McGuire, another OU graduate, headed for New Haven to study at Yale University. Lucy enrolled in the drama school. Almost immediately, Hugh took and passed the requisite language exams in German and Greek for his doctoral degree. A small, neat, young man, Hugh lived in a private home in New Haven, in a room that had a small, gas-fired hot plate, on which he sometimes warmed tomato soup. On the evening of October, 1938, Hugh, having heated soup, turned again to his studies of Ralph Waldo Emerson and to letter writing.[12]

One of those letters was to his good friend Dick Disney. The tone was, on its face, cheery and confident, with Hugh exclaiming that "nothing can keep me from that Ph.D." He indicated that he had seen Lucille for a very brief while that evening, and she had never been more charming. The academic year would hurry by, he declared, and then "she will be mine. With a Ph.D., Lucille, and a job teaching, what more could I ask?"[13]

He evidently set aside the letter for a spell to delve into Emerson. When he returned to his correspondence, he asserted that "Emerson understood." Man did not change over the ages, aspiring to accomplish all he could, Hugh wrote, "and the beauty of it is that he reaches them! Each with his limitations reaches up and grasps a segment of eternity." Hugh closed by declaring that he liked to dream and believed that "the future as I paint it is glorious." As indicated by his scrawl, the gas was already affecting his penmanship.[14]

The next morning, another resident smelled gas fumes and went to check in Hugh's room. Hugh's body was crumpled on the floor, lifeless. Dick, who was at a basketball game when informed of his brother's death, on receiving the news—like the other members of the family—went into a state of shock.[15]

When Nick received word of his son's death, he immediately left for Connecticut. As the train approached Hartford, Nick remembered that his column for the *Oklahoma Daily* was about due and he proceeded to write about the losses he and Esther had experienced—the baby Lee and Hugh. He wrote of a young couple who planted a garden; one morning, they discovered that their "most vigorous" flower was beginning to wilt. Within three days, a dreaded disease had devoured that flower. Eventually, other flowers came their way, receiving the greatest of care, but, as they grew and matured, "the pride of the garden," whose growth was "luxuriant" and whose promise was great, was cut down unexpectedly.[16]

Along with Lucille McGuire, Nick took care of arrangements for the burial in a cemetery in Hartford. A memorial service was held at the First Presbyterian Church in Norman, with orations by

Pastor John B. Thompson and Dr. John Mosely, the president of Central State University. Mosely indicated that Hugh was the kind of individual who accepted responsibility, "the kind of teacher that college presidents go gunning for." The inscription on his headstone read, "Scholar, Gentleman, Christian." A poem was delivered by Jewel Wurtzbaugh, a favorite English teacher of Hugh's. A tribute was spoken by Dick Disney.[17]

The "official party line," as his sister Anne later indicated, was that Hugh had been asphyxiated by gas that had leaked from a faulty fixture on his hot plate. Later, Nick indicated to her that, in his estimation, Hugh, "a very intense kind of person," had taken his own life. Nick reported that Hugh had been deeply distressed about the apparent termination of his engagement to Lucille McGuire, whom "he was terribly fond of." She, evidently, had become involved with another man, and Hugh feared he had lost her for good. "Hugh was this very sensitive personality," Anne pointed out, "a creative and sensitive and artistic kind of thing." Consequently, Nick reasoned, based on a conversation he had with Lucille when he went back East, that Hugh simply could not cope with the ending of their relationship and committed suicide. Nick never said anything regarding his suppositions to Esther, fearing such news would make her even more distraught.[18]

If Nick's analysis was correct, Hugh, in writing his last letter, had obviously couched it in a manner that he hoped would prevent his family from discovering what he had done. He had hoped, unrealistically, to ease their pain.

CHAPTER NINE

NICK
THE
HERETIC

The late 1930s was a period when the nation's political landscape shifted markedly. Following the 1932 presidential election, which brought Franklin Delano Roosevelt and his New Deal advisers into the Oval Office, widespread support had existed for the construction of a welfare state. Roosevelt's personal charisma and the appeal of liberalism had resulted in a succession of electoral triumphs, through the 1936 presidential campaign. But a series of events shortly after Roosevelt's second inauguration allowed for a resurgence of conservative forces determined to prevent the expansion of the welfare state.

Roosevelt's attempt to pack the Supreme Court—he called for presidential authority to appoint as many as six new justices in place of those jurists who reached the age of seventy and refused to retire—proved to be politically disastrous. His image was also hurt by the administration's identification with the labor movement as sit-down strikes were waged against recalcitrant employers by the new Congress of Industrial Organizations. It was further damaged by FDR's decision, made with the economy having rebounded markedly since its lowest ebb, to cut government spending: he mistakenly believed that private entrepreneurs could pick up the slack, but another sharp downward turn resulted. Roosevelt's invincibility was called into question and political foes achieved remarkable gains in the 1938 congressional elections.

Unease on the home front was intensified by the quickening pace of events overseas. Right-wing aggressor states were on the march. Republican Spain was about to fall to the Falangists of Francisco Franco and Germany was carving up Czechoslovakia, the lone democratic state in Eastern Europe, while Austria was now firmly in Fascist hands. Italy had completed its conquest of Ethiopia. Japan's incursions against China were likewise proceeding at a bloody pace.

Many were increasingly disturbed by developments in Soviet Russia, which had been viewed since its inception by many leftists as a progressive force, even a remarkable experiment in creating a workers' state. Throughout the decade, however, and particularly during the final few years, news of purge trials involving Old Bolsheviks—even former leaders of the Communist nation—had filtered out of the USSR. Some dismissed the reports as the work of counterrevolutionaries; others saw the developments as a perversion of the ideal of socialism. Stories about Soviet machinations during the Spanish Civil War only further fed suspicions, or brought outright certainty, that something was rotten under Stalinist rule.

The advocates of Communist or Fascist solutions for the problems in the United States remained a minority throughout this troubled period, although the Communist Party of the United States garnered more support than ever and right-wing groups like the German-American Bund and the Silver Shirts numbered followers in the tens of thousands. Because of the disturbing events at home and overseas, calls were heard for the establishment of investigative committees to ferret out information about extremist organizations. As early as 1930, a committee led by Representative Hamilton Fish looked into the practices of the Communist Party. In 1934, Congressmen John McCormack and Samuel Dickstein induced the House of Representatives to establish a special committee to examine "Nazi propaganda activities" and the spread of "subversive propaganda." The Fish Committee had been apprised of stories running the gamut from "responsible to fantastic allegations of communist deceit and treachery" and the McCormack-Dickstein hearings featured charges that Nazi witnesses had engaged in treasonous practices. Then in 1938, the Dies Committee investigated the Bund and the Silver Shirts, but focused most of its attention on the Communist Party, the CIO, and the Roosevelt administration. The antics of the Dies Committee were particularly irresponsible, as its members effectively went after the American Left and attempted to depict the New Deal as connected to a Communist conspiracy.[1]

The U.S. Congress was not the only legislative body that targeted suspect groups. Starting in 1939, the state legislature in Oklahoma City, which had a history of holding investigative hearings into political matters, conducted a series of hearings into purported Communist undertakings in Oklahoma. Twenty years previously, an earlier Red scare in the state had resulted in the passage of a criminal syndicalism act, intended to prevent "industrial or political revolution," and another measure prohibiting the display of a Red flag. In 1923, the legislature passed an act that required teachers at all schools, public and private, to take an oath of allegiance, indicating they would support and defend the state and federal constitutions. In 1935, the state senate unanimously backed a bill to bar Communists from the ballot, although the house did not follow suit. Interestingly, the membership of the Communist Party in Oklahoma at this point was fewer than three hundred.[2] Over the course of the next three years, calls to combat Communism in the state were at least matched by exhortations to investigate those with Fascist sympathies, including those at Oklahoma A&M and the University of Oklahoma. But less than a month after his victory in the gubernatorial campaign, Leon C. "Red" Phillips, who had earlier made his mark as a staunch opponent of both Roosevelt's New Deal administration and Governor E. W. Marland's "little New Deal" for Oklahoma, spoke in Norman and challenged the Communists in the state, now purportedly numbering 600 or so. "Our citizens," he declared, "will not stand for Communists in Oklahoma. I have an ambition for such a unity of feeling among our citizenship that I know they'll never do much here." As H. E. Anderson, special agent in charge of FBI operations in Oklahoma City, indicated in a special report to Director J. Edgar Hoover, Governor Phillips made his confidential files available to governmental operatives. Phillips purportedly gathered the information to help ferret out Communism in institutions of higher learning in the state. Among those discussed in the report, entitled "Communist Activities in United States, Subversive Activities," were John B. Thompson and Nick Comfort.[3]

On January 6, State Representative H. Tom Kight, of Claremont, urged the amending of the state criminal syndicalism act through the outlawing of sit-down strikes and the forbidding of Communists to serve as elected public officials. Kight did not stop there, however. He soon attacked Nick Comfort: the trauma caused by the death of his son Hugh the previous fall was now to be followed by another trying season. Always controversial, Comfort was soon viewed as outside the pale altogether by such governmental figures as Representative Kight and Governor

Phillips, who were determined to chalk up political points by attacking both him and the School of Religion. A column Comfort wrote for the *Oklahoma Daily* of January 7, 1939, possibly triggered the first of a succession of attacks. Comfort warned of "the military octopus" that was "entwining itself about every expression of American culture and placing a sucker on every artery of American life." The movement was operating by stealth in effect, thereby avoiding needed public scrutiny.[4]

Oklahoma, Comfort continued, was engulfed by a growing military presence. Great armories were cropping up all over; military convoys could regularly be spotted and thousands of Oklahomans were receiving summer military training. The major state universities had compulsory ROTC programs, some high schools had military training of their own, a military academy was in place, and military organizations were present in all the major urban areas.[5]

Comfort believed this resulted from the American president's preparedness campaign. Consequently, the U.S. military was heading "toward the center of the vortex of international military preparedness." All of this was occurring "under a cloak of self-righteousness." The people of the United States "were so dumb" to reason that their nation could construct a vast military apparatus for defense purposes only; such a belief, Comfort wrote, had been used throughout the ages by those desiring more armaments. The familiar litany rang out that our people, unlike others, were honorable, well-intentioned, blessed by God, desirous of simply living in peace, and determined only to withstand the onslaught of "the scheming, dangerous, ravaging barbarian."[6]

At the very least, Comfort reasoned, Americans should recognize that such fallacious reasoning always resulted in disaster. All knowledgeable

Americans, he asserted, viewed with disdain "Germany's military madness." Likewise, "every thinking European" beyond the borders of Nazi Germany was plotting to rein in that state's "vaulting ambitions." Probably thoughtful Germans also were cognizant of the suicidal nature of Hitler's aggression. It was clear, Comfort declared, that military preparedness did not guarantee national security.[7]

Rather, "the world's preparedness madness is simply a prelude to disaster." No one doubted this, yet ignorance or disinterest characterized Americans who viewed the march of other nations to their "certain doom." Instead, they seemed bound to "stumble into the maelstrom mumbling inanities about our righteousness, the cussedness of the rest of the world, and the necessity of preserving our democracy by meeting force with force."[8]

Comfort exclaimed,

> In God's name, when will we learn that militarism is the denial of democracy? Oh! How long? How long will it take men to learn that war is the antithesis of Christianity? It is not the German in German militarism that makes it bad, nor is it the Japanese in Japanese militarism that makes it to be dreaded. It is the militarism that is poison in both Germany and Japan. Militarism always has and always will of necessity mean regimentation, unreasoning obedience, class consciousness, force as final arbiter, surrender of individual rights and conscience, mass movement, dictatorship.

Comfort viewed it as no accident that German religious leaders and academics had become puppets or been forced out of their country. He saw that as the inevitable by-product of full-blown militarism and something that the United States could also experience unless the military spirit were curbed.[9]

Comfort advised his countrymen to look at what was happening in their own land long enough to halt "the military craze" that was enveloping the United States. The issue was simple for Comfort: "If we meet militarism with militarism, we become the victims of the very thing we are supposedly attempting to destroy." Among other steps that should be immediately undertaken, he believed, was an end to military preparedness.[10]

Not surprisingly, such an analysis was not well received by many Oklahomans. By early 1939, international tensions were even more tightly drawn. Japanese encroachments upon China were continuing; Italy held sway over Ethiopia; Germany had taken effective control of Austria. The Spanish Civil War had come to a disastrous close and the Czech democracy was more imperiled than ever. President Roosevelt, imbued with Wilsonian internationalism, was determined to revise the neutrality laws. Speaking before Congress on January 4, Roosevelt warned that the neutrality acts might actually assist an aggressor and penalize the victim.[11]

Along with the worsening state of international affairs, the peace forces in the United States seemed more divided than they had been since the end of World War I. The peace movement of the 1920s was marked by the willingness of activists to submerge differences to present a united front. Through the middle part of the 1930s, a comparable approach resulted in the robust antiwar movement that arose on college and university campuses. However, ideological differences—which had always existed in the antiwar camp—increasingly caused the peace coalition to fray, with Communists, anti-Stalinists, advocates of collective security, and isolationists increasingly unable to find common cause.[12]

Among those in Oklahoma particularly riled by what he perceived to be only the latest of Nick's shenanigans was Representative Kight. The state legislator was still disturbed that the dean of the

Nick
the
Heretic

School of Religion had so recently attended the biracial Southern Conference of Human Welfare convention in Birmingham. Kight no doubt also was perturbed by the fact that Comfort had invited George O. Pershing, a member of the Young Communist League, to speak in Norman, which had resulted in something of a public furor. Police in Oklahoma City arrested Pershing at his room in the Huckins Hotel and spirited him off to the city jail, where he was held incommunicado for nine hours. The *Oklahoma News* on January 26 charged that the police action violated fair play and was an example of "half-cocked Americanism."[13]

The following day, a public hearing was held at the state capitol concerning the criminal syndicalism measure that Kight had proposed. Representative S. E. Hammond, of Okmulgee, indicated that church people in his district wanted to know if such a measure would be applied to sit-down strikes only. Kight responded that radicals were attempting to infiltrate the churches. He went on to assert that a school of religion at one of Oklahoma's leading universities was "so much out of harmony with the intent of every law of this state, that you can't help but believe that it is communistic." When asked what institution he was referring to, Kight replied, "There is only one such school in the state, the University of Oklahoma." In response to Kight's charges, Comfort demanded an open meeting that might publicly vindicate the School of Religion. He considered this request to be reasonable as Kight's allegations had been widely reported across the state. Only through such an encounter, Comfort declared, could "we . . . have the democracy which is so dear to both of us" and the School of Religion cleared of the scurrilous charges. Comfort assured Kight that he would endeavor to have the meeting conducted in a cordial and instructive manner.[14]

Kight refused to convene a hearing, accusing Comfort of having breached confidentiality in releasing his letter to the school newspaper. Due to Comfort's actions, Kight declared, "I have not sufficient confidence in your integrity to further confer with you." Kight said he had formed his own conclusions regarding Comfort's involvement at the Birmingham conference, where the minister had called for "seating the races together."[15]

Comfort emphatically denied having betrayed any confidences. He asked Kight if such a "cry of betrayal of confidence" were merely "a trumped up and flimsy attempt to avoid an open hearing on your slanderous accusations concerning the School of Religion?" He exhorted Kight not to "get cold feet now" and to allow for a public hearing. There, the state representative would be compelled to either prove that the school was "communistic" or to acknowledge that misrepresentations had been made.[16]

If Kight truly were unwilling to meet with him personally, Comfort went on to say, then he could name a hundred individuals with unsullied reputations who would defend the honor of the School of Religion. The bottom line, as Comfort saw it, was that "you have either through ignorance or deliberate malice sought to destroy the Oklahoma School of Religion. It is an outrageous thing that you have done." Kight's accusations that the school opposed private ownership of property, marriage, and religion, and viewed children as property of the state, were "so monstrous that the maintenance of your self-respect and the confidence of even the most prejudiced people in the state" demanded the public confrontation. Furthermore, Kight could not cloud the issue, Comfort asserted, by discussing something as "tame" as his involvement with the Southern Conference for Human Welfare. Comfort indicated that he would be happy to defend his participation in the conference at any point, but declared that the issue of integration was "a far cry" from the charges Kight had made. He closed by urging Kight to "come on now" and display his "vaunted high respect" for democratic processes.[17]

In the midst of the squabble between Comfort and Kight, Governor Phillips again picked up the anti-Red cudgel, lambasting what he perceived to be the teaching of Communism or Nazism in Oklahoma public schools and calling for an investigation of the state universities. Phillips insisted that certain instructors at the University of Oklahoma and Oklahoma A&M College were proselytizing on behalf of these foreign *isms* and should be dismissed from their positions. OU president Bizzell declared that he would welcome an investigation of the charges the governor had made. He also declared that faculty at state schools "do not have the right to propagandize students with any alien theory of government." Bizzell then indicated that he would talk to Phillips about the accusation, but he did not believe that there were any Communists among the OU faculty.[18]

Since Bizzell had assumed the presidency of the University of Oklahoma, he had been one of Nick Comfort's strongest supporters and one of the earliest backers of the School of Religion. He was also a man who respected Nick enormously and did his best to deflect criticism from his friend on more than one occasion. When Bertrand Russell gave a lecture at the university, and Bizzell and his wife held a dinner in his honor at the president's house, Nick and Esther were among the invited guests. Another time, a group of professors from the university was being readied for a photograph. The photographer suggested that Nick should position himself on a lower step, so that he would be seen looking up at Bizzell. The president wryly responded, "Nick Comfort doesn't look up to any man."[19]

Now Bizzell himself was on the receiving end of some heated criticism. An impatient Governor Phillips soon lashed out at the university president, accusing him of carrying out a "whitewash," which Bizzell vehemently denied. At a special meeting of the OU board of regents, Bizzell reported that no evidence had been found to back the charges of Communist affiliation.[20]

One member of the state legislature, James C. Nance, later explained what he considered to be the source of Oklahoma's version of the Red scare during the late 1930s, asserting that "corporate monopolies" were behind the campaign. These business interests were determined, he said, that liberal instructors not lead students to adopt antibusiness beliefs or to support governmental welfare programs.[21]

Friends, former students, and allies did their best to provide moral support to Nick and the School of Religion. An editorial in the *Oklahoma Daily* stated that many in Norman were simply "laughing out loud" at Kight's charges. The editorial writer of the student paper declared that the university and local communities well recognized that Nick Comfort had probably done more than any other individual in the state "to encourage liberal thought." Furthermore, in the eyes of his supporters, the educator was one of the few individuals who supported freedom of thought not only for those he agreed with but also for his opponents. The success of the Norman Forum was largely attributed to Comfort, who was praised for his courageous proposal for teacher's pensions and his championing of oppressed minorities. The editorial indicated that the University of Oklahoma faculty included several liberals, but that unlike Nick, few "would risk their necks." The editorial observed that Comfort was quick to speak out when he saw injustice arise, was a true friend of democracy, and taught Christian ethics in the classroom.[22]

One letter addressed to Comfort blasted the "Ism Witch Hunt" of Governor Phillips and the "inquisition" of State Representative Kight. The governor, the writer declared, evidently required "a new Bogie, thus the Red Baiting episode," and he also seemed to favor only the ideological perspective of publishers like E. K. Gaylord and Eugene Lorton of the *Tulsa World;* that is, "the Stone Age conceptions of the Bourbons." The correspondent urged Comfort to "stay in and Pitch. Pitch for the right of freedom of thought and action." Phillips and Kight, on the other hand, seemed to back the activities of the House Un-American Activities Committee, as did those who desired to besmirch "all progressives and forward movements."[23]

In other correspondence, Oklahoma City attorney B. M. Parmenter suggested that the attack against Comfort was linked to the earlier one against George Pershing. Comfort had reason for good cheer, because there existed "an abundance of citizens who will support you as against this very unjust attack." Indeed, the lawyer declared, "this surely is a time for the good and sound thinking people of this country to be alert against vicious and unwarranted attacks upon citizens."[24]

The Reverend James Smith Griffes, of the First Presbyterian Church of Poteau, Oklahoma, wrote that "someone was 'after your head!'" It seemed clear to Griffes that Governor Phillips was either woefully lacking in knowledge about Communism, "sorely afraid of Christian teaching," or deliberately attempting to agitate the public for political gain. Griffes offered to provide whatever assistance he could. Elizabeth Irwin, fired from a teaching post in Oklahoma City because of her political views, was another who wrote to encourage Comfort. Martin A. Klingberg, minister of the First Presbyterian Church in Nowata, Oklahoma, informed Comfort that he paid no heed to the charges by Phillips and Kight. "Don't you let these ignorant, half-baked political ignoramuses bother you one bit. Apparently they are afraid of coming out in the open, and personally, I think you have them on the run." Saying he was certain that Nick's presbytery would come to his assistance if necessary, Klingberg stated, "There are plenty of your friends all over the state who won't let you down either."[25]

Without a doubt, Nick Comfort viewed the attacks by Governor Phillips and State Representative Kight as more than sharp-edged criticisms of himself or the Oklahoma School of Religion. They seemed all too symptomatic of the growing eruption of "fear, suspicion, class antagonism and blind hysteria." He believed the time to handle such "maladies" was when they were in their relative infancy. In starker form, he watched with disdain and alarm as 18,000 German-American Bundists, spewing out anti-Semitic diatribes, met in Madison Square Garden to demonstrate their solidarity with German Nazism. It was clear to Comfort that these native fascists exhibited total loyalty to an individual who was out to subvert all democratic principles and processes. Through "word, symbol, and action," such loyalty was displayed. In Comfort's eyes, this amounted to more than an attempt at revolution; it was a betrayal of everything that Americans most revered.[26]

In his weekly piece in the *Oklahoma Daily*, he declared that he held civil liberties in as high regard as any man; however, when a group openly asserted that it had collected millions for propaganda purposes and began to train storm troopers to demonstrate allegiance to an authoritarian government, it had "gone far beyond the realm of free speech, free press, and free assemblage." Such American fascists were active rebels and should be treated as such.

Comfort did not, however, indicate what that treatment should be.[27]

To counteract the native fascists necessitated a large educational campaign and a recognition of the deficiencies in the U.S. economic, political, and social order. It also required that his countrymen keep their wits about them and refuse to give in to "prejudice, hatred, blind hysteria." The people of the United States had to possess the courage of their convictions and the willingness to defend the same.[28]

In the spring of 1939, a small group of political figures demonstrated their support for Comfort and the Oklahoma School of Religion. Gomer Smith, an Oklahoma City attorney, former vice president of the Townsend Clubs (which had helped lead the fight for old-age pensions) and a seemingly perennial candidate for statewide office, said he and his wife viewed with interest "the unfair publicity" heaped upon Comfort and the School of Religion. Smith affirmed that "we are for you and will be glad to do anything we can to help." State Representative Cecil A. Myers of Beckham County, a former student of Comfort's, congratulated him on his "very great" work and declared his readiness to defend the school. State Representative Ripley S. Greenhaw of Washita County assured Comfort that he possessed "the utmost confidence" in the School of Religion.[29]

Zula J. Breeden, of Breeden & Breeden Oil and Gas Leases and Royalties, wrote to Comfort, indicating that her blood pressure had risen "to unprecedented heights" thanks to Kight's scurrilous charges. Breeden informed Comfort that she had headed for the capitol to let Kight know he was not about to move on to higher electoral office "on your shoulders if the Mothers of the Alumnae" of the University of Oklahoma "had anything to say and I assured him they would have something to say at the polls." Both of her boys, graduates of OU, were livid "at the unwarranted attack," and like other members of the Breeden family stood ready to aid Comfort if needed.[30]

Newspaperman Lawrence Thompson termed Comfort "the most interesting member of the University of Oklahoma faculty." He spoke of the School of Religion operating "on a shoestring" since its inception a dozen years earlier. The journalist clearly recognized the nurturing impact Comfort had had on the institution and the 3,251 students who had enrolled in its classes: "If it weren't for Comfort, the school probably would never have been established. Too, strangely enough, if it weren't for Comfort it probably would be comfortably endowed right now." He assured his readers that Comfort was no Communist, no Red, but rather "a forthright and frank speaker, a dyed-in-the-wool liberal." Comfort was something of an unusual instructor who actually encouraged the students in his classrooms to think. Comfort was a different kind of minister who believed that religion should involve how one lived, and not amount to "a lot of mumbo-jumbo that sounds nice but doesn't have any application to ordinary every day life."[31]

That way of thinking, reporter Thompson declared, got Comfort "into hot water"; after all, he downplayed the importance of "the frills of religion, the creeds and the ceremonies"; he gave short shrift to religious teachings of a controversial nature, underscoring instead "the importance of living honest, decent and helpful lives." The result, nevertheless, was that trouble assuredly came his way. At the end of the past semester, for example, one student had informed him, "Dean Comfort, I'm sorry, but you are going to hell."[32]

Journalist Thompson went on to say that Comfort was able to report that most students eventually acknowledged that matters they once considered beyond dispute were open to different perspectives. They were willing to admit that the way one lived was more important than arguing about church doctrine. Thompson suggested that many churches throughout the state would never consider allowing Nick Comfort to preach in their establishments because of the issues he might discuss. In fact, during the past week he had talked to young people in Oklahoma City about marriage, sex, venereal disease, contraception, and the like. But "even the students who are horrified by his views like him," Thompson noted. Alumni of his classrooms included full-fledged ministers, missionaries, a hospital administrator, university professors, newspapermen, and a Broadway actor, Van Heflin.[33]

It was clear that Comfort's determination had at the very least enabled the School of Religion to survive during a period when many college departments of religion and seminaries were being sharply scaled back. This was in line with a general reduction of funds available to religious organizations. Somehow, the Oklahoma School of Religion managed to avoid the fate suffered by so many religious institutions.[34]

On July 31, Oscar Presley Fowler, director of education at the Oklahoma State Reformatory, congratulated Comfort for the "noble work" he was performing in Norman. Fowler found Comfort's efforts to present God as a rational figure to be far healthier than the "stupid" and "positively immoral" approach adopted by so many small-town ministers. He found equally important Nick's dissemination of both birth control information and materials on curbing venereal diseases. Fowler believed that the state of Oklahoma should be commended for allowing such an individual to head a religious program at the university.[35]

The new academic year was to witness a wholesale change in the public perception of Nick Comfort, even at the University of Oklahoma, where he had long been regarded as one of the most popular figures around. His "So This Is Life" column in the Oklahoma Daily, begun in 1935, continued to be widely read and generally provided favorable publicity for the School of Religion. It helped to keep the School of Religion at the forefront of affairs affecting both the university community and the State of Oklahoma, which admittedly soon proved to be something of a mixed blessing. And most importantly to Nick, it allowed him to possess a teaching ministry with a much larger audience than would have otherwise been possible. That in turn enabled him to continue spreading the word of social Christianity to many folks in the state.

For a good while, the message Nick put forth was warmly received, at least by most students and faculty at the university. In mid-August 1936, he had been accorded the distinct honor of being asked to deliver the baccalaureate sermon at the university. The title for his text was "The Challenge of Religion and Education." He opted to make it somewhat controversial, declaring that "Oklahoma politics smells to heaven." In June 1937, the graduating class of the university, many of whom had either attended his classes or read his column in the school newspaper, dedicated their yearbook, *The Sooner,* to Nick. It contained a picture of him and words of dedication from him to the class: "For you the universe focuses on this instant. So far as you are concerned, God's plans pivot on this moment. Make the most of the present. Live!"[36]

The attacks by Kight and Governor Phillips, along with a host of earlier ones, however, undoubtedly caused some to view Comfort with unease or in a different light than they had previously. So too did the turn of events, at home and abroad, starting in the summer of 1939. The signing of a nonaggression pact by the foreign ministers of Nazi Germany and Communist Russia in August stunned many, and led to the collapse of the Popular Front. That alliance of liberals and leftists had, at least on its face, supported reform in the Western democracies and anti-Fascist unity following the destruction of the Weimar Republic and Hitler's ensuing aggression. The outbreak of World War II soon followed, with the invasion by Germany and Russia of Poland and the Baltic states. These developments led to a hardening of positions in both the antiwar and preparedness camps.[37]

During this period, President Roosevelt wielded his full prestige to bring about a repeal of the arms embargo required under the 1935 Neutrality Act. Isolationists, led by Senators William E. Borah, Gerald P. Nye, and Robert M. La Follette Jr., joined with Socialist Party leader Norman Thomas, former President Herbert Hoover, and legendary aviator Charles A. Lindbergh to block the administration's efforts. Backed by the Non-Partisan Committee for Peace through Revision of the Neutrality Act, President Roosevelt got what he wanted in the form of the Neutrality Act of 1939. That measure resulted in the termination of the arms embargo and helped to make the United States the "arsenal of democracy," able to funnel weapons to England and France.[38]

By this point, former allies in the peace campaign were adopting a variety of stances regarding the matter of collective security. In the manner of Reinhold Niebuhr, a number of leading theologians discarded pacifist and social gospel perspectives. Niebuhr carried enormous weight among American intellectuals, but Comfort and a number of pacifist groups were not impressed. John Nevin Sayre and

Devere Allen continued to believe that noncombatants might remain out of the fray were they to adopt liberal trading policies, disarm, lend support for world government, and champion the cause of internationalism.[39]

Such an analysis was one which largely matched Comfort's. In early October, he twice wrote in the *Oklahoma Daily* analyzing why and how the American people could remain outside of the European conflagration. It appeared clear to him that England and France were not primarily concerned about defending democracy and doing battle with totalitarianism. Had such been the case, their embargo against delivering arms to the Spanish Republic and their handing over of Czechoslovakia to the Nazis, "lock, stock, and barrel," would not have occurred. Nor would Hitler's move into the Rhineland or Austria have taken place. By their actions, the two European states had indicated that they were concerned about "their own preservation" only, and possibly, the extension of their empires.[40]

Furthermore, ample opportunities had existed for England to establish alliances with Russia that would "have cut Hitler's throat." However, Neville Chamberlain and other English leaders had been, and still remained, too tilted toward Nazism to deal forthrightly with the Russian Communists. The result was that Russia felt compelled to emphasize balance-of-power concerns. In addition, as Comfort saw it, the English and French governments were not much better than the one in Berlin.[41]

Comfort was certain that Europe would not settle her internecine quarrels if war were to come. Furthermore, U.S. involvement in something he saw to be Europe's fight would do little good. Rather, a forceful, neutral stance would more likely result in "a just peace." The greatest role the United States could undertake, he believed, would be to serve as the repository of democratic values, a model for all others.[42]

Even if Hitler hoped to eradicate democracy altogether, Comfort continued, "there is not one chance in a thousand that he could ever get around to the United States." Were this nation to head into war once more, democracy would be more endangered than by German aggression. Indeed, the military itself posed the largest threat to American democracy. "At every point the war machine is the antithesis of democracy." Another war might well spell the demise of the American system of government.[43]

Happily, Comfort declared, the United States did not seek war. In fact, "the cry of 'Never again' by the 'burnt babies' from Herbert Hoover to the dirtiest bum runs through the land." This he considered a hopeful sign that the United States could remain outside of the worldwide conflict. Comfort explained how this could be accomplished. A 100 percent free-trade policy with all other nations should be put into effect. A cash-and-carry trade policy with the belligerents should be carried out. It should be made clear that U.S. citizens and their possessions located in troubled spots would receive no protection, with an exception made only for government officials. The same would hold true for American business enterprises. The manufacture of war munitions should be nationalized and sales to other nations prohibited. Those who supported a rapid military buildup should be viewed with suspicion. Each justification for entering the war should be carefully examined to uncover possible economic influences. Even apparently hostile actions against the United States should be looked at carefully and thoughtfully. An altruistic patriotism, involving a willingness to give to other peoples more than one could possibly receive in kind, should be put into practice. In contrast, "national boasting, chip-on-the-shoulder attitude, imperialistic tendencies, false pride, show of brute force, mob psychology, jingoism and cheap sloganism" should be avoided whenever possible. Efforts to construct a nation that afforded its people the opportunity to thrive should be systematically undertaken. Such a nation would boast citizens determined to defend it against all encroachments and be more secure than any other.[44]

Comfort's determined antiwar stance undoubtedly did not sit well with the many Oklahomans who supported President Roosevelt's mobilization effort or who were caught up in it themselves. Many, like the administration in Washington, now believed that U,S. entrance into the World War II was all but inevitable. Recognizing large differences between the Allied and Axis states, they reasoned that the interwar isolationism that at times had so influenced U.S. foreign policy must be discarded altogether. Those, like Comfort, who thought otherwise were increasingly viewed as foolhardy or as endangering the very security of both the Western democracies and the United States.

Every bit as controversial was Comfort's involvement with the Oklahoma Youth Legislature (OYL), whose constitution called for the inclusion of all young people, no matter their race, color, or political persuasion. The OYL affirmed only its belief in fundamental American liberties as contained in the Bill of Rights and the U.S. Constitution. Nevertheless, Nana Beth Stapp, the provisional chair of the state council of the OYL felt compelled to respond to accusations that its members were "a bunch of wild and woolly Communists, foreign agents from Moscow, with knives in our teeth and bombs in our beards." She closed her keynote address to the third annual session of the OYL in late December 1939 by declaring that the organization stood at "the center of progressive youth activities" in the state. Its members sought "peace, progress, democracy, and liberty." If such was "treason," she indicated, "make the most of it!"[45]

On January 9, 1940, Comfort delivered a speech before the youth legislature in the state capital. He warned the young people in attendance that American ideals and practices were threatened by foes, both within the United States and outside of her borders. "It is a day of shibboleths and hypocrisy in public life." Never before, he said, had there existed such a need "for clear thinking and courageous action." The responsibility that the American people held was a heavy one, for "we are helping decide the destiny of the world." The United States, as the most influential actor in the Western Hemisphere, possessed tremendous importance due to its natural wealth, geographical locale, diverse populations, and wide range of religious, political, and technological influences.[46]

At present, democratic practices, Comfort continued, were "being junked on every hand." Such was true in Communist Russia, Nazi Germany, and militarist Japan. These same nations sought worldwide supremacy and, should they prevail, would make democracy more tenuous. Still, they were not the greatest threat to the United States, and neither were their satellite states; nor were the overt champions of such governments who resided in the United States. The latter posed a small danger only, for once they displayed their true colors every genuine American would pay them little heed. "An above-board follower of Lenin, Hitler, Mussolini or the Mikado stands about as much chance in the United States as would a bootlegger at a W.T.C.U. meeting."[47]

Rather, the greatest foes of the United States, Comfort argued, were those who continually employed "constitutional shibboleths but by their actions trample the constitution into the dust." The attempt to exclude blacks and Communists from the youth legislature was a perfect example of simple-minded, but purportedly patriotic, action. The young people who joined in this effort were not enemies of their country, but they were "misguided and ignorant of the gravity of the error they have made." A constitution would not be ushered in through unconstitutional means. Such prejudice was subverting institutions and entire nation-states throughout the globe. Furthermore, exclusionary practices were inherently wrong.[48]

Comfort warned that abridging the rights of one group provided a means to do the same to others. He considered it irrelevant if one agreed with the Communists or not. "I do not;" he declared, "emphatically I do not!" But as an American he felt obliged to defend their constitutionally based right to express their ideas and program. He also asserted that blacks resided in this nation "through no fault of their own," and insisted that racial discrimination contradicted core American ideals as well as the concept of the brotherhood of man. "What hypocrites we are, to get into a lather about Hitler's treatment of Jews," he wrote, "and then permit such flagrant race discrimination within our own state."[49]

Comfort's speech before the Oklahoma Youth Legislature triggered a vociferous response from members of the state chapter of the American Legion, among others. They demanded his dismissal as chaplain of the Oklahoma Central State Hospital, a post he had held for nearly fifteen years. The same day Comfort spoke before the OYL, the commander of the Oklahoma chapter, Dr. A. B. Rivers, of Okmulgee, avowed that national unity was essential and that "no good American citizen" could "bosom a Communist in one hand and uphold the Constitution of America in the other." Rivers accused Comfort of being a Communist, but later denied having made such a charge.[50]

The fact that Rivers would hurl such accusations Comfort's way struck his friend J. Rud Nielsen as "tragi-comical" at best. Only a short time before, another acquaintance of Nick's had indicated that he "was more like Jesus Christ than any other person I've ever known."[51]

It took a great deal to anger Nick Comfort, but Rivers's fusillades had done precisely that. He had long been, in the words of a close friend, "one of the ablest, most sensitive and imaginative chaplains" for the kind of institution Central State was. At times, he would request a session with "one of the really wild, hopeless cases." Nick would take the patient down a corridor to a window, slightly opened to allow the afflicted person to gaze at his own image in a mirror that was hung outside. Now, Comfort drafted a letter to Rivers, indicating that he could not comprehend "your brand of patriotism." After Rivers had called for his resignation, Comfort had written to the head of the Oklahoma chapter, inquiring whether that was a position that the organization had officially taken or was one man's opinion alone. No response was forthcoming. Instead, Rivers went to Central State Hospital, insisting that Comfort be dismissed from his post there. He had not tried to contact Nick, even though he was at Central State during the very time Rivers was on the hospital grounds.[52]

Now, Comfort had questions of his own for his accuser. Was it fair or in the best American tradition to level charges at someone without any factual basis for the same? Comfort challenged Rivers to give one example in which he had championed Communism in any fashion. If Rivers were unable to do so, then a public acknowledgment of the falsity of the accusation was in order. Comfort queried his tormentor if he were not able to differentiate between defending the constitutional rights of all groups and supporting the positions they stood for. "Haven't you wit enough to see," he wondered, "that the heart of Americanism is to defend constitutional procedure?" In exhorting college youth to disturb meetings of Communists, Comfort asked, had not Rivers's zeal and that of Deputy Adjutant Milt Phillips surpassed "the bounds of reason and true patriotism?" In charging Comfort with seeking to disrupt peaceful relationships between blacks and whites in Oklahoma, was not Rivers crippling the Constitution?[53]

Comfort ended by suggesting a public meeting "where we can thrash out our differences." A $1 admission could be charged and the proceeds equally divided between the School of Religion and the American Legion. Comfort saw such an encounter as "the test of our belief in democracy." He closed with the following farewell: "Yours for democracy and freedom." On February 17, Comfort sent an edited version of this letter to Rivers, who replied that he had never accused the minister of being a Communist but refused the request for either a debate or a retraction.[54]

Comfort subsequently sent to the state capitol a letter in which he declared that his political, social, and religious tenets were "an open book" for all Oklahomans. He proudly declared that he had always fought "without fear or favor to anyone" for what he considered right, and would continue to do so. Such a stance, he recognized, had produced powerful antagonists, who included among their ranks certain members of the American Legion. In his desire to further American democracy and the ideal of the brotherhood of man, Comfort declared, he took a back seat to no man.[55]

In the midst of his clash with the Legionnaires, another series of events took place that must have further weakened Comfort politically. On February 11, a front page headline in the Sunday edition of the

Norman Transcript read, "Church Women Condemn Norman's Negro Attitude." Female members of the First Presbyterian Church, including Esther Comfort, regularly gathered to observe an annual day of prayer for women around the globe. That year, Esther was a member of the planning committee. Reasoning that it was "unChristian" to pray for women throughout the world while black women were unable to spend a single night in Norman, she proposed a resolution expressing shock at the oppression accorded minority groups anywhere, including within the boundaries of the United States. Her resolution further declared that the Norman Federation of Church Women would "go on record as protesting against continuing slavishly to follow an unchristian un-American tradition" and in asserting that the "unwritten" discriminatory code in Norman that abridged the Bill of Rights "no longer exists." Thus, "the regime of intimidation by means of which this tradition has been maintained is ended." Other members of the community were urged to support such a stance.[56]

Esther was not about to present such a proposition without Nick's approval and she asked him to read it. He did so and urged her to go forward with it, fully aware that he would be accused of having drafted it. Mary DeBardeleben, who taught Bible classes for the School of Religion, successfully moved that the resolution be adopted, although a number of women refused to vote.[57]

The following morning, Nick was called into President Bizzell's office. When asked about the resolution, Nick replied that he had only given his consent to it. Bizzell responded, "You can't tell that to the men on Main Street."[58]

The *Oklahoma Daily* continued to support Comfort at this point, and he informed the director of Central State that he would remain in good humor and strive to "cause you and the hospital as little trouble as possible." However, on February 28, the state board removed him from his hospital position. The board cleared Comfort of the Communist charges, but reasoned that as the hospital cared for veterans and was aided by the American Legion, the wishes of the organization had to be heeded. It also denied that Comfort's speech before the Oklahoma Youth Legislature had resulted in his ouster. The following day, Comfort thanked the board for acknowledging that he was not a Communist and disclosed that he would no longer contest the ouster, refusing "to fight force with force." But he warned that the Legion chapter was doing damage to democratic freedoms in the state.[59]

In a final salvo, Comfort wrote to Rivers, bemoaning what he considered to be the undemocratic and anti-American activities carried out by the American Legion to bring about his dismissal. Comfort asked whether the inability to confront one's accusers and the lack of substantive evidence for the accusation did not violate democratic precepts. He called for the chapter to acknowledge its bigotry and "willful denial of brotherhood, justice, and constitutional rights to man." He also castigated the group's incitement of students to engage in a "Red hunt" at Oklahoma A&M College. Why, he asked, did the Legionnaires consider themselves to be the guardians of what should be discussed in public schools and on public platforms? How did their "desired dictatorship differ from those of Stalin and Hitler?"[60]

As in the previous year, support for Comfort poured forth from across the state. A group of university students circulated a petition that strongly condemned Comfort's dismissal. One admirer suggested that only a few "zealots" in the American Legion, and certainly not all of its members, had sought his head. "We know that no one with a thimble full of brains thinks you are un-American." John Lokey, on the staff of the *Post-Democrat* in Wilson, Oklahoma, expressed his appreciation for Nick's courage and regretted the troubles that he, "one of the few stimulating men on the campus," was encountering. No matter what the Legionnaires charged, this former student declared, Nick Comfort would not "teach communism or much of anything else except a philosophy of life and living which I have come to appreciate more and more as each day I live." Newspaperman R. M. McClintock suggested that "utility-oil wolves" had pressured Governor Phillips to have Comfort removed from the chaplainship of Central State Hospital.[61]

"As a fellow-victim of the Phillips purge," McClintock recognized the "calamity" that could befall one with a small income who lost any part of it, referring to the $36 a month pay Comfort had drawn for his work at Central State. No doubt this was particularly true in Comfort's case. He had recently written to Lew Wentz, the Tulsa oil millionaire, asking for assistance in procuring funds for the Oklahoma School of Religion. Nick indicated that he had received virtually no salary the past three months due to uncertainties about the status of the institution.[62]

Dr. Thomas L. Wilson, an osteopathic physician in Tulsa, congratulated Comfort on his opposition to the American Legion's "dictatorial action" concerning "the so-called subversive activities." Wilson implored Nick to "Keep up the fight" and declared that "red hunting" was a diversionary tactic to deflect attention away from the nation's real problems, such as high levels of unemployment among young people. The Reverend Herman H. Lineman, superintendent of the Congregational and Christian Churches, a division of the Board of Home Missions, assured Comfort that he was providing "a splendid, even if difficult, example of consistent Christian living in a situation in which the penalties are pretty sure to be exacted sooner or later." An old friend in Norman, comparing Nick's troubles with the crucifixion of Jesus and the poisoning of Socrates, deplored the "witch-hunts" that made it more dangerous for citizens to think, and still more perilous to express their thoughts. Another correspondent considered himself hopeful "that democracy and human brotherhood may be expanded when we can have an occasional minister and teacher with vision, intelligence, ideals, and courage like yours." He claimed that the American Legion had become as closed-minded and bigoted as the Ku Klux Klan. Students at the University of Oklahoma circulated a petition to demonstrate their indignation at the way Comfort had been treated.[63]

In response to an inquiry from black former soldiers regarding his dismissal, Comfort defined communism as he saw it. The reality, he declared, was that the idea of common property was of ancient origins. A number of primitive people held property in common; the Essenes practiced a brand of almost pure communism, as did the early Christians. Benedictine monks in the sixth century A.D. and Jesuits in Paraguay eleven centuries later adopted communistic practices. So, too, did the eighteenth-century Shakers, an offshoot of the Quakers. But Russia was the first nation to turn to Communism as a guiding principle. Comfort then examined Soviet Communism. It amounted to "rule by the masses with the elimination of the wealthy and privileged classes." It was generally "anti-religious and usually atheistic." In theory, it called for the ideal of dictatorship of the masses, but that had not been brought about. The Russian Communists had used violence to come to power and to retain it. Desiring to spread Communism worldwide, they called for the overthrow of other governments through "force, trickery, or any other method," including fifth-column activities.[64]

Needless to say, Comfort declared, he was opposed to "the Russian style of communism." The Legionnaires would know of this if they bothered to read his writings or listen to him speak. They then would realize that he believed wholeheartedly in American democracy and the Bill of Rights, both of which should be "applied without reference to creed, color, or social and economic status."[65]

For a couple of months, the furor over Nick Comfort seemed to abate. Then a series of columns he produced for the *Oklahoma Daily* caused additional trouble for him. His praising of the second Southern Conference for Human Welfare undoubtedly infuriated many. His adherence to the increasingly controversial antiwar movement and his bitter denunciation of the U.S. mobilization effort produced still more difficulties. By now, the Keep America Out of War Congress, championed largely by Socialists and pacifists but also by isolationists like Chester Bowles and John T. Flynn, stood as the lone national antiwar coalition still in existence in the United States. Well-regarded churchmen like Reinhold Niebuhr, John C. Bennett, and Sherwood Eddy, in contrast, spoke of "America's Responsibility in the Present Crisis." The Reverend H. S. Coffin and the Reverend Francis J. McConnell joined William Allen White's "Interfaith Committee for Aid to the Democracies."[66]

Continuing to believe that the governments of England and France were insufficiently democratic, Comfort, like the members of the Keep America Out of War Congress, remained a noninterventionist, despite heightened Fascist aggression and successes. As the Nazi blitzkrieg swept over more of Europe, he suggested once again that little distinguished the German, British, Italian, French, and Russian regimes. All, he declared, were "diametrically opposed to the democratic procedure." To aid any would thereby be providing assistance to avowed opponents of democracy or imperialists. The leading European states were all imperialistic, oppressive, and brutal, he believed, and "fattened on the blood of crushed people."[67]

If the United States truly wanted to make the world safe for democracy, he went on to say, it should provide direct assistance to the suffering peoples in all lands and not to those who kept them ground under with some version of an iron heel. Were we to deliver medical care, clothing, and foodstuffs to the infirm, wounded, and deprived in Japan and Germany, he asked, would their leaders be able to rally the masses to wage war against the United States? To those who might consider such a proposal utopian, Comfort reminded them that the attempts to construct societies based "on hate, fear, and force" had obviously failed.[68]

On May 19, as the president's defense program continued to face heavy criticism, Comfort published a column in the *Oklahoma Daily* that condemned what he termed "a fit of hysteria" regarding an imminent threat to the nation. Nick declared that Germany would never attack the United States; the notion was "so preposterous that it would seem that only an imbecile or a madman could seriously consider it." Unfortunately, it seemed that "bush-league editors" around the state believed in precisely that. Certainly, he acknowledged, the United States needed to be adequately armed for purposes of self-defense. The Army Air Corps appeared best suited for such protection, while moneys spent on the other branches of the armed forces were likened to funds "poured into a rathole."[69]

After the fall of Denmark and the German incursion into Norway, Comfort commented on the furnishing by the United States of war materiel to the Allied powers: that, he said, would at least bring about a stalemate, if not outright victory for the

Allies. But America's greatest interests, he insisted, involved the Western Hemisphere and maintenance of the democratic ideal.[70]

Reaction to this column in particular was rapid and hostile. One self-proclaimed "foreign born patriot" termed Comfort's failure to extol the preparedness program an insult to all "red blooded" Americans. This writer asked, "If you don't like the country why don't you leave or are you one of the fifth columnists running at large?" Comfort's essays, he stated, were a "disgrace (to) the newspaper profession." Comfort needed to "put your ear to the ground and listen to the comment on your theories. It is voiced by more than one person."[71]

Governor Phillips angrily demanded that the *Oklahoma Daily* should drop Comfort's column. If the governor favored such tactics, Comfort responded, "then he should go over and join Hitler." However, Nancy Royal, editor-elect of the school newspaper, revealed that she would confer with Dean Comfort regarding whether his column would be continued. President Bizzell suggested that his old friend limit the column to religious matters only, but Comfort refused to submit to what he considered to be censorship. As Nick informed the press, "If I write a column, it will have to be printed as I write it and on the subjects I choose." The changed mood on the University of Oklahoma campus was demonstrated by the seemingly inevitable decision in late May to drop Nick's "So This Is Life" column.[72]

The ongoing clash between Governor Phillips and Comfort was an intriguing one, given that the two men might be considered mirror opposites. They both were products of the American heartland of the late nineteenth century. Phillips grew up in Worth County, Missouri, Comfort in rural northeastern Texas. Each was attracted to the ministry, although Phillips eventually opted for the law. Both were imbued with frontier qualities—particularly that of rugged individualism—no matter the degrees, licenses, and titles they acquired along the way. They stood on opposite sides of the political and ideological divide, Phillips being bitterly opposed to the New Deal–spawned welfare state, which he saw as sapping the spirit of those who received federal assistance, while Comfort read the depression-era developments through the lens of the social gospel ministry.

Given the changes Oklahoma was about to experience, the two men might well be considered transitional figures between frontier days past and a soon-to-arrive modern state. In a very real sense, Leon C. Phillips and E. Nicholas Comfort were the last in a breed of prominent individuals who were shaped by the frontier in which they grew up and the urban centers in which they acquired their educations and made their mark as noteworthy Oklahomans. They just happened to be transplants from neighboring states. Perhaps the marked similarities, as well as the differences between the two men, help explain the passion with which they viewed one another. In their contrasting visions of their adopted state of Oklahoma, they possessed sharply divergent views of both its future and the heritage of the frontier from which they sprang.

The loss of his column with the *Oklahoma Daily* transformed Nick's relationship with the student body and faculty at the University of Oklahoma. No longer did he possess a forum that allowed him to speak on matters dear to his heart to the full university community, all the while ensuring that the Oklahoma School of Religion was an important institution to reckon with in Norman and throughout the state. The "So This Is Life" essays and opinion pieces—and they were often both—had been one of the school newspaper's most popular features and helped to make Nick a revered and beloved figure on campus. Through his column, Nick had articulated the gospel of social Christianity, calling for all to treat their fellow men, particularly those less fortunate, with respect, and to appreciate the need for civic responsibility. Time after time, he had invoked the doctrines of the social gospel and its guiding tenets, the fatherhood of God and the brotherhood of man. Most happily for him, he had been able to proselytize on behalf of social Christianity to those he saw in greatest need of such guidance, the young people who promised to become future leaders of the Sooner State or the nation.

Shorn of both his newspaper column and his position at Central State Hospital, Nick now became even more involved with the faltering antiwar movement. He seemed to be deliberately waving a red flag in the face of his critics. In the summer, Cooperative Books, which put out a series edited by Winifred Johnston, of Norman, published Nick's *Christ-Without-Armor: Uncensored Essays on the Democratic Way*. Johnston also printed pamphlets for the series written by John Dewey, Freda Kirchwey, Oswald Garrison Villard, and Oscar Ameringer. The title of Comfort's work was deliberately chosen, for two reasons. First, it placed Jesus in the antiwar camp. Second, the title asserted that the selections in the little volume had not been censored. *Christ-Without-Armor* contained a number of Nick's most controversial selections from his *Oklahoma Daily* columns and his speech before the Oklahoma Youth Legislature.[73]

The less-hospitable atmosphere in Oklahoma was also exemplified by a series of events that unfolded in the summer of 1940. In June, a radio preacher in Oklahoma City called for a public book-burning of Communist writings. In July, a police raid was carried out against the Progressive Book Store, run by Robert Wood, state secretary of the Communist Party. Then in August, assistant district attorney

John F. Eberle orchestrated the arrest in Oklahoma City of fourteen leaders of the Communist Party. They were held incommunicado for several days: their names were withheld from the press and they were denied the right to speak to relatives or friends. A full weekend passed before Momon Pruiett, a well-regarded criminal defense attorney in the state capital, was able to file a writ of habeas corpus. Shortly thereafter, charges were filed against the Oklahoma City Fourteen, as they came to be known, and this group thereby became the first individuals indicted under the 1923 criminal syndicalism act. Eberle announced that the greatly increased activity of party members had resulted in the prosecution. "They have brought in outside workers, have been making a large number of contacts, and have had a lot of money to spend in their work here." Four party members were eventually tried and convicted, receiving the maximum ten-year sentences. The prosecution's case largely relied on some seven thousand books seized in the raid on the Progressive Book Store, along with documentation of the defendants' party membership. One of the attorneys for the accused was himself arrested in the midst of the trial, held incommunicado, with his briefcase sifted through by Oklahoma State Highway Patrolmen. A court of appeals later overturned the lower court's rulings, and the proceedings against the other ten defendants were dismissed.[74]

During this period, Comfort served as a sponsor for both the Emergency Peace Mobilization of the Committee to Defend America by Keeping Out of War and the Declaration Against Conscription, which warned that a peacetime draft "smacks of totalitarianism." The Emergency Peace Mobilization declared that strict neutrality provided the best defense and urged members to guard the rights of labor, religious groups, racial minorities, and civil liberties in general, and to support social reform. Its officers included Jack McMichael, Joseph Cadden, Harriet Pickens, and James B. Carey. Among its sponsors were Oscar Ameringer, editor of the *American Guardian,* published in Oklahoma City; Joseph Curran, president of the National Maritime Union; author Theodore Dreiser; journalist George Seldes; artist Rockwell Kent; Howard Lee, executive secretary of the Southern Conference for Human Welfare; Congressman Vito Marcantonio; and the Reverend Claude C. Williams. Nick's good friend John B. Thompson, pastor of the First Presbyterian Church in Norman, was named temporary chairman of the committee.[75]

Because Comfort had been listed incorrectly on the national brochures as dean of the University of Oklahoma, he wrote to the organizations requesting that the mistake be rectified. He asserted that the university administration was "highly militaristic" and was strongly opposed to his position; furthermore, a pervasive resentment against his stand existed throughout the state. Therefore, it was highly unfair that he be associated so directly with OU.[76]

Comfort was affiliated with the Committee on Militarism in Education, whose executive board of officers included historian Merle E. Curti, Norman Thomas, Oswald Garrison Villard (former editor of *The Nation*), and John Nevin Sayre. He was also invited to join the Committee to Defend America by Waging Peace, which was orchestrated by the Campaign for World Government, whose international co-chairs were Lola Maverick Lloyd and Rosika Schwimmer.[77]

In early October 1940, Comfort sought to establish an Oklahoma Committee on Civil Liberties to record abuses of political rights. Several recent developments in the state had demonstrated to him the need for just such an organization: a professor at

Southeastern State College, Streeter Stuart, was dismissed from his position for writing a letter to his congressman urging opposition to a conscription bill. Through employment of the seldom-used 1923 criminal syndicalism measure, individuals, due to their affiliation with the Communist Party, had received jail sentences. And the antimilitary position of the Jehovah's Witnesses had caused some two hundred such believers to be arrested. In another case, the American Legion had petitioned the courts to take three children from their parents after the youngsters were expelled from school for refusing to salute the U.S. flag.[78]

On October 19, investigators from the Dies House Un-American Activities Committee met in Oklahoma City and questioned ministers Nick Comfort, John B. Thompson, and Paul S. Wright about their political views. When an interrogator moralized about the impropriety of a liberal "sticking his neck" out, Comfort replied: "Young man, it's a shame to see a nice fellow [such] as you working for such a rotten boss like Martin Dies." The three churchmen—who became known as the Dies Committee Three—issued a paper claiming that the Dies committee call was "trumped up," and was designed to intimidate or stigmatize those individuals who attempted to uphold constitutional freedoms and democracy itself during a time of great strife.[79]

The members of the First Presbyterian Church in Ada, Oklahoma, expressed their belief "in the absolute loyalty" of the Dies Committee Three regarding basic American liberties. They also spoke for the personal integrity of these "true Christian gentlemen." A grade-school principal asserted that the questioning of Comfort by the Dies Committee "was a rotten and disgraceful thing." He declared it was "shameful" that "a man who really still believes in the deep principals [sic] of Democracy is not allowed to express himself without being called to one side and told to watch his step."[80]

Six faculty members, directly or indirectly affiliated with the University of Oklahoma, including Comfort once more, called for the creation of a state civil rights' committee at an upcoming conference on constitutional liberties. Comfort's old antagonist Governor Phillips asserted that the professors had no business dealing with such an organization, declaring that they were employed to teach and should not become involved with issues that did not concern them. He remarked that the six individuals were "apparently sadly misinformed" and indicated that perhaps there was insufficient work "to do down there in Norman." Despite the protestations of the governor, the six participated in the conference, which resulted in the formation of the Oklahoma Federation For Constitutional Rights. Dr. A. B. Adams, dean of the College of Business Administration at the University of Oklahoma, quickly proclaimed that such a stand against the U.S. government should not be tolerated.[81]

Meantime, the Comforts' son Dick, who had transferred to Oklahoma A&M College in 1939 and married Winona Wise in Amarillo the following year, was also becoming involved in social activism. He had decided to follow in his dad's footsteps and study at Union Theological Seminary in New York City. While in Manhattan, Dick became chairman of the rural commission of the American Youth Congress, which increasingly was dominated by fellow travelers and Communists. Dick believed that the civil liberties of certain individuals were being abridged because of their political and religious beliefs and that the civil rights of black Americans were also being given short shrift "in a land of 'so-called' democracy." He urged other young people to make Congress aware "that we are determined to keep out of war" and would oppose every move to pull the United States into the world conflagration.[82]

Perhaps in response to the latest controversies surrounding Nick Comfort, the board of regents of the University of Oklahoma, on January 8, 1941, voted to exclude the listing of courses offered by the School of Religion in campus publications. Comfort responded by charging that the regents were bowing to "outside pressures." He declared, "This is another step in the personal fight on me by Governor Phillips and the American Legion."[83]

At least partially in response to the actions of the Oklahoma Federation For Constitutional Rights, the state legislature in early 1941 initiated an investigation into "all subversive activities at the University of Oklahoma." The investigating committee—the so-called Little Dies Committee—was chaired by Senator Joe Thompson, who had been among those leading the call for Communists to be barred from the ballot box. James C. Nance, who, representing McClain and Cleveland Counties in the state senate counted the University of Oklahoma in his district, favored the investigation but feared the direction it might take. He urged the committee not to undertake a "fishing or smelling expedition" to besmirch the state's leading university. "I don't want the University shown up in the press of the nation as a breeding ground for reds. Two men down there were done an injustice two years ago when they were accused of being reds and radicals." One of those individuals was Nick Comfort. OU President Bizzell insisted that he would not allow anyone who believed in Communism to serve on the faculty and declared his readiness to help the committee in its investigations.[84]

While Bizzell was hoping that his acquiescence would lent itself to a rational discussion of the matter in question, the tone at the state capitol was more charged than ever. Among those called before the so-called Little Dies Committee was Comfort, now a familiar figure at legislative investigations. Also receiving a subpoena on February 4 to appear before the committee was John B. Thompson, now chairman of both the American Peace Mobilization and the Southern Conference for Human Welfare. In fact, most of the thirty-five individuals ordered to appear before the committee were associated with the Oklahoma Federation For Constitutional Rights. Governor Phillips, whose preinaugural accusations had helped to set the stage for the ensuing events, termed the committee "wholesome and proper" and promised to deliver the names already at his disposal to the Federal Bureau of Investigation; in fact, he had already done so. He again declared that pro-Communist sympathies were too common at public universities in the state and condemned "freak theories" that could also be heard in churches, undoubtedly referring to both Comfort and Thompson.[85]

Friends who remembered that trying period avowed that Comfort "was completely unawed" by the proceedings. While waiting to testify at this inquiry, Nick "lay upon a table and slept the sleep of the just. Who were these sycophants who dared to astigmatize as political heresy the honest thoughts of honest men? Theirs was rather a duty to clean the Augean stables of the filth which had accumulated since statehood, to give to the people of Oklahoma the kind of a government which human beings deserved!" The friend who told the story of that day reported that Nick had to be awakened in order to undergo the interrogation. This was not surprising to anyone who knew him well, for, as Cortez Ewing put it, "there was in him a complete lack of fear— fear of circumstances, fear of administrative officials, or fear of consequences."[86]

Ken Lowe later reminisced that when Nick actually appeared before the committee "he was so plain-spoken that the hearing became a comedy." At long last, he was being afforded an opportunity to respond to allegations delivered against him and the Oklahoma School of Religion. Comfort declared that he was a prime instigator in the creation of the civil liberties group and indicated that he would remain in the organization if informed that Communists were also involved. Comfort condemned what he considered to be the unjust arrests of Communists and the dismissal of Professor Stuart. Comfort denied that he was a Red, blasted the criminal syndicalism act as unnecessary, and asserted that it was absurd to make the display of a Red flag during a political gathering illegal.[87]

During the hearings, State Senator Paul Stewart of Antlers declared that members of the Oklahoma Federation For Constitutional Rights were "damn red." Upon the hearing's conclusion, he stated, "I would say that those university faculty members are slightly pink and possibly a little above the word 'slightly.'" Senator Julius Cox, of Boise City, reported that the hearings had indicated that many university professors had been educated back East where liberal political views abounded. Furthermore, many of these individuals "are teaching liberalism at the University and perhaps in some instances there is a pinkish tinge." However, he expressed doubts that the legislators had spoken with any actual Communists.[88]

On May 7, 1941, the Oklahoma Little Dies Committee report expressed no fears of the "theoretical crackpot fool" and the conscientious objector, whose own actions ensured that they were isolated from the mainstream. The Oklahoma Federation For Constitutional Rights, the report proclaimed, had been constructed by outside, subversive elements. The report indicated that the Oklahoma Federation exuded "nothing but a fellow traveler spirit," fostered dissatisfaction among the people of the state, and impeded the national defense effort. Thompson was singled out as "a bad and un-american influence," and the American Peace Mobilization was damned as subversive, as declared by the Dies Committee. It was recommended that the full state senate charge the Oklahoma Federation For Constitutional Rights with being an "un-american and subversive" organization. In contrast, the American Legion, the Dies Committee, and the district attorneys who prosecuted the Oklahoma City Fourteen were praised.[89]

Public institutions of higher learning in the state were given a "clear and completely favorable report," but the dismissal of one controversial figure, Maurice Halperin, from the Department of Modern Languages at OU, was called for. So too was a severance in the relationship between the University of Oklahoma and the Oklahoma School of Religion."[90]

The report also urged the passage of pending legislation calling for Communist Party activities to be curbed or even prohibited, as well as the establishment of detention centers for "organizers and agitators" to be housed in the event of an emergency. Soon three anti-Communist bills were sailing through the statehouse, preventing Communists or advocates of criminal syndicalism or violent revolution from holding public office and denying recognition to any organization that urged a seizure of political power.[91]

Upon the release of the report, Comfort simply stated, "I don't know what the committee's talking about." However, the call for Professor Halperin's dismissal demonstrated "how shallow this committee's report is." The federation's response accused the committee of anti-Semitic behavior in its questioning of Halperin. The organization claimed that the attempt to dismiss the professor lacked any evidentiary basis. It was, they said, an example of "dictatorial procedure," and demonstrated "religious and racial intolerance." The federation questioned why the state legislators considered themselves too regal to be criticized by members of the public that had elected them. When the committee proposed the absolute separation of the Oklahoma School of Religion from the University of Oklahoma, President Bizzell again came to its rescue, and, by inference, to Nick Comfort's as well, terming the school "one of the most satisfactory in the country." Rescinding its earlier action, the OU board now moved "to renew and strengthen the connections with Comfort" and to resume listing the School of Religion in the OU schedule of classes. This was clearly intended by the regents to serve as a statement that university operations would not be dictated by the state legislature.[92]

The conclusion of the hearings by the Little Dies Committee did not result in a tempering of the political climate in Oklahoma. The Communist Party and the Ku Klux Klan now went toe-to-toe. One Communist leaflet, issued in mid-July, insisted that the defendants in the criminal syndicalism cases were avowed foes of Hitler and were needed in the fight against Fascism. A handful of days later, a KKK parade led by Grand Dragon J. W. Reed ended up on university grounds. One Klan pamphlet, which referred to Comfort, Thompson, and four other witnesses who had appeared before the Little Dies Committee, attacked the Oklahoma Federation For Constitutional Rights, the American Peace Mobilization, and the Southern Conference for Human Welfare. Another Klan paper promised "to ferret out and to expose the insidious activities of those who would destroy our American government."[93]

The controversies that had abounded in the past two years had resulted in a far less hospitable atmosphere for both Comfort and the Oklahoma School of Religion. Previously esteemed by the community in Norman, particularly faculty and students at the University of Oklahoma but also throughout much of the state, Comfort was increasingly viewed in a different light. Some, especially certain fundamentalists and right-wing elements, had always looked upon him with distrust; now, because of the turmoil that seemed to swirl constantly around him, a number of other individuals, including some well-placed ones, considered him and the School of Religion to be outside the pale of respectability.

The disdain of the few troubled Nick not at all, and he would have dismissed the concerns of less-adventurous people but for one fact: their mounting number. In the face of the series of highly publicized and embarrassing incidents, fewer Oklahomans would be receptive to the message Comfort was trying to convey in his writings, at the pulpit, in the classroom, and before governmental investigative committees. Bereft of his column in the *Oklahoma Daily*, he now lacked a vehicle to reach out to the wider university community, let alone the whole state. At the very least, this ensured that his educational ministry was far more circumscribed than it had been. At worst, the most recent controversies endangered the actual existence of the School of Religion, the fount of his teaching ministry. At best, the School of Religion—if it continued to survive at all—would exist only in a tenuous fashion, with no endowment fund established and little in the way of permanent facilities.

His recognition of the plight of the School of Religion disturbed Comfort greatly. Following more than a decade and a half of operations in Oklahoma, his desire to convey the word of God to young people in the state had in no way slackened. However, his ability to continue teaching the social gospel and its fundamental precepts, the fatherhood of God and the brotherhood of man, as well as the continued viability of the Oklahoma School of Religion, soon would appear more precarious than ever.

CHAPTER TEN

FROM PEARL HARBOR TO THE PROGRESSIVE PARTY

Comfort, like many others in the antiwar camp, was jolted by the Japanese attack on Pearl Harbor on December 7, 1941 and the declaration of war by the U.S. Congress that followed. For some time, like many in the remaining segments of the prewar antiwar movement, he seemed to refrain from commenting on international events. Perhaps significantly, his daughter Elizabeth, still two years from receiving her degree at the University of Oklahoma, was photographed, with other students, listening attentively as an organizer spoke on behalf of conscientious objectors. Nick himself lent moral support to wartime conscientious objectors.[1]

In the summer of 1941, the sixteen-year tenure of William Bizzell as president of the University of Oklahoma had come to an end. Comfort, his political base whittled away, was seen by many in the Sooner State as out of step with what they perceived to be in the best interests of both Oklahoma and America. The FBI continued to receive reports that referred to Comfort as one of the known Communists at the University of Oklahoma campus. Nick was termed a "bosom friend" of John Thompson, whom the bureau had recommended for custodial detention in "warranted" circumstances. Both men were denounced as "radical Presbyterian ministers" who had "achieved a certain notoriety in the past due to their association with Communist Front organizations."[2]

In a somewhat less controversial vein, Comfort concentrated more of his attention on an issue long dear to his heart. As early as 1937, Nick—who had then just been appointed to the Norman School Board—became involved with a campaign to bring about a program for teacher retirement in Oklahoma. Serving as president of the Oklahoma Association for Teachers Retirement, he was determined to protect the interests of all teachers, "without reference to color or position." Ineligible for such benefits himself— he was an instructor at a private institution—Comfort nevertheless believed deeply in the worth of a free public school system. He reasoned that good teachers were absolutely essential "for the secure existence of a society of free people" and that quality public schools must be maintained. As president of the association, he tirelessly traveled the state at his own expense to organize groups that would promote necessary legislation. He did so during a period when even many teachers were all but oblivious to the problem.[3]

The initial drive supporting a teachers' retirement program went down to defeat, fueled by the continued hard times in Oklahoma, the apparent lack of interest of many teachers, and the opposition of leading politicians. But Nick persevered, and in July 1942, the voters in the state supported an amendment to the Oklahoma constitution that allowed for the formation of a teachers' retirement system. On July 1, 1943 the system became effective.[4]

In a sermon he delivered in the midst of the war entitled "American Ideals," Comfort philosophized about the future of the Republic. Once again he indicated why he considered education to be so important. In his wide-ranging talk, he referred to

244

From
Pearl Harbor
to the
Progressive
Party

"the Fountainheads of the American experiment,"
including the likes of Rousseau, Locke, and Milton.
He spoke of Jesus and the Hebrew prophets Moses,
Abraham, Amos, and Isaiah. He indicated that the
essence of the American system of government, in
the words of Jefferson, involved, among other things,
"equal and exact justice to all men, of whatever state
or persuasion, religious or political." Indeed, in
Jefferson could be found the sum total "of the political wisdom of Western Europe, Greece, Rome,
Persia, Babylon and Egypt." In Abraham Lincoln,
existed "nearest the incarnation of the American
Spirit that we have ever had."[5]

After delivering his history lesson, Comfort discussed the roads that the nation could now take. The
United States could move in the direction of "equal
and exact justice for all men" and amicable relations
with other nations. Or it could fall into "the morass
of imperialism, race domination, control by force, and
national strife."[6]

What the United States had to do, he continued,
was not simply to win the war but to lay the foundations for peace at home and overseas. No people, he
declared, had ever possessed the opportunity that the
American populace now did. Since ancient times,
"the seers of mankind" had been laying blueprints
for utopias. What emerged from those was the gospel
of Jesus. "Today we are called upon to demonstrate
that Gospel." The stage had been reached where
Jesus' precepts had to be adopted on an everyday
basis or "race suicide" would ensue.[7]

No longer possessing the public forums he had
once had in the *Daily Oklahoman* and the *Oklahoma Daily,* Comfort decided in late 1943 to launch
a new publication, the *Oklahoma Journal of Religion.* The journal, in the same manner as the
School of Religion, which owned and published it,
was said to be "blazing a spiritual trail in Oklahoma."

245

From
Pearl Harbor
to the
Progressive
Party

The first issue appeared in January 1944 and was, Comfort reported, "the fulfillment of one of my fondest hopes." The *Journal of Religion* was intended to serve as an instrument of the social gospel and a means for Comfort to broaden once more his educational ministry. The journal's tenets were to be the fatherhood of God and the brotherhood of man: these were its divining principles. He promised to call things as he saw them, "with good-will toward all and a sincere desire to hurt none, but so far as within me lies." The pages of the publication would be open to others interested in religious developments in the state of Oklahoma.[8]

246

From
Pearl Harbor
to the
Progressive
Party

Nick also looked into the possibility of writing a column that might appear in newspapers around the state. He thought that such a column, like the one he had written years earlier for the *Oklahoman*, might be carried in the religious section of the papers, or on Sundays. He hoped to provide "a constructive and non-sectarian" approach toward dealing with topics at hand. Apparently little interest was expressed in such a column: it was likely that either Comfort's name no longer possessed the luster it once had or that he was simply viewed as too controversial. Possibly he was increasingly seen as an outdated figure, much as Oscar Ameringer had been when he closed the *American Guardian* in 1942, a year before his death.[9]

For the next year and a half, Comfort concentrated his energies on trying to make the *Journal* succeed. The message of the paper was clearly that of the social gospel. For the Christian, Comfort declared, "the human race is one big family," regardless of the false barriers of race, class, education, or nationality. Belief in democratic processes was fundamental. Cooperation and responsibility were essential. The individual Christian was linked to all of his fellows, present and past, and possessed a duty to "give a full account of himself at all times and to all people."[10]

It was time, he wrote, for the good people of his adopted state to "get our heads together and pour our hearts out to each other." While American "propagandists" decried "German Jew-baiting" and "Jap jingoism about racial superiority," anti-Semitism and Jim Crowism remained ever present realities in Oklahoma. Comfort charged that once the war ended, it would be recognized that the greatest tragedy for Oklahoma did not involve events abroad or in Washington; rather, it concerned developments inside the state. The good people of Oklahoma needed to discard their sectarian ways and devise "a social organism" that would enable the state to appear as "a model of Christian brotherhood."[11]

By May 1944, Comfort felt compelled to ask his readers to come to the aid of his journal. He considered his latest enterprise to be vitally important— one that could help "to build the Kingdom of God in Oklahoma." He viewed the *Oklahoma Journal of Religion* as a unique venture in religious journalism, in the same way he considered the School of Religion to be a novel experiment in interdenominational religious instruction. But after the first four issues, which had been financed by local businessmen, funding had already begun to dry up.[12]

The *Journal* struggled for several months more—a hand-to-mouth existence, typical for Nick Comfort. Once more, the spirited nature of Nick's editorials and the inclusion of extensive articles on antiwar churches and the oldest all-black town in the country, likely did not make for new friends or allies.[13]

In June, he looked ahead to the postwar period, whose fate he felt certain would be largely determined by the United States, Soviet Russia, and Britain. He insisted that Russia was not "land hungry"

247

From
Pearl Harbor
to the
Progressive
Party

and had "been the most consistent great nation in her efforts to build world peace." Furthermore, her attempt to better the lot of the masses was "outstanding." She had traversed "one of the greatest experimental stages in the history of man," but was now evidently "leveling off to a long flight of individual liberty in personal affairs and group control in public undertakings." Russia wanted "a peaceful and just world" in which she would be allowed to distribute her great natural wealth equitably among her people. While Americans might not approve of certain aspects of the Soviet program, "its general outline," he asserted, "is in harmony with the deepest roots and highest branches of our own noble experiment in nation building."[14]

During World War II, the image of the Soviet Union was recast in the United States. Even relatively conservative publications like Henry Luce's *Time* and *Life* presented Stalin in a favorable light and the nation he ruled as an invaluable ally. This was a period when conservatives such as Bishop Fulton J. Sheen and Mississippi Congressman John Rankin lavished praise on the USSR. But, that said, it must have been hard-line fellow travelers or even Communist Party members who would have readily nodded their heads in agreement with Comfort's wartime reading of the USSR. To state it at the very least, simplistic analyses such as his were hopelessly naive. It was one thing to welcome the Soviet Union as a partner in the anti-Fascist alliance; it was something else entirely to suggest that "a long flight of individual liberty" was occurring in that land, which was still ruled by the Red version of the iron heel.[15]

In contrast, Comfort argued that Britain could not undertake an independent course of action. Her efforts to maintain "her tottering empire together" seemed wholly dependent on the sufferance of the other two Allies. Should they greet her with a firm

248

From
Pearl Harbor
to the
Progressive
Party

hand, attempts to resubjugate members of the British Empire would be abandoned. Or perhaps the British would realize that their empire might become part of an international confederation of nations, in which their country could perform a leading part. Britain, through "that bull-doggedness combined with her realism," might yet retain a stranglehold upon imperial possessions.[16]

249

From
Pearl Harbor
to the
Progressive
Party

The United States, the third member of the anti-Fascist alliance, Comfort asserted, was where "liberty, freedom, individual responsibility, social welfare, mass control, procedure based on fact and brotherhood have reached their fullest expression." Still, Americans remained afflicted with imperfections of their own and needed to aspire "toward completion (of) the Christianizing of all aspects of our life." Once again, Comfort declared that his own nation was face to face with its greatest opportunity. The world war had provided "a chance to demonstrate to all men the stuff we are made of"; the turn of events had "thrust us into the front rank of the nations." What would the American people do now? Would their nation uphold "the banner of justice, intelligence, honesty, and brotherhood" for all to see, or again adopt an isolationist stance?[17]

In the September issue of the *Journal of Religion,* Comfort again looked ahead and optimistically highlighted issues likely to emerge. The United States now possessed "an unprecedented opportunity to spread Christianity to the uttermost parts of the earth." What needed to be put to rest immediately was the notion that dominance would soon be in store for the United States; clearly, Comfort had no sympathy for those who spoke of an impending American Century. Similar ideas, he noted, had only led to tragedy. Instead, the people of the United States needed to demonstrate what Christians could accomplish. The United States, he wrote, "is the flowering out of man's hope for freedom." It was the embodiment of centuries' long struggles to obtain freedom of religion, freedom of conscience, and freedom of expression.[18]

To honor this nation's noble heritage required sharing with others "the finest fruits of our American experiment in the Democratic procedure." That demanded transformations of the economic order, racial practices, and international relations. To begin, all Americans should be afforded "a broad economic base on which each one can stand securely to do his part in building the brotherhood of man." American businessmen would thrive in the process, resulting in "a new economics of abundance" that would produce tremendous advances in living standards, education, and the general welfare of the people. Simultaneously, "a new day in race relations" had to take place. "The Christian idea of brotherhood demands equal pay for equal work without reference to sex or color," he indicated in a remarkably prescient statement.[19]

Equally important, other peoples had to be given the chance to chart their own course. "It is not our business to tell them what they must have or how to get it. Our business is to help set them free to move in whatever direction seems best to them." Were dealings between nations to change in such a manner, the possibility of international comity would be heightened immeasurably. That cooperation could be used for the good of the smaller nations as well as for their more powerful siblings. Thus, the opportunity that lay before the American people was unprecedented. It would require an affirmation that the slate should be wiped clean. All debts owed by combatants to the United States should be forgiven, provided the money were used to rebuild the debtors' war-torn lands. Equally important, those nations and the United States should join with others to establish

250

From
Pearl Harbor
to the
Progressive
Party

a world organization that would "guarantee the freedom, security and welfare of all."[20]

Comfort's declaration that large changes were in order on the home front, especially in the economic arena and concerning racial relations, was prophetic. So, too, was his pronouncement that the United States could not simply compel other nations to follow its lead. The failure to adopt such policies, of course, resulted in the continued presence of mass poverty in the world's richest land, terrible strife between blacks and whites, and the propensity of U.S. policymakers to view their country as a world policeman. That way, large tragedies lay ahead for the United States.

251

From
Pearl Harbor
to the
Progressive
Party

In October, Comfort indicated that none of the changes he envisioned would be possible if America's own soldiers were not treated with respect and dignity. That required not only that women remain true to the Johnnies soon to come marching home, but also that class tensions be abated and cooperation result. Political democracy had to extend into other realms, social, economic, educational, and religious. Likewise, the Indian, black, and white Johnnies had to find that the constant talk about "brotherhood, minority rights and protection" was not idle chatter.[21]

The *Oklahoma Journal of Religion* resulted in more kudos and brickbats for Comfort. A blistering letter dated March 5, 1945, reproved him for his "sympathetic attitude" toward "RED MARXIST RUSSIA." The note instructed Comfort to go to live in the Soviet Union, the "hellish land of rape, murder, pestilence, and the vicious creed of KARL MARX— RELIGION IS THE OPIUM OF THE PEOPLE," if he were so enamored with it. It expressed astonishment that Comfort could possess "the unmitigated gall to teach the Gospel of JESUS CHRIST," while exhibiting a tolerant view of Russia. It indicated perplexity regarding someone like Comfort, who sounded like a Southerner, but needed to act like one, too.[22]

Comfort was told to change his ways and reread the Bible, to discover what Christianity was all about. "COMMUNISM and CHRISTIANITY" have nothing in common—remember that!" In spite of anything that Comfort or "other left-wing preachers say," the simple fact was that nothing was more antithetical to Christianity than Communism. The letter declared that "the Reds" were busy achieving control in the United States while men were "being slaughtered by the millions for LIBERTY and CHRIST." Comfort too would recognize this if he weren't "so ignorant and cowardly," but he undoubtedly had no interest in "helping rescue the youth of this nation from this hellish MARXIAN ATHEIST COMMUNISM!" The letter warned that some "twenty million Republicans" felt similarly about "this Red Russian menace," and were determined to scrutinize what was being taught in the state universities. They wanted "less about this other stuff! So disgusting," and were fed up with wolves in sheep's clothing. The message was signed, "An irate listener, and an AMERICAN who believes in the DEMOCRACY OF GEORGE WASHINGTON AND THOMAS JEFFERSON and not in the hellish Economic tribulation and philosophy of Karl Marx!"[23]

In May 1945, a month after the end of the European campaign of the war, Comfort announced to his readers that this was the final issue of the *Journal*. He deeply regretted the closure, but he had determined that he would not implore friends for funds to keep the journal afloat. Running the journal had been "a lot of fun" and he regretted only that it "was no more outspoken for right and forceful in its condemnation of wrong."[24]

The termination of the *Journal* was another in the series of professional blows Comfort had experienced

252

From
Pearl Harbor
to the
Progressive
Party

over the past half-dozen years. It all but ensured that he lacked the means to speak to the people of Oklahoma as a whole and that the audience for his teaching ministry would be smaller than at any time since he had moved to Norman. Enrollment at the Oklahoma School of Religion remained small and the institution was increasingly viewed as little more than an adjunct to the University of Oklahoma. University administrators had come to look upon the School of Religion as more trouble than it was worth, undoubtedly due to the controversies that had raged around its director and others affiliated with the institution. They had already sought to distance themselves from the school's operations and, with its dwindling constituency, lacked motivation to help sustain it.

253

From
Pearl Harbor
to the
Progressive
Party

At the very time Comfort had to contend with the financial shortfall that doomed the journal, the school was afflicted with its own ongoing financial problems. Indeed, the fiscal difficulties that beset the *Journal* must have had a crippling effect on Comfort, now sixty years old. In early 1945, George L. Cross, president of the University of Oklahoma, wrote to Comfort expressing his concern about the "hand to mouth existence" of the School of Religion. Cross indicated that efforts to acquire more dependable funding were essential. During this period, Comfort was in touch with Lew Wentz concerning properties the school might be able to acquire. He also corresponded with Lloyd Noble regarding the long-envisioned chapel for the school.[25]

Thus, as late as the spring of 1945, Comfort was still concocting plans and devising strategies to ensure that the School of Religion would not merely survive, but thrive. The proposed chapel, he declared, would embody man's most Godlike representations in architecture, art, and music. The windows and murals of the chapel would paint the picture of "man's reach toward God" throughout the ages, with particular emphasis on developments in Oklahoma. Comfort believed that the time was ripe as never before for the School of Religion to undertake a building program. Such expansion would enable the school to provide "the most constructive and far reaching religious program" to be found anywhere in the United States.[26]

254

From
Pearl Harbor
to the
Progressive
Party

Within a matter of days after writing to Wentz and Noble, however, Nick decided to resign as dean of the Oklahoma School of Religion. He had become convinced that the school would never be able to raise the funds it so desperately needed if he continued to be involved with its operations. Perhaps others had indicated as much to him. He submitted his resignation at the meeting of the institution's board of trustees on April 18, 1945. He was owed more than $20,000 as compensation for salary never paid through December 31, 1944. During the meeting, he expressed his willingness to accept a payment of $2,500 and a deed to eighty acres of land situated in Cleveland County. He asked for that amount, as that was the sum required to pay off money he had borrowed from friends and from his life insurance when his salary had not been paid in full by the school. The land—secured by Nick as a gift to the institution—had been appraised at a mere $300. He also asked that his salary be maintained at the rate of $3,000 a year, from the beginning of 1945 until his resignation became effective. Comfort's proposals were termed generous, the deed was delivered to him, and a committee was established to come up with the funds to make the $2,500 payment and to pay his current salary.[27]

His resignation was made effective as of May 31, 1946. After eighteen years of many triumphs and a considerable number of setbacks Comfort was no longer in charge of operations at the school. He had yet to receive the $2,500 promised by the board, and he was owed another $1,631 for reduced paychecks over the course of the past seventeen months. This was troubling to Nick, who by September 5 had to pay back $1,200 he had borrowed on his life insurance.[28]

255

From
Pearl Harbor
to the
Progressive
Party

Apparently, still other provisions to the arrangement had been made between Comfort and the trustees. He had yet to meet the new director, but he believed that he had fulfilled his contractual obligations. "I have kept away from the School of Religion," he declared, "and kept my mouth shut concerning it and shall continue to do so." He offered to help the school in any way he could.[29]

On May 21, 1948, the Oklahoma School of Religion closed its doors. Eight days later, the board of regents of the University of Oklahoma voted unanimously to terminate all prior agreements with the School of Religion, including the listing of course offerings in the OU catalog. Comfort explained that a lack of funds had buried the institution he had devoted nearly twenty years of his life to. He thanked the more than six hundred people who had made donations, large and small, to the school. "I shall never cease to thank God for the cooperation of these friends in this pioneering venture." He was able to look happily back at the number of students, more than four thousand in all, who had taken courses offered by the school. To have worked with them was "one the greatest joys" of his life. But "to have this spring of spiritual life sealed over is one of the major tragedies of Oklahoma."[30]

The school "incarnated the American spirit of religious freedom," welcoming peoples of all faiths as well as those of none. However, it was the presence within the state of "the denominational spirit" that had helped to ensure the demise of this ecumenical endeavor.[31]

256

From
Pearl Harbor
to the
Progressive
Party

The School of Religion, Comfort declared, sought to teach in a very practical manner the religious tenets he most believed in: the fatherhood of God and the brotherhood of man. It envisioned brotherhood as requiring "economic, educational, moral, political, spiritual, and social democracy." This resulted in its dean and a number of its finest instructors being "branded as dangerous leaders with Communistic and revolutionary tendencies."[32]

The School of Religion also suffered from a "lack of leadership," said Comfort. The reality, he declared, was that its founder and longtime head "did not have the mental acumen, the moral stamina, the spiritual insight, willpower or . . . ability required for such an important undertaking. He was too small a man for such a big job. Had he been a big enough man he could have rallied the good and intelligent people of the state to the all-important task of keeping religious instruction abreast of our economic, political, scientific and social progress. Oklahoma's greatest need is a man big enough for this task. May God send him."[33]

It could be argued, as even his best friends on occasion did, that the Oklahoma School of Religion, which had largely been birthed, nurtured, and sustained throughout its existence by Comfort, had not proven to be what he hoped it might. The School of Religion never acquired the luster or reputation of the nation's finest religion programs, such as those at Yale, Princeton, and Chicago, notwithstanding the most strenuous efforts on Comfort's part. Had he been willing to curb his outspoken ways and avoid controversies, perhaps the school would have been able to survive, with his name attached to it. That would have required Nick to do something he never was able to do: compromise on matters of principle. It simply was not in Nick Comfort's nature to avoid controversies; he relished them, whether in the classroom, involving the institution he so loved, or regarding himself.

Others, like John B. Thompson, who was Nick's compatriot and probably his closest ally for many years, viewed the School of Religion as "a great dream and a great achievement." True, Comfort's dreams of grand buildings and a great chapel had not borne fruit. To Thompson, nevertheless, the school had been "blessed with the power and purity that seem to depend upon poverty of purse." Thompson believed that the School of Religion had indeed fulfilled its promise of "blazing a spiritual trial in Oklahoma," and Nick Comfort had instructed his students in the need for "courageous faith." Perhaps most importantly in his friend's eyes, Comfort had taught his students that a religion unable to confront the most pointed questions was simply "not worth having." As Nick had put it, "when you ask a man to park his intelligence outside the church you kill Christianity." He reasoned just as strongly that "fear of truth is the greatest weakness of religion in Oklahoma."[34]

The closing of the Oklahoma School of Religion must have been a crushing blow to Comfort, notwithstanding his generally optimistic nature. He now saw in ashes the dream he had long possessed of birthing, building, and sustaining an interdenominational educational institutional that would provide fellowship for its faculty, students, and the general community. He had viewed the school as an instrument of the social gospel. Now this vehicle was no more.

Everything that followed must have been something of an aftermath to Nick, sixty-four years old at the time of the closure, now lacking the institutional station he had devoted his most productive years to, and realizing that the Oklahoma School of Religion had shut its doors in part because of his own failings.

257

From
Pearl Harbor
to the
Progressive
Party

258

From
Pearl Harbor
to the
Progressive
Party

True, the increasingly conservative nature of the State of Oklahoma had little helped, particularly as the postwar period witnessed a new and virulent Red scare. Nor had the obliteration, in an almost Orwellian manner, of the state's radical elements and, as it seemed, its radical heritage. Continuing clashes between progressive, moderate, and fundamentalist elements inside and outside the religious community were also factors.

So, too, were ignorance and indifference regarding this attempt to create a religiously guided center for Oklahomans, which became more pronounced as the state experienced major changes due to World War II and its aftermath. The pouring into the state of federal money had helped at long last to terminate Oklahoma's version of the Great Depression. With the advent of Robert Kerr's tenure as governor in 1942, Oklahoma politics also became sometimes less contentious. The days of "Red" Phillips and Alfalfa Bill Murray were left behind, even while colorful figures like Gomer Smith continued to make runs for statewide office. To many, Comfort was increasingly viewed as a figure from an earlier time, when passions influenced political affiliations and even economic developments. In a state taking on the trappings of modernity, a man who continued to speak in tones that hearkened back to social gospelers Walter Rauschenbusch and George Herron and Socialist Oscar Ameringer was no longer considered at the cutting edge of the state's development.

Out of touch with the direction his adopted state's corporate moguls and politicians aspired toward, Comfort had clearly contributed to the demise of the School of Religion. And the recognition that his financial ineptitude and administrative incompetence had not well served the institution and his teaching ministry must have devastated him.

But even during the final months of the school's existence, Nick again served as a itinerant minister for a number of rural communities. He also remained politically engaged, receiving an inquiry in early 1947 from Harry F. Ward and Vincent Sheean asking him to sign a document condemning current moves to drive the Communist Party underground.[35]

He continued to suffer financially. For several months, correspondence flew back and forth between Comfort and the board of pensions of the Presbyterian Church regarding the School of Religion's failure to keep up full contributions to the church's service pension plan. Eventually the payments were made and Comfort's small pension was guaranteed, for the time being.[36]

Financial concerns and political activism kept Comfort busy for a full year and a half after his retirement from the school. In early 1948, he helped to write the state constitution for the Progressive Party. Revolving around the presidential candidacy of Henry Wallace, Roosevelt's former running mate, the Progressive Party attacked the cold warrior policies of Harry Truman, condemned the mounting infringements of political liberties, and urged expansion of the welfare state. In Oklahoma, the state party's constitution declared its support for legislation that would further "the economic and social needs of the people," augment democratic practices by "the full and free use of the franchise," and seek "a just and enduring peace throughout the world." The state branch of the party would work to eradicate "all discrimination based on race, color, creed, sex or national origin," to sustain the civil rights of all citizens, to defend the right of labor to bargain collectively, and to attempt to bring to fruition the Four Freedoms Roosevelt had promised during the war— freedom from want, hunger, fear, and war.[37]

259

From
Pearl Harbor
to the
Progressive
Party

260

From
Pearl Harbor
to the
Progressive
Party

The Progressive Party of Oklahoma included a small number of aging agrarian radicals. They managed to amass some eight thousand signatures, ostensibly five thousand more than were required to get the party on the ballot for the state primary on July 6. However, legal challenges were made by Gerald L. K. Smith, a rabid rightist and anti-Semite, and others. The state supreme court ruled that the party had neither established an organization nor crafted a platform prior to filing petitions. Thus, in November, the only choice for voters was between the two major party candidates.[38]

Nick declined to run as a congressional candidate on the Progressive Party ticket. In late July, he served as a delegate at the party's founding convention in Philadelphia and was involved in a series of campaign rallies in Oklahoma. Wallace's showing was not what his followers had hoped for. Badly hurt by claims that the candidate was "Red"—and by his own faux pas, which were not inconsiderable, and the adoption by Truman of a reform program prior to election day— the party vote proved highly disappointing.[39]

However, the reelection of Truman seemed to Comfort and many other observers to auger something of a welcome shift "considerably to the left of center." He found it hopeful that the people of the United States had seemingly rejected the exhortations of big newspapers and professional politicians and cast their ballots for "a man who will fight for his convictions." In an article that he sought unsuccessfully to have published in the *Atlantic* or the *New York Times* in early 1949, Comfort admitted that Wallace and the Progressive Party had shifted "too far to the left." Happily, in Comfort's estimation, the average American was fed up with "the Martin Dies– Parnell Thomas mania." Given the diversity of religious groups and the general satisfaction expressed by the U.S. public, Comfort declared in this unpublished article that "the demagogues" and "the military-plutocrat alliance" would have difficulty whipping up anti-Communist hysteria.[40]

It appeared to Comfort and others in the non-Communist Left that a new reform drive might now be possible. The president had been forced to take a stand in favor of civil rights. Labor seemed more politically vibrant than ever. Many Americans lacked social security. Popular support for national health insurance was present. Awareness of the devastating effects of soil erosion had never been keener. Farmers understood who was championing price supports on their behalf. The American people appreciated the need for conservation of natural resources. "A new sense of oneness as a people" was clearly apparent. The importance of equalizing educational opportunities was recognized by more and more Americans. Happily, they were realizing "that saber rattling and isolation are outmoded techniques for securing peace."[41]

Comfort's optimism could not have been more misplaced. The attempt by President Truman to expand the American welfare state with his own Fair Deal package was accorded a hostile or indifferent response by Congress. Anti-Communism, not New Deal–styled liberalism, dominated political discourse at the national level. And in early January 1949, a proposal requiring a loyalty oath of all teachers and students—it involved not being a Communist—sailed through the state assembly in Oklahoma City. Comfort fired off a letter to state senators who were about to consider the measure, urging them to vote against it. "The soul of American democracy," he declared, "is freedom of thought, speech, press, assemblage, politics, economics, and religion." To secure these liberties, the Founding Fathers had revolted from British tyranny, this generation's grandparents had waged the Civil War, and Americans had

261

From
Pearl Harbor
to the
Progressive
Party

fought in two world wars. Now, this non-Communist oath law struck at the heart of the most basic American freedoms.[42]

Loyalty, Comfort insisted, "cannot be coerced. Like love it comes from the heart." If the state's representatives desired loyalty from their citizenry, they should work to ensure justice, fair play, and the welfare of all. Should such a program be carried out, "communism would stand about as much chance in Oklahoma as a snow ball in hell." Moreover, the loyalty oath represented the very totalitarianism the legislature sought to shield young people from. But "why take a leaf from Stalin's book to protect us from his way?" It simply did not make any sense to "let the communists hoodwink us into adopting their tactics. We ought to be smarter than that." There were real dangers too in attempting to outlaw ideas. History had proven that the best way to disprove an idea was to counter it with a better one. "Truth is the only barricade against falsity" and "the only protection for democracy is more and better democracy."[43]

With his own stock considerably reduced from where it had stood during Oklahoma's earlier Red scares, Comfort's admonitions were little heeded; nor were protests that emanated from the campus of the University of Oklahoma. One writer in the *Oklahoma Daily* declared that the legislature should "have its collective head examined," but such opposition only fueled the ire of House members determined to require a loyalty oath in state schools. Representative D. C. Cantrell called for an investigation of Communist influence at the state's flagship university. A proposal by Ed Langley of Muskogee that such an investigation include all the state colleges was passed. The Cantrell hearings—which resulted in ten administration officials from the University of Oklahoma being called as witnesses—resulted in no

262

From
Pearl Harbor
to the
Progressive
Party

recommendations of any substance. While it was indicated that a few Communists students were at the university, they were said to be under "constant surveillance" by President George Lynn Cross, faculty members, and the FBI. No further action was deemed necessary.[44]

By now, Comfort was increasingly dissatisfied with the Progressive Party. His repeated condemnations of legislative measures that effectively outlawed the Communist Party made his own charges of Communist domination of the party more unsettling. Had he known that the party "would sink into a front for communist activity," he declared in mid-September 1949, he never would have joined it. Comfort proclaimed his intention to continue to his last breath to defend the rights of all, including Communists and Roman Catholics. However, "from sad personal experience," he noted, that both Communists and Catholics possessed "a loyalty center outside the United States" that frequently surpassed their allegiance to their own nation. Both sets of true believers, he reasoned, often advocated any means to achieve the goals they desired. Each group was "determined to rule or ruin" and had no appreciation of the kind of cooperation possible "outside its own predetermined dogmatisms."[45]

A meeting Comfort had just attended with officials of the Progressive Party of Oklahoma had convinced him that Communists wanted to "serve their own party ends without reference to the best interests of the masses of this state." To his dismay, his protests at the gathering had gone unheeded. Instead, the declaration by Carl von der Lancken, formerly state chairman of the party, that "in Russia and her satellites alone lies man's only hope," had been unreservedly accepted.[46]

Comfort declared that he was "unalterably opposed to totalitarianism in all its forms." He affirmed that

263

From
Pearl Harbor
to the
Progressive
Party

he possessed "no sympathy with Communist tactics," which he considered "so stupid" as to hold little attraction for thoughtful individuals. In a letter to an officer of the Progressive Party of Oklahoma, he wrote,

264

From
Pearl Harbor
to the
Progressive
Party

> The Communists' appeal to force is contrary to all that I hold dear. Their appeal to class struggle is a denial of my concept of the brotherhood of man. Their teaching that the end justifies the means is the antithesis of my notion of intellectual integrity and plain every-day honesty. Their doctrine of materialistic and economic determinism seems to me to ignore a chief characteristic of man; namely, his idealism. Their practical and dogmatic atheism seems to me to rob man of his most comforting, energizing, and reasonable source of power; namely, the belief in, and experience of, a good God who made and loves us all.

Comfort closed by declaring that he possessed no ill will toward anyone involved with the state branch of the Progressive Party. He simply determined that it was time to submit his resignation from the party and asked to have his name removed from the executive committee and materials associated with it.[47]

Nevertheless, Nick Comfort remained deeply concerned about political developments, both in Oklahoma and Washington, D.C. In mid-January 1950, he was appalled when students from the University of Oklahoma burned a cross in front of the Hillel Foundation, near the campus. The fiery cross was intended to protest a talk delivered there by the state leader of the Communist Party. Clearly, the political atmosphere at OU had dramatically shifted from the period in which Comfort had been something of an icon there. The hurling of epithets regarding Jews, blacks, and Communists disgusted him. For democracy to exist in this country, he argued, every individual must be allowed to assemble peaceably and to speak freely about public issues.[48]

It is noteworthy that the incident occurred in Norman, where—if anywhere in Oklahoma at this point—progressive voices might still be found. It also antedated Joseph McCarthy's meteoric rise to national prominence and the outbreak of the Korean War—two developments that further colored the political atmosphere, ensuring that anyone suspected of even harboring sentiments in favor of the Communist Party, let alone active involvement with it, would be treated as a pariah.

265

From
Pearl Harbor
to the
Progressive
Party

Perhaps as a means to leaving the state for a while, Nick considered enrolling at Harvard or Yale. He corresponded with his friend Frank Milton Sheldon, now minister of the Centre Congregational Church in Lynnfield Centre, Massachusetts. Sheldon indicated on April 3 that "a man of your ability" should be able to find a place to preach in close proximity to those august institutions, and possibly have a parsonage to live in. Sheldon, writing shortly following McCarthy's emergence in early 1950, declared that the United States was probably going to fail in both Germany and China, because "we do not believe enough in democracy." Now, "we have even become intellectual witch hunters trying to determine what people think." Were Jesus to visit the United States, Sheldon declared, McCarthy would call him a Red.[49]

Comfort, for his part, now seemed no happier with Harry Truman's presidency than with "the recent insane rantings of Joe McCarthy and the suicidal policies of the yellow bellied rascals who hide behind him." In a long open letter to the president, quite possibly never delivered, Comfort displayed an embittered quality, previously little displayed. He condemned the graft that he saw to be afflicting the administration. Comfort also blasted Truman's get-tough approach with the Soviets, which he believed demonstrated "what a midget conception you have of how to deal with men in a realistic creative way."

266

From
Pearl Harbor
to the
Progressive
Party

He assailed what he perceived to be Truman's "boasting, defiance, and saber rattling" that had transformed the United States into "the most feared nation on earth." He compared Truman unfavorably with his predecessor, arguing that the president had squandered the hopeful and brave atmosphere that FDR had exuded, with blinding fear replacing it. That fear, Comfort wrote, involved distrust of one's countrymen as well as the so-called Other. Consequently, the FBI, congressional investigative committees, and McCarthy were in their element. During this period, as J. Rud Nielson pointed out, a number of scientists from the University of Oklahoma were asked, both at legislative hearings and more informally, to discuss their dealings with Nick Comfort.[50]

Fear of Communism had now returned in full force to Oklahoma, with the state legislature passing a stringent measure requiring the taking of a loyalty oath, with nary a dissenting vote. Police in Oklahoma City charged Communists with disorderly conduct after discovering in an open field a gathering in possession of literature that condemned the Korean War and the atomic bomb. The police chief, in explaining the charge, declared it necessary because the city lacked an ordinance forbidding such activities. Later in the decade, additional measures were proposed at the state legislature calling for additional loyalty oaths, the outlawing of the Communist Party, and the issuance of prison sentences to those who advocated revolution.[51]

These developments did not go completely unchallenged. Opposition to the 1951 loyalty oath was particularly pronounced, with the *Oklahoma Daily* and several faculty members at the University of Oklahoma condemning the violations of civil liberties. Also in Norman, the YWCA, the YMCA, and Students for Democratic Action, an adjunct of the liberal Americans for Democratic Action, passed resolutions attacking the loyalty oath requirement. The Methodists of the Wesley Foundation in Norman and the Presbyterians of the Westminster Foundation in Stillwater both denounced the oath requirement as violative of religious freedom. Student polls undertaken at Oklahoma A&M expressed widespread dissatisfaction with the provision.[52]

Notwithstanding such opposition, which required a measure of courage considering the temper of the times, Comfort undoubtedly viewed the events at the state capitol with sadness. Events in Washington, D.C. were no happier. Repressive legislation was drafted, including the McCarran Internal Security Act that provided for the establishment of six detention camps, one of them in Oklahoma, to house accused subversives in times of national emergency.[53]

267

From
Pearl Harbor
to the
Progressive
Party

CHAPTER ELEVEN

HEADING FOR
COMFORT
HILLS
AND BEYOND

Norman, like so many other parts of Oklahoma, had undergone sweeping changes during World War II, with the arrival of two U.S. naval installations, looming presences referred to as the North Base and the South Base. The northwestern corner of the South Base was situated near the southeastern corner of 2000 Chautauqua. The Comforts had themselves experienced large changes during the war. Dick Comfort, having completed his studies at Union Theological Seminary in New York City, had gone on to Vanderbilt University, where in 1946 he received a Ph.D. in sociology. Anne finished her undergraduate studies at the University of Oklahoma and entered the medical school in Oklahoma City. There, the very day she registered for her first classes, she met her future husband, Clay Courtright. They were married on May 29, 1948. Elizabeth had graduated from the art school at OU in 1943 and gone to Manhattan to continue her studies. On April 17, 1944, she married Johnny Dixon, who had been a fellow art student in Norman.[1]

Elizabeth and Johnny lived for a time in the little house at the western edge of 2000 Chautauqua. Johnny was inducted into the U.S. Armed Forces and commuted to Oklahoma City to serve as a military policeman. Later, he was sent to Louisiana for boot camp and then was ordered overseas. On April 5, 1945, just before the war in Europe came to an end, he was killed in action, shot while marching with his regiment through a German forest. Soon afterwards, Elizabeth moved to Taos, New Mexico, to resume her art studies and Anne went to stay with her for several months. In Taos, Elizabeth met Peggy Pond Church, the poet and essayist, and her son, Theodore. On July 5, 1947, Elizabeth and Ted were married. Eventually, they moved to Albuquerque, and Ted worked as an engineer at the Sandia Base.[2]

The Comfort residence at 2000 Chautauqua, where Elizabeth had stayed during part of the war, was opened up to others because of the severe housing shortage. At the end of 1947, Nick and Esther decided to sell the house and went to live in a small teacherage that he constructed on the grounds of the country school where he was working, sixteen miles southeast of Norman. One reason for selling 2000 Chautauqua was to help pay for Anne's medical studies.[3]

Following Hugh's death, Nick had established a memorial fund to which donations could be sent. He now planned to use that fund to build a residence on the property he had obtained from the School of Religion (chapter 10). The property, which Nick and Esther referred to as Comfort Hills, was where Nick intended to build their retirement home. In summertime, he would go out to Comfort Hills with Anne, arriving on Monday and staying through Saturday afternoon. They constructed terraces and ponds.[4]

The land itself, which had come so cheaply, was wasteland that had been overfarmed and suffered from soil erosion. The mineral rights had already been sold off, although Nick received small sums from oil companies from time to time, to avoid potential legal liability for any damage that might be inflicted on the surface and for rights of way. Nick's dream was to restore the land and, consequently, aided by a governmental reclamation program, he worked to have it terraced. He built dams on gullies and placed brush as part of the restoration project. Nick could scarcely await the morning hours when he could go out to do battle against the gullies. He planted bluestem, rye, and vetch to help revitalize the land. He also grew tomatoes and watermelons. He hauled horses out to Comfort Hills, or had Anne or Dick ride them to the farm, so that more work could be completed. They had to travel through Norman on the horses, which often were spooked by the experience.[5]

Eventually, Nick was able to purchase a tractor and a bulldozer to carry out some of the heavier chores. He seemed to love riding the bulldozer to knock over trees. "Mother was just scared spitless every time he would take off on the bulldozer," worrying that he might end up in a ditch.[6]

In May 1948, Nick and Esther moved out to Comfort Hills. Nick renovated a small house, already situated on the property, with materials from the teacherage and elsewhere, all of which were eventually covered with red sandstone from the fields. Large rocks were used, too—the now sixty-four-year-old, self-taught architect positioning them, thanks to his still strong back. The structure thus had a distinctive patchwork quality to it, much as had the house at 2000 Chautauqua. Initially, the new domicile had a flat roof, which invariably leaked when it rained; later, a sturdy roof with an attic was added. Not until 1953 was the house completed.[7]

As always, the Comforts got by on a shoestring. In May 1949, Nick began receiving a pension from the Presbyterian Church—$22.04 a month. He also started getting a small social security check. The monthly social security coverage was effective once

Nick discovered a way to make the additional $50 he needed to become eligible. He asked the head engineer at the University of Oklahoma, who happened to be an old friend, if work were available. Subsequently, attired in faded blue jeans and sporting an old felt hat, Nick went around the campus with other elderly folk, cleaning up whatever needed to be attended to. One day, he spotted a faculty friend ahead of him, reached over, and tilted the professor's hat down over his face. The startled academic turned around to see Nick grinning widely. In a situation that might well have embarrassed another individual, Nick, characteristically, made light of it, and of himself.[8] On occasion, Comfort continued to receive $50 here, $100 there, from corporations drilling for oil and gas. They sometimes paid him an additional amount to do a bit of work for them. They also purchased water from one of the ponds he had built on his farm.[9]

Nick was determined to do whatever he had to in order that he and Esther could avoid falling into "the sugar teats of old age pension and poverty relief." He remained blessed with a strong body and an alert mind, although one that he declared to be only "three leaps ahead of the moron."[10]

By the fall of 1949, having just purchased a new Dictaphone, he again attempted to sell magazine pieces or short stories, trying numerous publications. Evidently, he found no takers. However, he did manage to sell some apricots, peaches, and chickens. He also continued teaching in a nearby, one-room country school. He purchased new art and writing materials and was determined to help mold "first-class scribes and regular geniuses in art." That would be the case, he said, only if the materials produced such a result, "for I have neither, as you know, in my soul." The latter assessment he confided to Anne, whom he addressed as Fuzzy-Wuzzy.[11]

The very day that Nick wrote to Anne regarding his latest set of plans, Esther had substituted for him in his classroom. But "Mammy says I'm not very complimentary of her noble efforts," he reported. To demonstrate his appreciation, he had taken her a box filled with strawberries and a hydrangea plant, dyed in blue. "Don't you think," he asked, "that's showing appreciation with a vengeance?" He wondered what "the old gal" could desire "more than a tummyful and all decorated with beautiful flowers." Undoubtedly, he declared, she wanted "a dress or possibly some chewing gum."[12]

In his twilight years, Nick continued to preach the message of the social gospel at the First Presbyterian Church in Norman and from other pulpits at churches around the state, whenever the opportunity arose. Among the more moving of his sermons was one he delivered on "growing old with flexibility, cheerfulness and serenity." He spoke of life being good, as "the universal good" in fact. Its continuation, he declared, was "the one struggle that seems worthwhile; yes, most worthwhile, as far as man's imagination can reach in space, time, or even eternity." As man grew philosophically and metaphysically, he invariably had to "involve even God in this ultimate quest for life in all its final meanings."[13]

In this sermon—he used such occasions as the latest expression of his once vibrant teaching ministry—Nick discussed a good friend who had recently been hospitalized. He recalled this man as a young professor on campus, "brilliant, attractive, supple and gay." While in his friend's hospital room, Nick happened to glance up at a nearby mirror that displayed "the reflection of an onion-headed old man whose face was wrinkled, whose eyes were dimmed and who was holding his hand to his ear for a trumpet." It was Nick's own reflection.[14]

While "our arms may grow old and stiff," Nick declared, "our minds may remain young." It was important to remain "supple, flexible and alive, intellectually, morally and religiously." Indeed, he wrote, "at seventy a person ought to be at his best." By that point, he will have experienced pitfalls along the way. He will have come to recognize, too, however, "that change is one of the inevitable laws of life." Fundamental beliefs had to be constantly rethought.[15]

Such old folks, like himself, Nick asserted, had come to certain definite realizations. Fretting, fuming, and fussing did no good at all. God was on the side of right, which was "the only sure and certain way." Truthfulness was absolutely essential and would lead to "joy, peace and contentment." Love was God's greatest expression and brought man into closest "communion with nature, man, and God." He continued:

> It has been wonderful to live on God's good earth. The heartaches and sorrows have softened us. The gossip of busybodies has chastened us. Our failures and mistakes have humbled us. The companionship of friends and loved ones has been sweet. The struggle for knowledge has enlightened us. Our reach toward God has strengthened us. May God in his goodness and wisdom lead us all on toward a more nearly perfect day.[16]

Nick's greatest joy remained Esther, their children, including the two who had lost their lives, and their children's spouses. One Christmas season, in a letter to Janet, Dick, Elizabeth, and Anne, he spoke of looking into the eyes of one's own children and becoming "lost in wonder, bewilderment and reverence for what you saw there." What you were experiencing, he declared, was "something of the wonders of God in making childhood the fountain for all that is beautiful, pure and good." Looking into the faces of one's children, he stated, caused a "cleansing and purifying" of the heart. Children helped to "redeem us from our sins by showing us afresh what we should and can be."[17]

His own children had grown into "fine, wholesome boys and girls." They were mischievous, shrewd, and gay, and possessed "discernment far beyond your age." Then, before Nick and Esther knew it, their children "had blossomed into young womanhood and young manhood," possessors of "a fine solidity of character." Now, Nick and Esther were allowed to "bask in the glow of your full maturity . . . revel in the warmth of your love . . . are made strong by your wisdom. We are given reassurance by your tender care."[18]

Eventually, Nick's strong, sturdy body began to wear out. Afflicted with high blood pressure, he suffered a pair of minor, paralytic strokes. Right after the initial stroke, he headed by bus to Texas to visit his sister and brother-in-law, Cova and Harry Kahl, for what he believed might be the last time. He did so without informing Esther that he had experienced a stroke, feeling that she would call a halt to his excursion. On the way home, he stopped off to see his eldest daughter, Janet, and her husband, Tom Losey, in Dallas.[19]

The first stroke left Nick partially hemiplegic. Afterwards, his left side remained weakened, particularly his arm and leg. Nevertheless, he continued to farm at Comfort Hills, wielding his tractor and bulldozer as best he could. He also engaged in his own program of physical therapy, using physiotherapeutic equipment he had constructed. But he appeared "more nervous, more agitated," than he had before; he no longer seemed to be "quite the calm person he had been." His daughter Anne reasoned that he was now "less secure, more helpless." Esther likewise was distraught at the turn of events. Unable to drive, she worried about what might happen were Nick to suffer another stroke at the farm. She was concerned about the distance from town and the possibility that if Nick were stricken while in the fields the tractor might turn over on him.[20]

In the summer of 1955, Janet and her son Nicky Losey drove her parents to see Elizabeth and Ted Church in Albuquerque. As the summer closed, Nick and Esther decided that they should not attempt to go through another winter in Oklahoma. Anne and Clay Courtright had temporarily settled in Rochester, Minnesota, for Clay to pursue a fellowship in dermatology at the Mayo Clinic. With the idea in mind of selling the Oklahoma farm and moving to Rochester, Nick and Esther wrote to their daughter and son-in-law to ask them what they thought. To the Courtrights, the idea was "fantastic" and Nick and Esther readied for the move. Dick, then living in Parkville, Missouri, came and took the Comforts to Kansas City, to the home of Uncle Charles Obee. Then in September, Elizabeth and Ted drove them the rest of the way to Rochester and helped them to set up in an apartment close to the Courtright home.[21]

Shortly thereafter, Anne started working at the state hospital and the Courtrights moved closer to that facility. The Comforts then relocated to a small apartment nearby, Esther taking care of Anne and Clay's children, Karen and Alan, during the day. Occasionally, Nick joined Esther and the children at the Courtright home, but he often remained in the apartment, spending a considerable amount of time reading. Particularly this was so following yet another stroke. Now, when he needed to go to the Mayo Clinic, he hailed a taxi. There, he did a good deal of therapy—including work on his speech, which had become impaired—but little progress resulted.[22]

In February 1956, Nick returned to Norman to retrieve books and other materials. With the help of friends, he selected several thousand books, correspondence, and journals, including a rare collection of magazines from the Civil War era, which he donated to the library at the University of Oklahoma. A fair number of other books and materials had already been passed on to family members and friends. A dinner was held in Nick's honor at the First Presbyterian Church. Photographs reveal the frail state of Nick's health at the time.[23] Janet drove up from Dallas to help Nick board a plane for Rochester. He had already sent along his most cherished books and other materials he wanted.[24]

On February 7, 1956, Nick wrote a letter to J. Rud Nielsen in Norman, expressing his frustration regarding the lack of "intellectual companionship" for him up north. He unsuccessfully sought to find, among the medical staff at the Mayo Clinic, a kindred soul who might share his religious perspective. His dealings with local ministers, whom he considered to be "very largely dead-heads," were similarly unsuccessful. The local Lutherans, for example, were engaged in their own heresy trials; they seemed oblivious to scientific thought and rational discourse. "How men can live with such closed minds," he exclaimed, "is a mystery to me," referring to individuals who nevertheless were ready to tell others how to contend with all the problems of the universe.[25]

Thus, to the very end, Nick remained a believer in ecumenicalism and a staunch opponent of hidebound denominationalism. He failed to understand how small-mindedness could guide those who held themselves out as men of God. He continued to believe in universalism, reasoning that any other approach would result in distrust, pettiness, and a determination to prove oneself superior to all others.

That way, in his estimation, lay more strife, hatred, or worse.

Early on the morning of February 27, Nick suffered another stroke, a massive one that left him speechless. The last words he spoke were "Call Anne." Nick was taken to the local hospital by ambulance, where, within hours, he died.[26]

Dick and Winona Comfort and Elizabeth went to Rochester for the cremation. A service was performed at the Rochester Presbyterian Church. Nick's treasured books were sent back to the university library in Norman.[27]

During a memorial service held in Norman on April 29, friends and colleagues fondly remembered Nick Comfort. They referred to him as "a complete man" who was somehow able to serve simultaneously as citizen, preacher, and teacher. Mourners applauded Comfort's teaching ministry, declaring that he had widened the reach "of his church and classroom to encompass the public. Like Mahomet, he went to the mountain." Those honoring Comfort praised his convictions and ideals, proclaimed him "an uncommon man" and a true democrat, termed him fearless and "a devoted patriot" who dearly loved the indigenous radical spirit that he was determined to keep alive in the Southwest. Those eulogizing him lauded his genuine friendship, great energy, and "magnificent freedom of mind," characterizing him as "untamed," a prophet, a giant, an authentic individual. Many expressed their admiration for his belief in the social gospel, especially its invoking of the fatherhood of God and the brotherhood of man. One longtime friend declared that Comfort "was a devoted churchman who came remarkably near to practicing what he preached." Nearly a quarter of a century after his death, another friend fondly recalled how

Comfort "loved his fellow man" and "wanted to fight for all his principles. That was his whole life."[28]

One of his closest friends, J. Rud Nielsen, acknowledged that Nick's career had hardly been successful in the conventional sense. The Oklahoma School of Religion, his great dream, for which he had made such enormous sacrifices, had closed after "even those trickles of money without strings" that sustained it for so long could be found no more. Had Nick been willing to compromise, Nielsen declared, repeating a frequent refrain, a school or building would now undoubtedly be named after him. "But he was never willing to evade controversial issues. As a result, he had to suffer for his convictions over and over again; but he never complained and never lost heart. No matter what his troubles were, he was always cheerful and ready to encourage others by word or deed."[29]

The closing of the Oklahoma School of Religion had been Nick's greatest disappointment. A personal setback for him, what it portended for the state of Oklahoma was of still larger significance. The failure of the School of Religion, despite its director's energy, dedication, and commitment, suggested that an interdenominational religious center faced enormous obstacles in Oklahoma, particularly one headed by a controversial figure. The demise of the School of Religion and the termination of Nick Comfort's educational ministry left a considerable vacuum— one that has never since quite been filled. The fate of the School of Religion also indicated that adherence to the social gospel was, more than ever, a tenuous proposition in a state that had undergone such changes as Oklahoma had. Those changes included not simply the disappearance of once-potent radical groups and well-known figures, but the weakness of liberal or progressive forces of any sort.

Comfort's passing coincided with the much greater prominence attained by another practitioner of the social gospel, the Reverend Martin Luther King Jr. It was during 1956, the year Nick died, that Dr. King achieved fame and notoriety for his role in the Montgomery bus boycott, waged to challenge Jim Crow edicts in that Alabama city. The two men, like brothers of a different color, shared a good deal in common. They both struggled diligently on behalf of social justice, racial harmony, and world peace. Each was a believer in the power of nonviolence to transform the human condition, but neither believed that change would come without a struggle. Both were sons of states of the old Confederacy, who left the regions in which they were born—the American Southwest, in the case of Comfort, the Deep South, in the case of King—to attend august educational institutions and returned to do work near the places of their birth, to spread the gospel as they perceived it. King, of course, became a far more widely known figure than Comfort, but his life, like that of Nick's, suggests ties that bound these two men of different hues and circumstances together. That is additionally fitting given Comfort's color-blind nature and King's determination to avoid racial discord— qualities that caused them to stand apart from strident voices seeking to keep black and white apart.

The social gospel, through which men of the church utilized their pulpits to sustain the cause of social reform, best encapsulates the philosophy of Presbyterian pastor and educator E. Nicholas Comfort. He strove throughout his career to further civil liberties, civil rights, economic democracy, and peace. Considering civil liberties to be the cornerstone of the American democratic system, Comfort continually defended—invariably, at considerable cost—the rights of castigated political and religious dissidents. He believed protection of the civil rights of racial minorities to be an essential part of the quest to create the brotherhood of man. Yet political freedoms alone were incomplete, Comfort argued, without corresponding economic rights, and thus he called for a degree of redistribution of wealth to aid the most impoverished. Consistently, he warned that democracy and his envisioned brotherhood of man could never exist in a militaristic state; consequently, he devoted long hours to the antiwar movement.

Because of his ideas and actions, this proponent of the social gospel, like so many other American reformers and radicals of his era, confronted considerable opposition and criticism. Working in a state with an increasingly conservative political environment and a strong fundamentalist religious orientation, Nick Comfort challenged archaic political and church doctrine. While he repeatedly endeavored to help bring about the Christian brotherhood of man, Comfort was unfairly castigated as an instigator of class warfare, a subversive, and a Red.

Buttressed by his strongly held beliefs, Comfort steadfastly held to his democratic and libertarian ideals. In the process, he unerringly followed the tradition of the homegrown radicalism of the American Southwest. In doing so, he made a notable contribution to his native region. At considerable cost to himself and his family, he accomplished precisely what he had set out to do so many years before: to bring religious instruction of a progressive cast to the young people of Texas and Oklahoma. Despite having to live on a financial precipice throughout the years of his ministry, and notwithstanding the invectives, scurrilous charges, and hate-filled rhetoric that came his way, he created a religious institution that helped to spread the social gospel to thousands of students and many others as well. The two-decade long life of the Oklahoma School of Religion was a remarkable achievement, given the economic uncertainties, fundamentalist hostility, and reactionary political atmosphere that so frequently beset it. In a very real sense, the Reverend Nick Comfort's educational ministry had succeeded in spreading his version of the social gospel to untold thousands whose lives were thereby enriched.

Moreover, in a time when few other leading figures in the region were willing to condemn in a forthright manner Jim Crow, militarism, the abridgment of civil liberties, mass poverty, and economic inequalities, Comfort did so readily, forcefully, and often eloquently. In a period when most influential ministers, educators, and political spokesmen veered sharply away from the indigenous radicalism of the Southwest, Comfort never even considered doing so. Only journalist Oscar Ameringer, another Oklahoman-by-choice, was as steadfast as Comfort in championing, in humane and generous fashion, ideas and groups so far out of the mainstream. With the death of Ameringer in 1943 and Comfort thirteen years later, something was lost in Oklahoma—something not since recaptured. It was not simply a void or vacuum that occurred on the left side of the political spectrum, although that certainly took place. Nor was it merely the demise of remarkable progressive institutions like the *Oklahoma Leader,* the *American Guardian,* and the Oklahoma School of Religion. Rather, it was the disappearance of an optimistic tenor of a spiritual variety, whether driven by the social gospel or by Socialism, which demanded that Oklahomans live up to the promises once so abundant in a still young state. Comfort and Ameringer appealed to the best in their fellow Oklahomans, urging movement in the direction of fuller democracy and greater equality. What they sought, what they envisioned, and what they demanded was nothing more or less than social justice. Consequently, their passing bespoke the end of an era, in which dreams were dreamed that the fatherhood of God and the brotherhood of man could come about. These then were individuals, no matter their failings, who were themselves irreplaceable.[30]

Heading for
Comfort
Hills
and Beyond

NOTES

Preface

1. Ken Lowe, "Broken Images," July 30, 1961, p. 2, Index, Oklahoma School of Religion Collection, Western History Collections, Univ. of Oklahoma, Norman, Oklahoma (hereinafter referred to as OSORC).

2. Cortez A. M. Ewing, "Nick Comfort's Attitude Toward Public Affairs," Memorial Service Transcript, p. 4, Janet Losey Collection; interview with Elizabeth Delatore, November 15, 1979; interview with Winifred Johnston, November 16, 1979; J. Rud Nielsen, untitled, Memorial Service Transcript, p. 7.

3. Today, an individual with the progressive mind-set of a Nick Comfort would undoubtedly be even more inclusive in his employment of phrases such as the fatherhood of God and the brotherhood of man. However, to recapture Comfort's perspective, his usages will be used throughout this book.

4. *"An Oklahoma I Had Never Seen Before": Alternative Views of Oklahoma History*, ed. Davis D. Joyce (Norman: Univ. of Oklahoma Press, 1994), p. xii.

5. Nick Comfort, "So This Is Life," *Oklahoma Daily*, November 21, 1937, p. 1 ; John B. Thompson, "A Personal Appreciation," Memorial Service Transcript, p. 11.

1. A Passion for Learning

1. Interview with Janet Losey, Dallas, Texas, August 8, 1994; Esther Comfort, Family History, "Remembering,"

283

October 7, 1966, pp. 3–4.

2. Esther Comfort, "Remembering," pp. 1–2.

3. Interview with Janet Losey; Nick Comfort to Tom Miller, December 6, 1926, p. 1, OSORC, Box XXV, Pers. Corr.

4. Esther Comfort, "Remembering," p. 1; Nicholas Comfort, "Autobiography of Nick Comfort," p. 1, Janet Courtright Collection.

5. Nicholas Comfort, "Autobiography," p. 1.

6. Ibid., pp. 1–2.

7. Ibid., p. 2; Nick Comfort, "," p. 4, Janet Losey Collection.

8. Esther Comfort, "Remembering," p. 3; Nick Comfort to Tom Miller, December 6, 1926, p. 1.

9. Comfort, "My Life Stream," p. 4; Esther Comfort, "To the East Coast," p. 41.

10. Nick Comfort, "My First School," p. 12.

11. Interview with Dick Comfort, April 1, 1994, San Antonio, Texas; Nick Comfort, "," p. 4.

12. Comfort, "The Prize," p. 1, Anne Courtright Collection.

13. Ibid., pp. 1–2.

14. Ibid., p. 2.

15. Ibid., p. 3.

16. Ibid.

17. Ibid., pp. 3–4.

18. Ibid., pp. 4–5.

19. Comfort, "The Stranger," p. 2.

20. Interview with Janet Losey.

21. Comfort, "E. Nicholas Comfort," p. 1, Anne Courtright Collection.

22. Comfort, "So This Is Life," February 13, 1938,

23. Ibid.

24. Ibid.

25. Ibid.

26. Comfort, "The Stranger," p. 2; Esther Comfort, "Remembrance," p. 4.

27. Comfort to Tom Miller, December 8, 1926, p. 1; Comfort, "The Stranger," p. 2.

28. Ibid., pp. 2–3.

29. Ibid., pp. 3–4.

30. Ibid.

31. Ibid., p. 4.

32. Comfort, "My Life Stream," Janet Losey Collection, p. 3.

33. Comfort, "The Stranger," p. 3a.

34. Ibid., pp. 3a–4.

35. Ibid., p. 4.

36. Ibid., pp. 4–5.

37. Ibid., p. 5.

38. Comfort, "," p. 6; Nick Comfort, "E. Nicholas Comfort," p. 2, Anne Courtright Collection; Esther Comfort, "Remembering," pp. 6–7.

39. Comfort, "E. Nicholas Comfort," p. 1.

40. Comfort, "," p. 6.

41. Cortez A. M. Ewing, "Nick Comfort's Attitude Toward Public Affairs," p. 3, April 29, 1956, Index, OSORC.

2. The Making of a Social Gospel Minister

1. Esther Comfort, "Remembering," p. 8; Janet Losey interview.

2. Esther Comfort, "Remembering," pp. 20–22; D. S. Stephens to Esther Obee, n.d., Box III, Misc. & Pers. Corr., OSORC.

3. Comfort, "E. Nicholas Comfort," pp. 3–4, Anne Courtright Collection.

4. Esther Comfort, "Remembering," p. 21; Donald K. Gorrell, *The Age of Social Responsibility: The Social Gospel in the Progressive Era, 1900–1920* (Macon, Georgia: Mercer Univ. Press, 1988), p. 100.

5. Transcript from Kansas City University, October 21, 1947, OSORC, Box V, Pers. & Bus. Corr.

6. Esther Comfort, "Remembering," pp. 8–9.

7. Ibid., pp. 24–25.

8. Ibid., pp. 25–26.

9. License to Administer the Ordinance, Methodist Protestant Church, September 17, 1910, Anne Courtright Collection; Gorrell, *The Age of Social Responsibility*, p. 4.

10. For an examination of the Social Gospel, see Ronald C. White Jr. and C. Howard Hopkins, *The Social Gospel: Religion and Reform in Changing America* (Philadelphia: Temple Univ. Press, 1976); Henry F. May, *Protestant Churches and Industrial America* (New York: Octagon Books, 1963); C. Howard Hopkins, *The Rise of the Social Gospel in American Protestantism, 1865–1915* (New Haven: Yale Univ. Press,

1967); Robert H. Craig, *Religion and Radical Politics: An Alternative Christian Tradition in the United States* (Philadelphia: Temple Univ. Press, 1992); Ferenc Morton Szasz, *The Divided Mind of Protestant America, 1880–1930* (University, Alabama: The Univ. of Alabama Press, 1982); Robert Moats Miller, *American Protestantism and Social Issues, 1919–1939* (Chapel Hill: Univ. of North Carolina Press, 1958); Donald Meyer, *The Protestant Search for Political Realism, 1919–1941* (Middletown, Connecticut: Wesleyan Univ. Press, 1988); Paul A. Carter, *The Decline and Revival of the Social Gospel: Social and Political Liberalism in American Protestant Churches, 1920–1940* (Ithaca, New York: Cornell Univ. Press, 1954).

11. Craig, *Religion and Radical Politics*, pp. 12–13.

12. Interview with Janet Losey.

13. Gorrell, *The Age of Social Responsibility*, p. 341; White and Hopkins, *Social Gospel*, pp. 151, 247–48.

14. D. S. Stephens to Comfort, July 15, 1912, pp. 1–2.

15. Ibid., pp. 1–4.

16. Stephens to Comfort, August 15, 1912, pp. 1–2.

17. Joseph J. Stotler, To whom it may concern, August 28, 1913, OSORC, Box III, Misc. & Pers. Corr.; Mrs. D. S. Stephens to Comfort, July 18, 1915, OSORC, Box III, Misc. & Pers. Corr.

18. Dillenback Certificate, Anne Courtright Collection; Comfort, "E. Nicholas Comfort," p. 2.

19. Esther Comfort, "Remembering," pp. 26–28.

20. McCormick Theological Seminary Transcript, August 29, 1947, OSORC, Box V, Pers. & Bus. Corr; Esther Comfort, "Remembering," pp. 28–29.

21. Nick Comfort to Alice Comfort, March 2, 1916, OSORC, Box III, Misc. & Pers. Corr.; A. Fitch to Nick Comfort, April 27, 1916, OSORC, Box III, Misc. & Pers. Corr.; Arthur J. Covell to Comfort, December 26, 1916, OSORC, Box III, Misc. & Pers. Corr.; Covell to H. L. Elderdice, January 5, 1917, OSORC, Box III, Misc. & Pers. Corr.; Elderdice to Covell, n.d., OSORC, Box III, Misc. & Pers. Corr.

22. Arch McClure to Comfort, January 25, 1917, OSORC, Box III, Misc. & Pers. Corr.

23. University of Chicago Transcript, August 22, 1947, OSORC, Box V, Pers. & Bus. Corr.

24. Lefferts A. Loetscher, *The Broadening Church: A Study of Theological Issues in the Presbyterian Church Since 1869*

(Philadelphia; Univ. of Pennsylvania Press, 1957), pp. 90–91.

25. Esther Comfort, "Remembering," pp. 29–30.

26. James H. Tufts to the Adjutant General of the Army, August 9, 1918, OSORC, Box III, Misc. & Pers. Corr.; Harlan L. Feeman, To whom it may concern, August 12, 1918, OSORC, Box III, Misc. & Pers. Corr.; E. W. Hart to the Adjutant General, August 13, 1918, OSORC, Box III, Misc. & Pers. Corr.

27. Registration Certificate, September 12, 1918, OSORC, Box III, Pers. Corr. & Misc.; Esther Comfort, "Remembering," p. 32; Esther Comfort, "Glimpses Through the Years," p. 190; Westminster College Teacher's Contract, September 21, 1919, OSORC, Box III, Misc. & Pers. Corr.; Comfort, "E. Nicholas Comfort," p. 2; "Esther Obee Comfort and E. Nicholas Comfort," December 3, 1958, p. 1, Anne Courtright Collection.

28. Esther Comfort, "Remembering," p. 32; Tufts to Comfort, July 31, 1920, OSORC, Box III, Pers. Corr. & Misc.

29. Esther Comfort, "Remembering," pp. 32–34.

30. Ibid.

31. Ibid., p. 35; interview with Janet Losey.

32. Esther Comfort, "Remembering," p. 35; interview with Dick Comfort; interview with Anne Comfort Courtright. Pueblo, Colo., October 23, 1994.

33. Esther Comfort, "Remembering," pp. 36–37; Nick Comfort to church member, n.d., OSORC, Box III, Misc. & Pers. Corr.

34. White and Hopkins, *Social Gospel*, p. 243; Gorrell, *Age of Social Responsibility*, p. 339.

35. William P. Merrill to Nick Comfort, April 5, 1920, OSORC, Box III, Pers. Corr. & Misc; Charles Chatfield, *The American Peace Movement: Ideals and Activism* (New York: Twayne Publishers, 1992), p. 53.

36. R. R. Elliott to Comfort, May 22, 1920, OSORC, Box III, Pers. Corr. & Misc. James A. Whitmore to Comfort, August 26, 1920, OSORC, Box III, Pers. Corr. & Misc.

37. Nick Comfort to A. J. Green, September 28, 1920, p. 1, OSORC, Box III, Misc. & Pers. Corr.

38. Ibid., pp. 1–2.

39. Ibid., p. 2.

40. Ibid.

41. Ibid., pp. 2–3.

42. Ibid.

43. Gorrell, *The Age of Social Responsibility*, pp. 325–26.

44. Esther Comfort, "To the East Coast," pp. 38–40; interview with Janet Losey.

45. Esther Comfort, "To the East Coast," pp. 40–41.

46. Ibid., pp. 48–50.

47. Comfort, "Why the Presbyterian Church," pp. 1–3, Anne Courtright Collection.

48. Ibid., pp. 3–4.

49. Ibid., pp. 5–6; Ernest Trice Thompson, *Presbyterians in the South: Volume Three: 1890–1972* (Richmond, Virginia: John Knox Press, 1973), p. 323.

50. Esther Comfort, "To the East Coast," pp. 41, 46; Richard Wightman Fox, *Reinhold Niebuhr: A Biography* (New York: Pantheon Books, 1985), p. 25; "A Generation of Pioneers," *The Outlook* 139 (January 14, 1925): 50–51.

51. Esther Comfort, "To the East Coast," pp. 41–42, 45.

52. Ibid., pp. 42–44.

53. Union Theological Seminary Transcript, August 12, 1947, OSORC, Box V, Pers. & Bus. Corr.

54. G. H. Tuthill to Comfort, August 22, 1923, OSORC, Box III, Misc. & Pers. Corr.; interview with Janet Losey; Esther Comfort, "To The East Coast," p. 48.

55. Theodore H. Aszman to Nick Comfort, February 1, 1924, pp. 1–2, OSORC, Box III, Misc. & Pers. Corr.

56. Kenneth Underwood, *The Church, The University, and Social Policy: The Danforth Study of Campus Ministries*, vol. 1 (Middletown, Connecticut: Wesleyan Univ. Press, 1969), p. 66; Glenn A. Olds, "Religious Centers," in *Religion and the State University*, ed. Erich A. Walter (Ann Arbor: Univ. of Michigan Press, 1958): 227–28.

57. Underwood, *The Church, The University, and Social Policy*, pp. 67.

58. Ibid., p. 1.

59. Aszman to Comfort, March 26, 1924, OSORC, Box III, Pers. Corr. & Misc.

3. At Home in Oklahoma

1. Esther Comfort, "To The East Coast," p. 51; Esther Comfort, "At Home in Norman," pp. 52–54; interview with Janet Losey.

2. Esther Comfort, "The Fruit Cellar," "And Other Things: Just Bits and Pieces," in Family History, February 22, 1967, pp. 107–08; interview with Janet Losey; Comfort to Martha M. Patten, August 13, 1929, p. 2, OSORC, Box XXV, Pers. Corr.

3. Comfort to C. A. Shaver, June 30, 1927, OSORC, Box XXVI, Pers. Corr.

4. Interview with Janet Losey.

5. Esther Comfort, "At Home in Norman," pp. 52–53; interview with Anne Courtright.

6. Esther Comfort, "At Home in Norman," p. 54; Esther Comfort, "Our Own Cyclone," pp. 114–15; Comfort to C. E. Sharp, May 17, 1925, OSORC, Box XXVI, Pers. Corr.

7. Interview with Anne Courtright; interview with Janet Losey; Comfort to Edward Schworm, July 6, 1925, OSORC, Box XXVI, Pers. Corr.; Comfort to C. A. Shaver, March 23, 1927, OSORC, Box XXVI, Pers. Corr.

8. Interview with Anne Courtright.

9. Ibid.

10. Ibid.

11. Ibid.

12. Ibid.

13. Ibid.; interview with Janet Losey; Esther Comfort, "More Fun," p. 117.

14. Interview with Janet Losey; interview with Anne Courtright; Esther Comfort, "The Slide," p. 116.

15. Esther Comfort, "Square Dancing," pp. 178–79; Comfort to C. A. Shaver, April 19, 1926, OSORC, Box XXV, Pers. Corr.; J. Rud Nielsen, Memorial Service transcript, p. 8; interview with Janet Losey; Comfort to Fenton Rote, May 8, 1925, OSORC, Box XXV, Pers. Corr.

16. Interview with Janet Losey; interview with Anne Courtright.

17. Esther Comfort, "Our Front Porch," pp. 138–39; interview with Janet Losey; interview with Anne Courtright.

18. Interview with Anne Courtright; interview with Janet Losey; Esther Comfort, "Dominoes, " pp. 157–58.

19. Interview with Anne Courtright; interview with Janet Losey; Esther Comfort, "Evenings for Talk," p. 121; John B. Thompson, "A Personal Appreciation," Memorial Service Transcript, p. 10.

20. Interview with Janet Losey.

21. Interview with Janet Losey.

22. Interview with Janet Losey; Nick Comfort, to Ira Westcott, March 6, 1925, OSORC, Box XXVI, Pers. Corr.

23. Esther Comfort, "The Fruit Cellar," pp. 107–08; interview with Janet Losey.

24. Interview with Janet Losey.

25. Ibid.

26. Esther Comfort, "Our Horses," pp. 152–56; Nick Comfort to Edward Schworm, July 8, 1925, OSORC, Box XXVI, Pers. Corr.

27. Interview with Anne Courtright.

28. Esther Comfort, "A Full House," pp. 133–34.

29. Comfort to Edward Schworm, July 6, 1925, OSORC, Box XXVI, Pers. Corr.

30. Esther Comfort, "Family Visits," pp. 140–41.

31. Esther Comfort, "Our Boys Camp Out," pp. 105–06.

32. Interview with Janet Losey; interview with Anne Courtright.

33. Interview with Janet Losey; interview with Clay Courtright.

34. Interview with Janet Losey; interview with Anne Courtright.

35. Interview with Janet Losey.

36. Ibid.

37. Interview with Anne Courtright.

38. Nick Comfort, "So This Is Life," November 21, 1937, p. 1; John B. Thompson, "A Personal Appreciation," Memorial Service Transcript, p. 11.

39. Worth Robert Miller, *Oklahoma Populism: A History of the People's Party in the Oklahoma Territory* (Norman: Univ. of Oklahoma Press, 1987); James R. Green, *Grass-Roots Socialism: Radical Movements in the Southwest, 1895–1943* (Baton Rouge: Louisiana State Univ. Press, 1978); Garin Burbank, *When Farmers Voted Red: The Gospel of Socialism in the Oklahoma Countryside, 1910–1924* (Westport, Connecticut: Greenwood Press, 1976); John Thompson, *Closing the Frontier: Radical Response in Oklahoma, 1889–1923* (Norman: Univ. of Oklahoma Press, 1986).

40. Miller, *Oklahoma Populism*, pp. 134–89, passim; Green, *Grass-Roots Socialism*, pp. 323–99, passim; Thompson, *Closing the Frontier*, pp. 188–89.

41. Charles C. Alexander, *The Ku Klux Klan in the Southwest* (Lexington: Univ. of Kentucky Press, 1965), pp. 129–58, 199–208; David M. Chalmers, *Hooded Americanism: The History of the Ku Klux Klan* (Chicago: Quadrangle Paperbacks, 1968), pp. 49–55; James R. Scales and Danney Goble, *Oklahoma Politics: A History* (Norman: Univ. of Oklahoma Press, 1982), p. 126.

42. Norman F. Furniss, *The Fundamentalist Controversy, 1918–1931* (New Haven: Yale Univ. Press, 1954); *Christian Century*, January 3, 1924,

43. Craig, *Religion and Radical Politics*, p. 132; Martin E. Marty, *Righteous Empire: The Protestant Experience in America* (New York: Dial Press, 1970), p. 218; Winthrop S. Hudson, *Religion in America: A Historical Account of the Development of American Religious Life* (New York: Macmillan, 1987), pp. 341–42; Loetscher, *The Broadening Church*, p. 116.

44. Thompson, *Presbyterians in the South*, pp. 324–25.

45. Loetscher, *Broadening Church*, pp. 40–47, 88–89.

46. Comfort, "My Life Stream," p. 9.

47. Comfort to J. H. Moses, July 6, 1925, OSORC, Box XXV, Pers. Corr.

48. Comfort to E. E. Watt, September 10, 1925, OSORC, Box XXVI, Pers. Corr.; Comfort to C. E. Sharpe, November 14, 1924, OSORC, Box XXVI, Pers. Corr.

49. Robert Michaelson, "Religious Education in Public Higher Education Institutions," in *Religious Education: A Comprehensive Survey*, ed. Marvin J. Taylor (New York: Abingdon Press, 1960), 306–15, passim; Clarence Prouty Shedd, "Religion in the American State Universities: Its History and Present Problems," in *Religion in the State University: An Initial Exploration*, ed. Henry E. Allen (Minneapolis: Burgess, 1949), p. 24.

50. Comfort to J. W. Sturgis, October 29, 1925, OSORC, Box XXVI, Pers. Corr.

51. Comfort to Hugh Anderson Moran, January 13, 1925, pp. 1–2, OSORC, Box XXV, Pers. Corr.

52. Ibid., p. 2.

53. Ibid.

54. Comfort to Shailer Mathews, March 4, 1925, OSORC, Box XXV, Pers. Corr.

55. Comfort to Kirby Page, February 3, 1925, OSORC, Box XXV, Pers. Corr; Charles Chatfield, *For Peace and Justice: Pacifism in America, 1914–1941* (Boston: Beacon, 1971), p. 179; Meyer, *Protestant Search*, pp. 48–50.

56. Comfort to Fenton Rote, March 6, 1925, OSORC, Box XXV, Pers. Corr.

57. Comfort to President, State Fed. of Labor, July 16, 1925, OSORC, Box XXVI, Pers. Corr.

58. Comfort to John Simpson, July 20, 1925, OSORC, Box XXVI, Pers. Corr.

59. Comfort to C. A. Shaver, April 19, 1926, OSORC, Box XXV, Pers. Corr.

60. Comfort, "So This Is Life," p. 1.

61. Comfort to Charlie Shaver, December 15, 1925, OSORC, Box XXVI, Pers. Corr.

62. Comfort to C. A. Shaver, February 1, 1926, OSORC, Box XXVI, Pers. Corr.

63. Address by Comfort before Council of Christian Religion, Oklahoma City, fall 1926, Anne Courtright Collection; Comfort to C. A. Shaver, December 8, 1926, p. 1, OSORC, Box XXVI, Pers. Corr.

64. Ibid., p. 2.

4. The Oklahoma School of Religion

1. Comfort, transcript of address before Council of Christian Religion, fall 1926.

2. Robert T. Handy, *The American Religious Depression, 1925–1935* (Philadelphia: Fortress Press, 1968), p. 11.

3. Comfort to Rev. Moseley, April 25, 1927, OSORC, Box XXVI, Pers. Corr.

4. Comfort to Harry C. Shiffler, June 9, 1927, p. 1, OSORC, Box XXVI, Pers. Corr.

5. Ibid., p. 2.

6. "History of the School of Religion," p. 1, Oklahoma School of Religion booklet, Box III, no name.

7. Ibid.; Comfort, "The School of Religion: A New Branch of University Training," *Sooner Magazine* (March 1930): 206; Comfort, "Aims of School of Religion Told in Special Story," *O.U. Campus News*, January 10, 1936, OSORC, Box XXVII, Newspapers.

8. Ibid., pp. 1–2; Comfort, "Aims of School of Religion Told in Special Story."

9. Ibid., p. 2; Comfort, "School of Religion."

10. Comfort, "School of Religion," pp. 206–08; Oklahoma School of Religion documents, no title, p. 17, OSORC, Box III, no name.

11. Oklahoma School of Religion documents, no title, pp. 19–20, OSORC, Box III, no name.

12. Comfort to John Nevin Sayre, April 4, 1927, OSORC, Box XXVI, Pers. Corr.

13. "History of the School of Religion," pp. 1–2.

14. Comfort to C. A. Shaver, December 19, 1927, OSORC, Box XXVI, Pers. Corr.

15. Esther Comfort, "At Home in Norman," p. 54.

16. Constitution of Oklahoma School of Religion, as amended May 23, 1930, pp. 1–2, OSORC, Box III, no name; Oklahoma School of Religion documents, no title, p. 19, OSORC, Box III, no name.

17. "School of Religion Makes Far–Sighted Plans for Blazing Spiritual Trail," *Norman Transcript*, n.d., OSORC, Box IV, Publicity.

18. Nick Comfort, "Radio Talk" transcript, WNAB, April 23, 1928, Anne Courtright Collection.

19. Ibid., pp. 1–6.

20. Foreword, Blazing a Spiritual Trail in Oklahoma, OSORC, Box III; Nick Comfort to W. H. Marback, December 4, 1928, OSORC, Box XXV, Pers. Corr.

21. Douglas Hale, "The People of Oklahoma: Economics and Social Change," in *Oklahoma: New Views of the Forty-Sixth State*, ed. Anne Hodges Morgan and H. Wayne Morgan (Norman: Univ. of Oklahoma Press, 1892): 32, 56–64.

22. Comfort, "Five Types of Schools of Religion at State Universities," Blazing a Spiritual Trail, p. 15.

23. Olds, "Religious Centers," pp. 227–28; Dumont F. Kenny, "The National Conference of Christians and Jews," in *Religious Education: A Comprehensive Survey*, ed. Marvin J. Taylor (New York: Abingdon Press, 1960): 410–11.

24. Olds, "Religious Centers," pp. 228–29.

25. Comfort to John A. Rice, November 18, 1928, OSORC, Box XXV, Pers. Corr; George Lynn Cross, *Professors, Presidents, and Politicians: Civil Rights and the University of*

Oklahoma, 1890–1968 (Norman: Univ. of Oklahoma Press, 1981), pp. 20–21, 25.

26. Comfort to Rice, November 18, 1928.

27. Furniss, *Fundamentalist Controversy*, p. 138; Loetscher, *Broadening Church*, pp. 155. Controversy concerning the Princeton Theological Seminary continued to trouble the northern branch for a while longer.

28. Furniss, *Fundamentalist Controversy*, pp. 142–47.

29. Comfort to J. C. Williams, March 21, 1929, OSORC, Box XXVI, Pers. Corr.; interview with Janet Losey.

30. Arch McClure to Comfort, February 9, 1929, OSORC, Box XXV, Pers. Corr.

31. Interview with Janet Losey.

32. Ibid.; Comfort to Archibald McClure, March 9, 1929, OSORC, Box XXV, Pers. Corr.; Comfort to J. C. Williams, March 21, 1929, OSORC, Box XXVI, Pers. Corr.; Comfort to W. T. Mayfield, July 15 1929, OSORC, Box XXV, Pers. Corr.

33. Comfort to J. C. Williams.

34. Hale, "The People of Oklahoma," pp. 56–58.

35. Ibid., pp. 58–60.

36. Comfort to Charlie Shaver, July 29, 1929, OSORC, Box XXVI, Pers. Corr.

37. Comfort to Martha M. Patten, August 13, 1929, OSORC, Box XXV, Pers. Corr.

38. Comfort to Wm. L. Young, December 2, 1929, p. 1, OSORC, Box XXVI, Pers. Corr.

39. Ibid., pp. 1–2.

40. Ibid., p. 2.

41. Ibid.

42. W. B. Bizzell to L. H. Wentz, January 15, 1930, OSORC, Box XXVI, Pers. Corr.

43. Comfort to A. W. Packard, February 20, 1930, OSORC, Box XXV, Pers. Corr.

44. Comfort, "The School of Religion: A New Branch of University Training," *Sooner Magazine* (March 1930): 206–07.

45. Ibid., p. 208.

46. J. F. Owens to Comfort, May 12, 1930, OSORC, Box II, Board of Trustees; J. F. Owens to E. L. Phillips, May 12, 1930, p. 1, OSORC, Box II, Board of Trustees.

47. Ibid.

48. Ibid., pp. 1–2.

49. Comfort to Raymond S. Rubinow, May 31, 1930, OSORC, Box XXV, Pers. Corr.; Comfort to G. K. Rogers, June 2, 1930, OSORC, Box XXV, Pers. Corr.

50. Comfort to William L. Young, August 2, 1930, OSORC, Box XXVI, Pers. Corr.

51. Comfort to H. L. Standeven, September 20, 1930, pp. 1–2, OSORC, Box XXVI, Pers. Corr.

52. Ibid., p. 2.

5. Dust Bowl Oklahoma

1. W. Richard Fossey, " 'Talkin' Dust Bowl Blues' A Study of Oklahoma's Cultural Identity During the Great Depression," *Chronicles of Oklahoma* 55 (spring 1977): 12–33.

2. W. David Baird and Danney Goble, *The Story of Oklahoma* (Norman: Univ. of Oklahoma Press, 1994), pp. 389, 394–95; Green, *Grass-Roots Socialism*, p. 417.

3. Ibid., pp. 417–18.

4. Green, *Grass-Roots Socialism*, pp. 397, 425–26.

5. Marvin J. Taylor, "Inter- and Nondenominational Agencies and Christian Education," in *An Introduction to Christian Education*, ed. Marvin J. Taylor (Nashville: Abingdon Press, 1966): 312.

6. Comfort to S. B. Williams, April 17, 1930, OSORC, Box XXVI, Pers. Corr.

7. Comfort to S. B. Williams, April 25, 1930, p. 1, OSORC, Box XXVI, Pers. Corr.

8. Ibid., p. 2.

9. Ibid.

10. Comfort to J. G. Puterbaugh, April 29, 1930, OSORC, Box XXV, Pers. Corr.

11. Comfort to S. B. Williams, May 6, 1930, OSORC, Box XXVI, Pers. Corr.

12. Comfort, "Answers to Religious Questions," *Daily Oklahoman*, September 21, 1930, p. 7C.

13. Comfort to J. D. Powell, November 12, 1930, OSORC, Box XXV, Pers. Corr.

14. Comfort, "Answers to Religious Questions," December 28, 1930, p. 6C; Furniss, *Fundamentalist Controversy*, p. 145.

15. Comfort, "Answers to Religious Questions," December 28, 1930, p. 6C.

16. Ibid.

17. Ibid.

18. Ibid.

19. Ibid.

20. Ibid.

21. Craig, *Religion and Radical Politics*, pp. 179–180; John Coleman Bennett, "The Social Gospel Today," in White and Hopkins, eds., *Social Gospel*, p. 290; Meyer, *Protestant Search for Political Realism*, pp. 207–08.

22. Scales and Goble, *Oklahoma Politics*, pp. 156–157; Keith L. Bryant Jr., *Alfalfa Bill Murray*, pp. 173–276 (Norman: Univ. of Oklahoma, 1968); Comfort to William H. Murray, January 12, 1931, OSORC, Box XXV, Pers. Corr.

23. Green, *Grass-Roots Socialism*, pp. 407–408.

24. Comfort to T. A. Williams, January 14, 1931, OSORC, Box XXVI, Pers. Corr.

25. Comfort to T. A. Williams, January 20, 1931, OSORC, Box XXVI, Pers. Corr.

26. Comfort to B. B. Sturgeon, March 4, 1931, OSORC, Box XXVI, Pers. Corr.

27. Comfort, "Answers to Religious Questions," *Daily Oklahoman*, June 14, 1931, p. 6C; Miller, *American Protestantism*, p. 232.

28. Miller, *American Protestantism*, pp. 75, 232–33.

29. Ibid., pp. 75–76.

30. Ibid., pp. 63–64.

31. Craig, *Religion and Radical Politics*, pp. 130–73.

32. Frank A. Warren, 3, *Liberals and Communism: The 'Red Decade' Revisited* (Westport, Connecticut: Greenwood Press, 1966). See also David Caute's *The Fellow-Travellers: Intellectual Friends of Communism* (New Haven: Yale Univ. Press, 1988), pp. 1–281.

33. Comfort, "Answers to Religious Questions," *Daily Oklahoman*, July 19, 1931, p. 4C.

34. Ibid.

35. Ibid.

36. Ibid.

37. Comfort to Fred Mays, July 25, 1931, OSORC, Box XXV, Pers. Corr.

38. Interview with Janet Losey.

39. Ibid.

40. Comfort, "Director's Report: From May 23, 1930 to Sept. 19, 1931," p. 1, OSORC, Box II, Board of Trustees.

41. Ibid.

42. Ibid.

43. Comfort to A. Frank Smith, April 9, 1931, OSORC, Box XXVI, Pers. Corr.; Comfort to A. Frank Smith, April 29, 1931, OSORC, Box XXVI, Pers. Corr.

44. Comfort to B. B. Sturgeon, July 21, 1930, OSORC, Box XXVI, Pers. Corr.

45. Comfort to Maude and Hugh Minor, September 14, 1931, OSORC, Box XXV, Pers. Corr.

46. Comfort to A. Frank Smith, October 1, 1931, OSORC, Box XXVI, Pers. Corr.

47. Ibid.

48. Comfort to R. E. L. Morgan, October 5, 1931, OSORC, Box XXV, Pers. Corr.

49. J. F. Owens to W. E. Rowsey, November 12, 1931, OSORC, Box XXV, Pers. Corr.

50. Fessenden A. Nichols to Comfort, November 30, 1931, OSORC, Box XXV, Pers. Corr.; Robert A. McCulloch to Comfort, December 1, 1931, OSORC, Box XXV, Pers. Corr.

51. John B. Thompson, "Personal Appreciation," Memorial Service Transcript, OSORC, Index.

52. Comfort to F. A. Nichols, December 3, 1931, OSORC, Box XXV, Pers. Corr.; Comfort to Percy H. Nickles, December 3, 1931, OSORC, Box XXV, Pers. Corr.; Percy H. Nickles to Comfort, December 4, 1931, OSORC, Box XXV, Pers. Corr.

53. Nickles to Comfort, December 4, 1931.

54. Comfort, "Answers to Religious Questions," *Daily Oklahoman*, December 20, 1931, p. 4C.

55. Ibid.

56. Ibid.

57. Comfort to Maude and Hugh Minor, January 27, 1932, OSORC, Box XXV, Pers. Corr.

58. Ibid.

59. Comfort to Jerome Shell, March 8, 1932, OSORC, Box XXVI, Pers. Corr.

60. Ibid.

61. Comfort to W. L. Young, March 8, 1932, OSORC, Box

XXVI, Pers. Corr.; John Lee Eighmy, *Churches in Cultural Captivity: A History of the Social Attitudes of Southern Baptists* (Knoxville: Univ. of Tennessee Press, 1972), p. 124.

62. Comfort to Carl Magee, May 27, 1932, OSORC, Box XXV, Pers. Corr.

63. Meyer, *Protestant Search*, pp. 166–67; Miller, *American Protestantism*, p. 75.

64. Comfort, "Answers to Religious Questions," *Daily Oklahoman*, July 3, 1932, p. 4C.

65. Ibid.

66. Ibid.

67. Harvey Klehr, *The Heyday of American Communism: The Depression Decade* (New York: Basic Books, 1984), pp. 80–81.

68. Comfort, "Answers to Religious Question," *Daily Oklahoman*, November 27, 1932, p. 3C.

69. Ibid.

70. Ibid.

71. *The Social Gospel in America: Gladden, Ely, Rauschenbusch*, ed. Robert T. Handy (New York: Oxford Univ. Press, 1966), p. 15; Handy, *The American Religious Depression, 1925–1935*, pp. 16–17; Robert Moats Miller, *American Protestantism*, pp. 63–64.

72. May, *Righteous Empire*, pp. 233–34.

73. Comfort, "Answers to Religious Questions," *Daily Oklahoman*, April 9, 1933, p. 5C.

74. Interview with Janet Losey; Comfort to Harry Wilson, June 2, 1933, OSORC, Box XXVI, Pers. Corr.

6. Turning Swords into Plowshares

1. Chatfield, *American Peace Movement*, pp. 62–63; Robert Moats Miller, "The Attitudes of the Major Protestant Churches in America Toward War and Peace, 1919–1929," *Historian* 19 (November 1956): 33–34; Miller, *American Protestantism*, pp. 317–44.

2. Chatfield, *For Peace and Justice*, p. 157; Comfort to John Nevin Sayre, January 3, 1927, OSORC, Box XXVI, Pers. Corr.

3. Ibid.

4. Comfort to Sayre, April 4, 1927, OSORC, Box XXVI, Pers. Corr.

5. Chatfield, *For Peace and Justice*, pp. 152–53, 155.

6. Chatfield, *For Peace and Justice*, pp. 152–58; Chatfield, *The American Peace Movement: Ideals and Activism* (New York: Twayne Publishers, 1992), p. 54.

7. Comfort to Sayre, May 23, 1929, OSORC, Box XXVI, Pers. Corr.; Chatfield, *For Peace and Justice*, p. 155; Sayre to Comfort, May 27, 1929, OSORC, Box XXVI, Pers. Corr.

8. Comfort to Kirby Page, February 27, 1930, OSORC, Box XXV, Pers. Corr.

9. Comfort to Tucker P. Smith, November 17, 1930, OSORC, Box XXVI, Pers. Corr.

10. Comfort to Elmer Thomas, December 18, 1930, OSORC, Box XXVI, Pers. Corr.; Comfort to W. B. Pine, December 18, 1930, OSORC, Box XXV, Pers. Corr; Chatfield, *For Peace and Justice*, pp. 152–56; Chatfield, *American Peace Movement*, pp. 62–63.

11. Chatfield, *For Peace and Justice*, pp. 202–12; Chatfield, *American Peace Movement*, pp. 80–81.

12. Comfort, "Answers to Religious Questions," *Daily Oklahoman*, April 6, 1930, p. 8C.

13. Ibid.

14. Ibid; Chatfield, *For Peace and Justice*, pp. 146–51.

15. Comfort, "Answers to Religious Questions," *Daily Oklahoman*, May 18, 1930, p. 7C.

16. Ibid.

17. Ibid.

18. Comfort to Kirby Page, January 8, 1931, OSORC, Box XXV, Pers. Corr.

19. Ibid.

20. Comfort to Tucker P. Smith, March 2, 1931, OSORC, Box XXVI, Pers. Corr.

21. Comfort, "Answers to Religious Questions," *Daily Oklahoman*, April 5, 1931, p. 5C.

22. Comfort, "Answers to Religious Questions," *Daily Oklahoman*, June 14, 1931, p. 6C; Paul A. Carter, *The Decline and Revival of the Social Gospel: Social and Political Liberalism in American Protestant Churches, 1920–1940* (Ithaca: Cornell Univ. Press, 1954), p. 134.

23. Lawrence S. Wittner, *Rebels Against War: The American Peace Movement, 1941–1960* (New York: Columbia Univ. Press, 1969), pp. 3, 5; Miller, *American Protestantism*, p. 331.

24. Comfort to Tucker P. Smith, July 21, 1931, OSORC, Box XXVI, Pers. Corr.

25. Ibid.

26. Ibid.

27. Ibid.

28. Comfort, "Answers to Religious Questions," *Daily Oklahoman*, March 13, 1932, p. 4C.

29. Ibid.

30. Ibid.

31. Comfort, "Answers to Religious Questions," *Daily Oklahoman*, April 9, 1933, p. 5C.

32. Comfort, "Answers to Religious Questions," *Daily Oklahoman*, January 21, 1934, p. 4C.

33. Ibid.

34. Ibid.

35. Ibid.

36. Miller, *American Protestantism*, pp. 333–36.

37. Ibid., p. 336; Charles Chatfield, *American Peace Movement*, pp. 63–64; Chatfield, *For Peace and Justice*, pp. 165–67.

38. Miller, *American Protestantism*, pp. 336–38.

39. Ibid., pp. 340–42.

40. Patti McGill Peterson, "Student Organizations and the Antiwar Movement in America, 1900–1960," in *Peace Movements in America*, ed. Charles Chatfield (New York: Schocken Books, 1973), pp. 122–26; Ralph S. Brax, *The First Student Movement: Student Activism in the United States in the 1930s* (Port Washington, New York: 1981); Eileen Eagan, *Class, Culture and the Classroom: The Student Peace Movement of the 1930s* (Philadelphia: 1982); Robert Cohen, *When the Old Left Was Young: Student Radicals and America's First Mass Student Movement, 1929–1941* (New York: Oxford Univ. Press, 1993); Robert A. Divine, *The Reluctant Belligerent: American Entry into World War II* (New York: John Wiley & Sons, 1979), pp. 10, 23–24, 28–30, 39–40; Wayne S. Cole, *Roosevelt & the Isolationists, 1932–45* (Lincoln: Univ. of Nebraska Press, 1983), pp. 146–55, 9; Chatfield, *American Peace Movement*, pp. 63–64; Miller, *American Protestantism*, pp. 342–43.

41. John Patrick Diggins, *The Rise and Fall of the American Left* (New York: W. W. Norton, 1992), p. 172; Chatfield,

For Peace and Justice, p. 260; Chatfield, American Peace Movement, p. 66; Eagan, Class, Culture, and the Classroom, pp. 57–71, 108–33; Wittner, Rebels Against War, pp. 19–22; Cohen, When the Old Left Was Young, pp. 81–86, 91–97, 134–87.

42. Eagan, Class, Culture, and the Classroom, pp. 153–68.

43. Comfort, "So This Is Life," January 12, 1936, p. 1; interview with Anne Courtright.

44. Comfort, "So This Is Life," Oklahoma Daily, March 22, 1936, pp. 1–2.

45. Chatfield, For Peace or Justice, pp. 271–72.

46. Comfort, "So This Is Life," March 22, 1936, p. 1.

47. Ibid., pp. 1–2.

48. "Peace Group to Petition for Vote on Declarations of War," Oklahoma Daily, April 23, 1937, p. 1.; Chatfield, For Peace and Justice, p. 272; Brax, First Student Movement, p. 104; Chatfield, American Peace Movement, pp. 66–67; Meyer, Protestant Search, p. 371.

49. Comfort, "So This Is Life," November 8, 1936, p. 1.

50. Ibid., p. 1.

51. Ibid., p. 1.

52. Ibid., pp. 1–2.

53. Bennett, "The Social Gospel Today," p. 286.

54. Comfort, "So This Is Life," November 29, 1936, pp. 1–2.

55. Comfort, "So This Is Life," December 6, 1936, pp. 1–2.

56. Ibid., p. 2.

57. Ibid.

58. "Peace Groups to Petition for Vote on Declarations of War," Oklahoma Daily, April 23, 1937, pp. 1, 4; Brax, First Student Movement, p. 78; Comfort, "So This Is Life," April 18, 1937, pp. 1–2; Eagan, Class, Culture, and the Classroom, pp. 169–93.

59. "Peace Groups to Petition," pp. 1, 4.

60. Comfort, "So This Is Life," September 19, 1937, p. 1.

61. Ibid.

62. Comfort, "So This Is Life," December 19, 1937, p. 1.

63. Ibid.

64. See the pointed analysis of Cohen, When the Old Left Was Young, pp. 94–97.

65. Cole, Roosevelt & the Isolationists, 1932–45, pp. 266–67; Justus D. Doenecke, In Danger Undaunted: The

Anti-Interventionist Movement of 1940–1941 as Revealed in the Papers of the America First Committee (Stanford: Hoover Institution Press, 1990).

66. Comfort, "So This Is Life," January 9, 1938, p. 1.

67. See David Caute, *The Fellow-Travellers: Intellectual Friends of Communism* (New Haven: Yale Univ. Press, 1988), pp. 180–85.

68. Ibid., pp. 1–2.

69. "Peace Day Is Peaceful on Campus," *Oklahoma Daily*, April 28, 1938, p. 1; Chatfield, *For Peace and Justice*, pp. 295–96; Eagan, *Class, Culture, and the Classroom*, pp. 193–201.

70. Meyer, *Protestant Search*, pp. 359–60.

7. So This Is Life

1. J. Rud Nielsen, untitled, Memorial Service Transcript, p. 7.

2. Cortez A. M. Ewing, "Nick Comfort's Attitude Toward Public Affairs," Memorial Service Transcript, pp. 4–5; J. Rud Nielsen, untitled, Memorial Service Transcript, p. 7.

3. Scales and Goble, *Oklahoma Politics*, p. 197.

4. Miller, *American Protestantism*, p. 64.

5. Comfort, "So This Is Life," March 24, 1935, p. ; Comfort, "Dean's Report, June 1, 1935, to Nov. 2, 1936," OSORC, Box II, National Intercollegiate Christian Council.

6. Esther Comfort, "The Columns," pp. 167–68.

7. Cortez A. M. Ewing, "Nick Comfort's Attitude toward Public Affairs," Memorial Service Transcript, p. 4.

8. Comfort, "So This Is Life," April 11, 1937, p. 1.

9. Comfort to Mr. Lay, December 28, 1936, OSORC, Box III, Pers. Corr. & Misc.

10. Comfort to E. P. Ledbetter, n.d., p. 1, OSORC, Box IV, Norman Forum.

11. Ibid., pp. 1–2.

12. Ibid., pp. 2–3.

13. Ibid., p. 3.

14. Interview with Anne Courtright.

15. Miller, *American Protestantism*, pp. 231–33.

16. Comfort, "So This Is Life," March 24, 1935, p. 2; Comfort, "So This Is Life," January 19, 1936, p. 1.

17. Comfort, "So This Is Life," February 2, 1936, p. 1.

18. Ibid.

19. Ibid.

20. Comfort, "So This Is Life," February 9, 1936, p. 1.

21. Comfort, "So This Is Life," February 16, 1936, p. 1.

22. Ibid.

23. Ibid., p. 2.

24. Ibid.

25. Comfort, "So This Is Life," February 23, 1936, pp. 1–2.

26. Warren, *Liberals and Communism*; Milton Cantor, *The Divided Left: American Radicalism, 1900–1975* (New York: Hill and Wang, 1978), pp. 114–18, 135–37.

27. Comfort, "So This Is Life," March 8, 1936, pp. 1–2.

28. H. L. Mitchell to Friend, December 16, 1936, OSORC, Box I, Southern Tenant Farmers Union; H. L. Mitchell, *Mean Things Happening in This Land: The Life and Times of H. L. Mitchell, Cofounder of the Southern Tenant Farmers Union* (Allanheld, Osmun: Montclair, N.J., 1979); Craig, *Religion and Radical Politics*, pp. 154–159, 161; John Egerton, *Speak Now Against the Day: The Generation Before the Civil Rights Movement in the South* (New York: Alfred A. Knopf, 1994), pp. 153–58.

29. Comfort to Treasurer, March 11, 1938, OSORC, Box III, Pers. Corr. & Misc.

30. Comfort, "So This Is Life," May 9, 1937, p. 1.

31. Ibid.

32. Ibid.

33. Baird and Goble, *The Story of Oklahoma*, p. 388. A contrasting image had been articulated by H. Wayne Morgan and Anne Hodges Morgan, *Oklahoma: A Bicentennial History* (New York: W. W. Norton, 1977), pp. 167–68; Robert Michaelsen, "Religious Education in Public Higher Education Institutions," p. 307.

34. Comfort, "So This Is Life," February 6, 1938, p. 1.

35. Ibid.

36. Comfort, "So This Is Life," May 1, 1938, p. 1.

37. Ibid., pp. 1–2.

38. Comfort, "So This Is Life," January 23, 1938, p.; Anthony P. Dunbar, *Against the Grain: Southern Radicals and Prophets, 1929–1950* (Charlottesville: Univ. Press of Virginia, 1981), pp. 187–189; Harvey Klehr, *The Heyday of*

American Communism: The Depression Decade (New York: Basic Books, 1984), p. 276; Thomas A. Krueger, *And Promises to Keep: The Southern Conference for Human Welfare, 1938–1948* (Nashville: Vanderbilt Univ. Press, 1967); Linda Reed, *Simple Decency & Common Sense: The Southern Conference Movement, 1938–1963* (Bloomington: Indiana Univ. Press, 1991); Egerton, *Speak Now Against the Day.*

39. Luther Patrick to Comfort, August 31, 1938, OSORC, Box I, Southern Conference for Human Welfare; Comfort to Luther Patrick, September 5, 1938, OSORC, Box I, Southern Conference for Human Welfare; Louise O. Charlton to Comfort, September 28, 1938, OSORC, Box I, Southern Conference for Human Welfare.

40. Comfort, "So This Is Life," October 2, 1938, p. 1.

41. Ibid., pp. 1–2.

42. Miller, *American Protestantism*, p. 309; Ronald C. White Jr., *Liberty and Justice: Racial Reform & the Social Gospel* (San Francisco: Harper & Row, Publishers, 1990).

43. Miller, *American Protestantism*, p. 310.

44. Southern Conference for Human Welfare, "Plans and Purposes," OSORC, Box I, Southern Conference for Human Welfare.

45. Ibid., p. 2; F. D.. Behringer to W. B. Emery, November 16, 1938, OSORC, Box I, Southern Conference for Human Welfare; Dunbar, *Against the Grain*, pp. 189–91; Klehr, *The Heyday of American Communism*, p. 276; Egerton, *Speak Now Against the Day*, pp 176–97.

46. "Oklahoma Develops New Race Attitude," *Harlow's Weekly*, November 26, 1938, p. 3; Dunbar, *Against the Grain*, p. 189; Robin D. G. Kelley, *Hammer and Hoe: Alabama Communists During the Great Depression* (Chapel Hill: Univ. of North Carolina Press, 1990), p. 185.

47. For an account of early Jim Crow practices in Oklahoma, see Jimmie L. Franklin, "Black Oklahomans and Sense of Place," in Davis Joyce, ed. *"An Oklahoma I Had Never Seen Before,"* pp. 266–72; Franklin, *Journey Toward Hope: A History of Blacks in Oklahoma* (Norman: Univ. of Oklahoma Press, 1982); Danney Goble, "The Southern Influence on Oklahoma," in Davis Joyce, ed., *"An Oklahoma I Had Never Seen Before,"* pp. 286–90; Goble, *Progressive Oklahoma: The Making of a New Kind of State* (Norman: Univ. of Oklahoma

Press, 1980), pp. 140–44, 219; and Philip Mellinger, "Discrimination and Statehood in Oklahoma," *Chronicles of Oklahoma* 49 (autumn 1971): 340–77.

48. Comfort, "So This Is Life," December 4, 1938, p. 1.

49. Dunbar, *Against the Grain*, pp. 189–90; Kelley, *Hammer and Hoe*, pp. 186–88.

50. Dunbar, *Against the Grain*, p. 191.

51. Green, *Grass-Roots Socialism*, pp. 432–35.

52. Comfort, "So This Is Life," April 21, 1940, p. 1.

53. Ibid.

54. Ibid.

8. A Death in the Family

1. Interview with Janet Losey.

2. Ibid.; interview with Anne Courtright.

3. Interview with Anne Courtright; H. E. Anderson to Director, October 9, 1939, John B. Thompson FBI File, #61-7559-4848.

4. Ibid; Esther Comfort, "The Question of Pride," p. 180.

5. Interview with Anne Courtright.

6. Ibid.

7. Interview with Dick Comfort; Esther Comfort, "The Oklahoma District Y.W.C.A.," pp. 169–72; Goble, "The Southern Influence on Oklahoma, pp. 284–90.

8. Esther Comfort, "The Oklahoma District Y.W.C.A.," pp. 170–71.

9. Interview with Janet Losey.

10. Esther Comfort, "At Home in Norman," pp. 56, 58; interview with Janet Losey.

11. Esther Comfort, "At Home in Norman," p. 58.

12. Ibid., p. 59; Comfort, "So This Is Life," November 6, 1938, p. 1.

13. Hugh Comfort to Dick Disney, n.d., Anne Courtright Collection.

14. Comfort, "So This Is Life," November 6, 1938.

15. Esther Comfort, "At Home in Norman," p. 60; interview with Dick Comfort.

16. Esther Comfort, "More about Hugh," p. 90; Comfort, "So This Is Life," October 30, 1938, p. 1.

17. Comfort, "So This Is Life," November 6, 1938; Esther Comfort, "More About Hugh," p. 98.

18. Interview with Anne Courtright.

9. Nick the Heretic

1. Robert Justin Goldstein, *Political Repression in Modern America: 1870 to the Present* (Cambridge: Schenkman Publishing Co., 1978), pp. 201, 213, 240–44.

2. James Arthur Robinson, "Loyalty Investigations and Legislation in Oklahoma," Ph.D. dissertation, University of Oklahoma, 1955, pp. 20, 29, 34–35.

3. Ibid., pp. 36–38.

4. Ibid., pp. 38–39; Comfort, "So This Is Life," January 7, 1939, p. 1.

5. Ibid.

6. Ibid.

7. Ibid.

8. Ibid.

9. Ibid., pp. 1, 3.

10. Ibid.

11. Divine, *The Reluctant Belligerent*, p. 60.

12. Charles F. Howlett and Glenn Zeitzer, *The American Peace Movement: History and Historiography* (Washington, D.C.: American Historical Association, 1985), pp. 28–32.

13. Comfort to Lewis, January 27, 1939, OSORC, Box I, Re-Comfort Investigation; "Half-Cocked Americanism," *Oklahoma News*, January 26, 1939, p. 4.

14. "Comfort and Kight Call Truce Until Conference," *Oklahoma Daily*, January 27, 1939, p. 1; Comfort to Tom Kight, January 27, 1939, OSORC, Box I, Re-Comfort Investigation.

15. Tom Kight to Comfort, January 30, 1939, OSORC, Box I, Re-Comfort Investigation.

16. Comfort to Tom Kight, January 31, 1939, OSORC, Box I, Re-Comfort Investigation.

17. Ibid.

18. Robinson, "Loyalty Investigations," pp. 40–41; "College Heads Welcome Inquiry into Ism Teaching in Their Schools, *Daily Oklahoman*, January 29, 1939, p. 1; George Lynn Cross, *Professors, Presidents, & Politicians: Civil Rights and the University of Oklahoma, 1890–1968* (Norman: Univ. of Oklahoma Press, 1981), pp. 112–14.

19. Esther Comfort, "Entertained with Bertrand Russell," pp. 108–109; Esther Comfort, "The Question of Pride," p. 180.

20. Robinson, "Loyalty Investigations," pp. 41–42.

21. Ibid., p. 44.

22. Ruth Robinson, "Word for Comfort," *Oklahoma Daily*, January 27, 1939, p. 1.

23. W. G. Lewis to Comfort, January 29, 1939, OSORC, Box I, Re-Comfort Investigation.

24. B. M. Parmenter to Comfort, January 31, 1939, OSORC, Box I, Re-Comfort Investigation.

25. James Smith Griffes to Comfort, February 1, 1939, OSORC, Box I, Re-Comfort Investigation; Elizabeth Irwin to Comfort, February 1, 1939, OSORC, Box I, Re-Comfort Investigation; Martin A. Klingberg to Comfort, February 1, 1939, OSORC, Box I, Re-Comfort Investigation.

26. Comfort, "So This Is Life," February 26, 1939, p. 1; M. J. Heale, *American Anticommunism: Combating the Enemy Within, 1830–1970* (Baltimore: Johns Hopkins Univ. Press, 1990), pp. 118–19.

27. Ibid.

28. Ibid., pp. 1, 2.

29. Gomer Smith to Comfort, March 24, 1939, OSORC, Box I, Re-Comfort Investigation; Cecil A. Myers to Comfort, March 27, 1939, OSORC, Box I, Re-Comfort Investigation; Ripley S. Greenhaw to Comfort, March 31, 1939, OSORC, Box I, Re-Comfort Investigation.

30. Zula J. Breeden to Comfort, April 11, 1939, OSORC, Box I, Re-Comfort Investigation.

31. Lawrence Thompson, "Dean Comfort Wants Young Men to Think," July 21, 1939, Janet Losey Collection.

32. Ibid.

33. Ibid.

34. Handy, *The American Religious Depression, 1925–1935*, p. 13.

35. Oscar Presley Fowler to Comfort, July 31, 1939, OSORC, Box I, Re-Comfort Investigation.

36. Comfort, "The Challenge of Religion and Education," transcript of baccalaureate sermon, University of Oklahoma, August 2, 1936, p. 6; Anne Courtright Collection; 1937 Sooner Yearbook, 3.

37. Norman Holmes Pearson, "The Nazi-Soviet Pact and the

End of a Dream," in *America in Crisis: Fourteen Crucial Episodes in American History*, ed. Daniel Aaron (New York: Alfred A. Knopf, 1952), pp. 327–48, 193–215; Milton Cantor, *The Divided Left: American Radicalism, 1900–1975* (New York: Hill and Wang, 1978), pp. 144–48.

38. Divine, *The Reluctant Belligerent*, pp. 70–78.

39. Chatfield, *For Peace and Justice*, pp. 311–17; Meyer, *Protestant Search*, pp. 360.

40. Comfort, "So This Is Life," October 1, 1939, p. 2.

41. Ibid.

42. Ibid.

43. Ibid.

44. Ibid; Comfort, "So This Is Life," October 8, 1939, p. 2.

45. Nana Beth Stapp, transcript of Keynote Address, Third Annual Session of the Oklahoma Youth Legislature, OSORC, Box I, Oklahoma Youth Legislature.

46. Comfort, transcript of address before youth legislature, Oklahoma City, January 9, 1940, p. 1, OSORC, Box I, Oklahoma Youth Legislature.

47. Ibid., pp. 1–2.

48. Ibid., pp. 2–5.

49. Ibid., pp. 4–5.

50. "Local Legion to Check in Red Squabble," *Norman Transcript*, February 25, 1940, p. 1; "Rivers Says Comfort Not Called Red," *Oklahoma Daily*, February 24, 1940, p. 1.

51. J. Rud Nielsen, untitled address, Memorial Service Transcript, p. 8; interview with Janet Losey.

52. Comfort to A. B. Rivers, n.d., OSORC, Box I, Oklahoma Youth Legislature.

53. Ibid.

54. Ibid., p. 5; Comfort to Rivers, February 17, 1940, OSORC, Box I, Re-Comfort Investigation.

55. Comfort to Gentlemen, n.d., OSORC, Box I, Re-Comfort Investigation.

56. Esther Comfort, "Norman in 1940," pp. 173–75.

57. Ibid., pp. 175–76.

58. Ibid., p. 176.

59. Comfort to Dave, February 19, 1940, OSORC, Box I, Oklahoma Youth Legislature; E. W. Smart to Comfort, February 28, 1940, OSORC, Box I, Re-Comfort Investigation; "Comfort Is Ousted by State Board," *Norman Transcript*,

February 29, 1940, p. 1; "Comfort Will Not Continue Ouster Fight," *Norman Transcript*, March 1, 1940, p. 1.

60. Comfort to Rivers, n.d., Box I, Re-Comfort Investigation.

61. "Petition Hits Removal of Nick Comfort," *Oklahoma Daily*, March 6, 1940, p. 1; Elmer Million to Comfort, n.d., OSORC, Box I, Re-Comfort Investigation; John Lokey to Comfort, March 1, 1940, OSORC, Box I, Re-Comfort Investigation; R. M. McClintock to Comfort, March 1, 1940, OSORC, Box I, Re-Comfort Investigation.

62. McClintock to Comfort, March 1, 1940; Comfort to Lew Wentz, February 21, 1940, OSORC, Box II, Correspondence Re-Finance.

63. Thomas L. Wilson to Comfort, March 2, 1940, OSORC, Box I, Re-Comfort Investigation; H. H. Lindeman to Comfort, March 2, 1940, OSORC, Box I, Re-Comfort Investigation; Charles N. Gould to Comfort, March 3, 1940, OSORC, Box I, Re-Comfort Investigation; Guy A. Lackey to Comfort, March 4, 1940, OSORC, Box I, Re-Comfort Investigation.

64. C. L. Jones to Comfort, March 1, 1940, OSORC, Box I, Re-Comfort Investigation; Comfort to C. L. Jones, March 6, 1940, pp. 1–2, OSORC, Box I, Re-Comfort Investigation.

65. Comfort to C. L. Jones, March 6, 1940, pp. 2–3.

66. Chatfield, *For Peace and Justice*, pp. 318–19; Meyer, *Protestant Search*, p. 360.

67. Comfort, "So This Is Life," April 21, 1940, pp. 1–2; Comfort, "So This Is Life," April 28, 1940, p. 2.

68. Ibid.

69. Comfort, "So This Is Life," May 19, 1940, p. 2.

70. Ibid.

71. A foreign born patriot to Comfort, n.d., OSORC, Box I, Re-Comfort Investigation.

72. "Governor Phillips Renews Attack on Dean Comfort," *Norman Transcript*, May 20, 1940, p. 1; "Nick Comfort Irks Phillips Through Column," *Oklahoma Daily*, May 21, 1940, p. 1; "Dean Refuses to Be Muzzled," *Tulsa Tribune*, May 24, 1940, OSORC, Box I, Re-Comfort Investigation.

73. Cross, *Professors, Presidents, and Politicians*, pp. 120–21; Nick Comfort, *Christ-Without-Armor: Uncensored Essays on the Democratic Way* (Norman: Cooperative Books, 1940).

74. Goldstein, *Political Repression in Modern America*, pp. 256–57; Robinson, "Loyalty Investigations," pp. 48–58.

75. Letter from Jack McMichael, June 15, 1940, OSORC, Box I, Peace Organizations; Joseph Cadden to Comfort, June 18, 1940, OSORC, Box I, Peace Organizations.

76. Comfort to Jack McMichael, July 19, 1940, OSORC, Box I, Peace Organizations.

77. Edwin C. Johnson to Comfort, July 12, 1940, OSORC, Box I, Peace Organizations; William B. Lloyd Jr. to Comfort, July 19, 1940, OSORC, Box I, Peace Organizations.

78. Comfort to Ben L. Morrison, October 1, 1940, OSORC, Box I, Oklahoma Committee on Constitutional Rights; "Communists and Negroes First Victims," Action Bulletin, October 26, 1940, OSORC, Box I, Re-Comfort Investigation.

79. "Ministers Quizzed by Dies Group," Daily Oklahoman, October 20, 1940, p. 1; "Three Pastors Charge Dies Call Trumped Up," ibid.; " 'Smear' Attack Charged by Presbyterian Pastors," Norman Transcript, October 20, 1940, pp. 1–2.

80. Harryle Miller to Comfort, October 21, 1940, OSORC, Box I, Re-Comfort Investigation; Bryan W. Biles to Comfort, October 21, 1940, OSORC, Box I, Re-Comfort Investigation.

81. "Six Faculty Members on Rights Group," Oklahoma Daily, November 10, 1940, p. 1; "Phillips Raps Six Profs in Rights Group," ibid., November 13, 1940, p. 1; "Six Profs to Attend Civil Rights Parley," ibid., November 15, 190, p. 1; "Adams Flays Subversive Actions," ibid., November 19, 1940, p. 1.

82. Richard Comfort to Friend, January 13, 1941, OSORC, Box I, Peace Organizations; Esther Comfort, "At Home in Norman," pp. 55–56. Klehr, The Heyday of American Communism, pp. 319–23.

83. Robinson, "Loyalty Investigations," p. 75.

84. Ibid., pp. 59–61; "Regents Give Full Support to Red Hunt," Norman Transcript, February 4, 1941, p. 1. See Cross, Professors, Presidents, & Politicians, pp. 122–27; Adam Coaldigger, "Hitler over Oklahoma," American Guardian, February 14, 1941, p. 4.

85. Robinson, "Loyalty Investigations," pp. 61–64.

86. Cortez A. M. Ewing, "Nick Comfort's Attitude Toward Public Affairs," Memorial Service Transcript, p. 4.

87. Ken Lowe, "Broken Images," July 30, 1961, OSORC, Index, p. 2; Robinson, "Loyalty Investigations," pp. 64–65.

88. Robinson, "Loyalty Investigations," pp. 69–70.

89. Ibid., pp. 69–73.

90. Ibid., p. 72.

91. Robinson, "Loyalty Investigations," pp. 72, 81–83.

92. Release by Comfort, May 8, 1941, OSORC, Box I, Oklahoma Commission of Constitutional Rights; "Ouster of Halperin Is Urged," *Norman Transcript*, February 4, 1941, p. 1; "Demand for Ouster of Halperin Is Denounced," ibid., February 11, 1941, p. 4; Lowe, "Broken Images," p. 2; Robinson, "Loyalty Investigations," p. 75.

93. Robinson, "Loyalty Investigations," pp. 76–77.

10. From Pearl Harbor to the Progressive Party

1. Chatfield, *For Peace and Justice*, pp. 325–26; Photograph of Elizabeth Comfort and other students sitting with David White, Fellowship of Reconciliation Southwest secretary, *Oklahoma Daily*, December 12, 1941, p. 2.

2. Roy Gittinger, *The University of Oklahoma: A History of Fifty Years, 1892–1942* (Norman: Univ. of Oklahoma Press, 1942), pp. 164–65; "Internal Security (C) Custodial Detention, October 29, 1942, p.7, John B. Thompson FBI File, #100-32736-5; "Internal Security-C Custodial Detention," April 5, 1943, p.9, John B. Thompson FBI File #100-32736-10.

3. Comfort to Lee K. Anderson, January 14, 1937, OSORC, Box IV, Norman Board of Education; Comfort to L. A. Hill, November 17, 1937, Oklahoma Association of Teachers Retirement Collection, Negro Teachers, Western History Collections, University of Oklahoma, Norman, Oklahoma; John Bender, "Tribute to Dean E. N. Comfort," Memorial Service Transcript, pp. 6–7.

4. Bender, "Tribute to Dean E. N. Comfort," p. 6.

5. Comfort, transcript of sermon entitled "American Ideals," pp. 1–3, n.d., Anne Courtright Collection.

6. Ibid., p. 5.

7. Ibid.

8. Comfort, "The Oklahoma Journal of Religion," *Oklahoma Journal of Religion* 1 (January 1944): 1.

9. Comfort to Joe McBride, January 31, 1944, OSORC, Box XXVI, Pers. Corr.

10. Comfort, "Christian Citizenship," *Oklahoma Journal of Religion* 1 February 1944): 1–2.

11. Comfort, "Let's Get Our Heads Together and Pour Our Hearts Out to Each Other," *Oklahoma Journal of Religion* 1 (April 1944): 1–2.

12. Comfort, "Dear Reader," *Oklahoma Journal of Religion* 1 (May 1944): 5.

13. Comfort, "Corn Community," *Oklahoma Journal of Religion* 1 (May 1944): 8–11; Comfort, "Boley," *Oklahoma Journal of Religion* 1 (July 1944): 8–11.

14. Comfort, "Looking Ahead," *Oklahoma Journal of Religion* 1 (June 1944): 1–2.

15. See Robert C. Cottrell, *Izzy: A Biography of I. F. Stone* (New Brunswick: Rutgers Univ. Press, 1992), pp. 110–11 and Cantor, *The Divided Left*, p. 158.

16. Ibid., p.1.

17. Ibid.

18. Comfort, "Our Chance," *Oklahoma Journal of Religion* 1 (September 1944): 1–3.

19. Ibid., pp. 1–2.

20. Ibid., pp. 2–3.

21. Comfort, "When Johnnie Comes Marching Home," *Oklahoma Journal of Religion* 1 (October 1944): 1–2.

22. An irate listener to Comfort, n.d., p. 1, OSORC, Box III, Misc. & Pers. Corr.

23. Ibid., pp. 1–2.

24. Comfort, "Thank You," *Oklahoma Journal of Religion* 2 (May 1945): 16.

25. George Cross to Comfort, March 8, 1945, OSORC, Box II, Correspondence Re: Finances of School of Religion; Comfort to L. H. Wentz, February 26, 1945, OSORC, Box II, Corr. Re: Finances of School of Religion; Comfort to Lloyd Noble, April 4, 1945, OSORC, Box II, Corr. Re: Finances of School of Religion.

26. Comfort to Lloyd Noble, April 4, 1945, OSORC, Box II, Corr. Re: Finances of School of Religion.

27. Comfort to Wentz, April 13, 1945, OSORC, Box II, Corr. Re. Finances of School of Religion; Comfort to Dear, August 21, 1946, OSORC, Box II, Corr. Re: Finances of School of Religion.

28. Ibid.

29. Comfort to Bruce, August 21, 1946, OSORC, Box II, Corr. Re: Finance of School of Religion.

30. Ray Parr, "Financial Starvation Closes Norman School of Religion," Anne Courtright Collection; "Resolution" by Board of Regents of the University of Oklahoma, May 29, 1948, OSORC, Box II. Untitled; Comfort, "Oklahoma School of Religion Closes," p. 1; OSORC, Box II, Untitled.

31. Comfort, "Oklahoma School of Religion Closes," p. 2.

32. Ibid., p. 3.

33. Ibid., p. 3.

34. John B. Thompson, "A Personal Appreciation," Memorial Service Transcript, p. 10.

35. Glenn C. McGee to Comfort, November 25, 1946, OSORC, Box III, Pers. Corr. & Misc.; Vincent Sheean and Harry F. Ward to Comfort, March 21, 1947, OSORC, Box V, Misc. Organizations.

36. Donald L. Hibbard to Comfort, October 21, 1947, OSORC, Box V, Pers. Corr. & Bus. Corr.; Hibbard to Comfort, December 10, 1947, OSORC, Box V, Pers. Corr. & Bus. Corr.

37. "The Need for the Peoples Political Party," OSORC, Box V, Misc. Material; "Constitution Progressive Party of Oklahoma," OSORC, Box I, Progressive Party of Okla.; Carl von der Lancken to Comfort, April 22, 1948, OSORC, Box I, Progressive Party of Okla; Lawrence Lader, *Power on the Left: American Radical Movements since 1946* (New York: W. W. Norton, 1979), pp. 19–55.

38. Curtis D. MacDougall, *Gideon's Army*, v. 2 (New York: Marzani & Munsell, 1965), pp. 435–37.

39. von der Lancken to Comfort, April 22, 1948, OSORC, Box I, Progressive Party of Okla.; "Delegate's Credential," National Founding Convention of the New Party, July 23–25, 1948, OSORC, Box I, Progressive Party of Okla.

40. Comfort, "Beware, Politicians, Beware," unpublished manuscript, 1949, Anne Courtright Collection; Cottrell, Izzy, p. 151; Norman D. Markowitz, *The Rise and Fall of the People's Century: Henry A. Wallace and American Liberalism, 1941–1948* (New York: Free Press, 1973), p. 296.

41. Ibid., pp. 4–12.

42. Comfort to Byron Dacus, February 12, 1949, Anne Courtright Collection.

43. Ibid.

44. Robinson, "Loyalty Investigations," pp. 88–97.

45. Comfort to Mary Morgan, September 12, 1949, OSORC, Box I, Progressive Party of Oklahoma.

46. Ibid., p. 1.

47. Ibid., pp. 1–2.

48. Comfort, "O.U. Students Give Communism a Boost," January 12, 1950, Anne Courtright Collection.

49. Frank Milton Shelton to Comfort, April 3, 1950, OSORC, Box XXVI, Misc. & Pers. Corr.

50. Comfort to Harry S. Truman, "An Open Letter," n.d., Anne Courtright Collection; J. Rud Nielsen, untitled, Memorial Service Transcript, p. 8.

51. Robinson, "Loyalty Investigations," pp. 131–56, 202; Goldstein, *Political Repression in Modern America*, pp. 350, 359–60.

52. Robinson, "Loyalty Investigations," pp. 144, 151–52.

53. Goldstein, *Political Repression in Modern America*, p. 324.

11. Heading for Comfort Hills and Beyond

1. George Lynn Cross, *The University of Oklahoma and World War I: A Personal Account, 1941–1946* (Norman: Univ. of Oklahoma Press, 1980), pp. 24–35; Esther Comfort, "At Home in Norman," pp. 56, 62–63; interview with Anne Courtright; Family History, p. 1, Anne Courtright Collection.

2. Interview with Anne Courtright; Esther Comfort, "At Home in Norman," pp. 63–64.

3. Esther Comfort, "At Home in Norman," p. 67; interview with Anne Courtright.

4. Interview with Anne Courtright.

5. Ibid.

6. Ibid.

7. Esther Comfort, "At Home in Norman," pp. 67–68; interview with Anne Courtright.

8. Donald L. Hibbard to Comfort, July 18,1949, OSORC, Box V, Pers. & Bus. Corr.; Esther Comfort, "Social Security," pp. 159–61.

9. "Release," June 20, 1949, OSORC, Box V, Pers. & Bus. Corr.; Comfort to Mr. LeRue, August 5, 1949, OSORC, Box V, Pers. & Bus. Corr.; A. D. Dooms to Comfort, August 24, 1949, OSORC, Box V, Pers. & Bus. Corr.

10. Comfort to Harry S. Truman, "An Open Letter," n.d., p.1.

11. Comfort to Anne Comfort, November 5, 1949, OSORC, Box V, Pers. & Bus. Corr.

12. Ibid., p. 2.

13. Comfort, transcript of sermon, "Growing Old with Flexibility, Cheerfulness and Serenity," n.d., Anne Courtright Collection.

14. Ibid., p. 2.

15. Ibid., pp. 2–3.

16. Ibid., pp. 3–5.

17. Nick and Esther Comfort, "Our dear, dear Children," n.d., Janet Losey Collection.

18. Ibid.

19. Esther Comfort, "At Home in Norman," p. 72.

20. Interview with Anne Courtright.

21. Esther Comfort, "At Home in Norman," p. 73; interview with Anne Courtright.

22. Interview with Anne Courtright; Esther Comfort, "At Home in Norman," pp. 73–75.

23. Esther Comfort, "At Home in Norman," pp. 75–77.

24. Ibid., p. 77.

25. J. Rud Nielsen, untitled, Memorial Service Transcript, p. 8.

26. Esther Comfort, "At Home in Norman," p. 77.

27. Ibid., p. 78.

28. John Bender, "Tribute to Dean E. N. Comfort," p. 5; Cortez A. M. Ewing, "Nick Comfort's Attitude," pp. 4–5; John B. Thompson, "A Personal Appreciation," pp. 10–12; J. Rud Nielsen, untitled, p. 7; Mitchell S. Epperson, "A Tribute to Nick Comfort," Memorial Service Transcript, p. 9; Lowe, "Broken Images," p. 2; interview with Dora McFarland, November 15, 1979.

29. J. Rud Nielsen, untitled, p. 8.

30. See Oscar Ameringer, *If You Don't Weaken*, ed. James Green (Norman: Univ. of Oklahoma Press, 1983).

SELECTED
BIBLIOGRAPHY

Primary Materials

Shortly after the Oklahoma School of Religion closed its doors, Nick Comfort proceeded to riffle through his personal correspondence and that of the institution he so loved. Distraught by the collapse of his life-long dream, Comfort was in the process of discarding those documents when an archivist at the University of Oklahoma was informed of what he was doing. Although some of the materials—especially a good deal of personal correspondence—had already been tossed out, much of it, fortunately, was spared.

The Western History Collections at the University of Oklahoma came to serve as the repository for the bulk of extant manuscript materials relating to the School of Religion and Nick Comfort. The Oklahoma School of Religion collection is located there, and contains a wealth of correspondence and a paper trail that allowed for a reconstruction of the history of the institution. Many of Nick Comfort's personal papers, ranging from grade transcripts to letters received from family members, friends, and foes are situated in that collection. So, too, are boxes of books from Comfort's personal library, donated to the archives.

Other manuscript materials—which will likely end up at the Western History Collections at some point—are held by three of Comfort's children, Dick Comfort, Janet Comfort Losey, and Anne Comfort Courtright. These include an invaluable family history by Esther Obee Comfort, articles, essays, sermons, autobiographical sketches, and copies of Nick's *Daily Oklahoman* columns. Photographs that capture the many sides of Comfort from boyhood to his declining years remain in the possession of his children. A small number of FBI documents relating to Comfort are available at the Western History Collections, culled from the John B. Thompson file.

In addition to the aforementioned writings, the bulk of Comfort's publications are available on microfilm. These include his "Answers to Religious Questions" column in the *Daily Oklahoman* (1930–1934) and his "So This Is Life" column in the *Oklahoma Daily* (1935–1940). Complete copies of the *Oklahoma Journal of Religion* (1944–1945) are held by the author, the Western History Collections at OU, and Anne Comfort Courtright.

Interviews conducted with Dick Comfort in San Antonio, Janet Comfort Losey in Dallas, and Anne Comfort Courtright in Pueblo, Colorado, proved to be illuminating. Transcripts and tapes of those interviews are at present retained by the author.

Books

Alexander, Charles C. *The Ku Klux Klan in the Southwest.* Lexington: Univ. of Kentucky Press, 1965.

Ameringer, Oscar. *If You Don't Weaken!* Norman: Univ. of Oklahoma Press, 1983.

Austin, C. Grey. *A Century of Religion at the University of Michigan: A Case Study in Religion and the State University.* Ann Arbor: Univ. of Michigan, 1957.

Baird, W. David, and Danney Goble. *The Story of Oklahoma.* Norman: Univ. of Oklahoma Press, 1994.

Brax, Ralph S. *The First Student Movement: Student Activism in the United States During the 1930s.* Port Washington, New York, 1981.

Brinkley, Alan. *Voices of Protest: Huey Long, Father Coughlin, and the Great Depression.* New York: Alfred A. Knopf, 1982.

Bryant, Keith L. Jr. *Alfalfa Bill Murray.* Norman: Univ. of Oklahoma Press, 1968.

Burbank, Garin. *When Farmers Voted Red: The Gospel of Socialism in the Oklahoma Countryside.* Westport, Connecticut.: Greenwood Press, 1976.

Cantor, Milton. *The Divided Left: American Radicalism, 1900–1975.* New York: Hill and Wang, 1978.

Carter, Paul. *The Decline and Revival of the Social Gospel, 1920–1940.* Ithaca: Cornell Univ. Press, 1954.

Caute, David. *The Fellow-Travellers: Intellectual Friends of Communism.* New Haven: Yale Univ. Press, 1988.

———. *The Great Fear: The Anti-Communist Purge under Truman and Eisenhower.* New York: Simon and Schuster, 1979.

Chalmers, David M. *Hooded Americanism: The History of the Ku Klux Klan.* Chicago: Quadrangle Paperbacks, 1968.

Chatfield, Charles. *The American Peace Movement: Ideals and Activism.* New York: Twayne Publishers, 1992.

———. *For Peace and Justice: Pacifism in America, 1914–1941.* Knoxville: Univ. of Tennessee Press, 1971.

———. *Peace Movements in America.* New York: Schocken, 1973.

Clark, Carter Blue. "A History of the Ku Klux Klan in Oklahoma." Ph.D. diss., University of Oklahoma, 1976.

Cohen, Robert. *When the Old Left Was Young: Student Radicals and America's First Mass Student Movement, 1929–1941.* New York: Oxford Univ. Press, 1993.

Cole, Wayne S. *Roosevelt and the Isolationists, 1932–1945.* Lincoln: Univ. of Nebraska Press, 1983.

Cook, Fred J. *The Nightmare Decade: The Life and Times of Joe McCarthy and the Senate.* Lexington: Univ. of Kentucky Press, 1970.

Cottrell, Robert C. *Izzy: A Biography of I. F. Stone.* New Brunswick: Rutgers Univ. Press, 1992.

———. "The Social Gospel of Nicholas Comfort," *The Chronicles of Oklahoma* 61 (winter 1983–84): 386–409.

Craig, Robert H. *Religion and Radical Politics: An Alternative Christian Tradition in the United States.* Philadelphia: Temple Univ. Press, 1992.

Cross, George Lynn. *Professors, Presidents, and Politicians: Civil Rights and the University of Oklahoma, 1890–1968.* Norman: Univ. of Oklahoma Press, 1981.

———. *The University of Oklahoma and World War II: A Personal Account, 1941–1946.* Norman: Univ. of Oklahoma Press, 1980.

Curti, Merle. *Peace or War: The American Struggle, 1636–1936*. New York: W. W. Norton, 1936.

DeBenedetti, Charles. *Origins of the Modern American Peace Movement, 1915–1929*. Millwood, N.Y.: KTO, 1978.

———. *The Peace Reform In American History*. Bloomington: Indiana Univ. Press, 1980.

Diggins, John Patrick. *The Rise and Fall of the American Left*. New York: W. W. Norton, 1992.

Divine, Robert A. *The Reluctant Belligerent: American Entry into World War II*. 2d ed. New York: John Wiley, 1979.

Doenecke, Justus D. *In Danger Undaunted: The Anti-Interventionist Movement of 1940–1941 as Revealed in the Papers of the America First Committee*. Stanford: Hoover Institution Press, 1990.

———. "Non-Intervention of the Left: 'The Keep America Out of the War' Congress.'" *Journal of Contemporary History* 12 (April 1977): 221–31.

Doran, Frank. "The Origins of Culture Areas in Oklahoma, 1830–1900." Ph.D. diss., University of Oregon, 1974.

Dunbar, Anthony P. *Against the Grain: Southern Radicals and Prophets, 1929–1950*. Charlottesville: Univ. Press of Virginia, 1981.

Eagan, Eileen. *Class, Culture and Classrooms: The Student Peace Movement of the 1930s*. Philadelphia: Temple Univ. Press, 1981.

Egerton, John. *Speak Now Against the Day: The Generation Before the Civil Rights Movement in the South*. New York: Alfred A. Knopf, 1994.

Eighmy, John Lee. "Religious Liberalism in the South During the Progressive Era," *Church History* 38 (September 1969): 359–72.

Floyd, Fred. "A History of the Dust Bowl." Ph.D. diss., Univ. of Oklahoma, 1950.

Fossey, W. Richard. "Talking Dust Bowl Blues: A Study of Oklahoma's Cultural Identity During the Great Depression." *The Chronicles of Oklahoma* 55 (spring 1977): 12–33.

Franklin, Jimmie Lewis. *Journey Toward Hope: A History of Blacks in Oklahoma*. Norman: Univ. of Oklahoma Press, 1982.

Furniss, Norman F. *The Fundamentalist Controversy, 1918–1931*. New Haven: Yale Univ. Press, 1954.

Gibson, Arrell M. *Oklahoma: A History of Five Centuries*. Norman: Univ. of Oklahoma Press, 1981.

Gittinger, Roy. *The University of Oklahoma: A History of Fifty Years, 1892–1942*. Norman: Univ. of Oklahoma Press, 1942.

Goble, Danney. *Progressive Oklahoma: The Making of a New Kind of State*. Norman: Univ. of Oklahoma Press, 1980.

Green, Donald, ed. *Rural Oklahoma*. Oklahoma City: Oklahoma Historical Society, 1977.

Green, James R. *Grass-Roots Socialism: Radical Movements in the Southwest, 1895–1943*. Baton Rouge: Louisiana Univ. Press, 1978.

Gregory, James N. *American Exodus: The Dust Bowl Migration and Okie Culture in California*. New York: Oxford Univ. Press, 1989.

Hale, Douglas. "The People of Oklahoma: Economics and Social Change." In *Oklahoma: New Views of the Forty-Sixth State*, ed. Anne Hodges Morgan and H. Wayne Morgan. Norman: Univ. of Oklahoma Press, 1982.

Handy, Robert T. *The American Religious Depression, 1925–1935*. Philadelphia: Fortress Press, 1968.

———, ed. *The Social Gospel in America: Gladden, Ely, Rauschenbusch*. New York: Oxford Univ. Press, 1966.

Heale, M. J. *American Anticommunism: Combating the Enemy Within, 1830–1970*. Baltimore: Johns Hopkins Univ. Press, 1990.

Hendrickson, Kenneth D. Jr. *Hard Times in Oklahoma: The Depression Years*. Oklahoma City: Oklahoma Historical Society, 1983.

Hopkins, Charles H. *The Rise of the Social Gospel in American Protestantism, 1865–1915*. New Haven: Yale Univ. Press, 1940.

Howlett, Charles F. and Glen Zeitzer. *The American Peace Movement: History and Historiography*. Washington, D.C.: American Historical Association, 1985.

Hudson, Winthrop S. *Religion in America*. 4th ed. New York: Macmillan, 1987.

Joyce, Davis D., ed. *"An Oklahoma I Had Never Seen Before"*: *Alternative Views of Oklahoma History*. Norman: Univ. of Oklahoma Press, 1994.

Kelley, Robin D. G. *Hammer and Hoe: Alabama Communists During the Great Depression*. Chapel Hill: Univ. of North Carolina Press, 1990.

Kenny, Dumont F. "The National Conference of Christians and Jews." In *Religious Education: A Comprehensive View*, ed. Marvin J. Taylor. New York: Abingdon Press, 1960.

Klehr, Harvey. *The Heyday of American Communism: The Depression Decade*. New York: Basic Books, 1984.

Krueger, Thomas A. *And Promises to Keep: The Southern Conference for Human Welfare, 1938–1948*. Nashville: Vanderbilt Univ. Press, 1967.

Lader, Lawrence. *Power on the Left: American Radical Movements Since 1946*. New York: W. W. Norton, 1979.

Loestcher, Lefferts A. *The Broadening Church: A Study of Theological Issues in the Presbyterian Church Since 1869*. Philadelphia: Univ. of Pennsylvania, 1957.

MacDougall, Curtis. *Gideon's Army*. 3 vols. New York: Marzani and Munsell, 1965.

Marchand, Roland. *The American Peace Movement, 1887–1914*. Princeton, N.J.: Princeton Univ. Press, 1972.

Markowitz, Norman D. *The Rise and Fall of the People's Century: Henry Wallace and American Liberalism, 1941–1948*. New York: Free Press, 1973.

Marty, Martin E. *Righteous Empire: The Protestant Experience in America*. New York: Dial, 1970.

Mathews, John Joseph. *Life and Death of an Oilman: The Career of E. W. Marland*. Norman: Univ. of Oklahoma Press, 1951.

May, Henry. *Protestant Churches and Industrial America*. New York: Harper and Brothers, 1949.

McReynolds, Edwin C. *Oklahoma: A History of the Sooner State*. Norman: Univ. of Oklahoma Press, 1954.

Mellinger, Phillip. "Discrimination and Statehood in Oklahoma." *Chronicles of Oklahoma* 49 (1971): 340–78.

Meredith, Howard L. "A History of the Socialist Party in Oklahoma." Ph.D. diss., University of Oklahoma, 1969.

Meyer, Donald. *The Protestant Search for Political Realism,*
1919–1941. Middletown, Conn.: Wesleyan Univ. Press,
1988.

Michaelson, Robert. "Religious Education in Public Higher
Education Institutions." In *Religious Education: A*
Comprehensive Survey, ed. Marvin J. Taylor. New
York: Abingdon Press, 1960.

Miller, Robert Moats. *American Protestantism and Social*
Issues, 1919–1939. Chapel Hill: Univ. of North Carolina
Press, 1958.

————. "The Attitudes of the Major Protestant Churches in
America Toward War and Peace, 1919–1929." *The*
Historian 19 (November, 1956): 13–38.

Miller, Worth Robert. *Oklahoma Populism: A History of the*
People's Party in the Oklahoma Territory. Norman:
Univ. of Oklahoma Press, 1987.

Mitchell, H. L. *Mean Things Happening in This Land: The*
Life and Times of H. L. Mitchell, Cofounder of the
Southern Tenant Farmers Union. Montclair: Osmun,
Allenheld, 1979.

Morgan, Anne, and H. Wayne Morgan. eds. *Oklahoma: New*
Views of the Forty-Sixth State. Norman: Univ. of
Oklahoma Press, 1982.

Morgan, H. Wayne, and Anne Hodges Morgan. *Oklahoma: A*
Bicentennial History. New York: W. W. Norton, 1977.

Olds, Glenn A. "Religious Centers." In *Religion and the State*
University, ed. Erich A. Walter. Ann Arbor: Univ. of
Michigan Press, 1958.

Pearson, Norman Holmes. "The Nazi-Soviet Pact and the End
of a Dream." In *America in Crisis: Fourteen Crucial*
Episodes in American History, ed. Daniel Aaron. New
York: Alfred A. Knopf, 1952.

Reed, Linda. *Simple Decency and Common Sense: The*
Southern Conference Movement, 1938–1963.
Bloomington: Indiana Univ. Press, 1991.

Robinson, James Arthur Robinson. "Loyalty Investigations
and Legislation in Oklahoma." University of Oklahoma, M.A. thesis, 1955.

Robinson, Jo Ann O. *Abraham Went Out: A Biography*
of A. J. Muste. Philadelphia: Temple Univ. Press,
1982.

Scales, James R., and Danney Goble. *Oklahoma Politics: A History.* Norman: Univ. of Oklahoma Press, 1983.

Schmidt, Karl M. *Henry A. Wallace: Quixotic Crusade, 1948.* Syracuse: Syracuse Univ. Press, 1960.

Shedd, Clarence Prouty. "Religion in the American State Universities: Its History and Present Problems." In *Religion in the State University: An Initial Exploration,* ed. Henry E. Allen. Minneapolis: Burgess, 1949.

Strout, Cushing. *The New Heavens and New Earth: Political Religion in America.* New York: Harper and Row, 1974.

Szasz, Ferenc Morton. *The Divided Mind of Protestant America, 1880–1930.* University, Alabama: Univ. of Alabama Press, 1982.

Taylor, Marvin J. "Inter- and Nondenominational Agencies and Christian Education." In *An Introduction to Christian Education,* ed. Marvin J. Taylor. Nashville: Abingdon Press, 1966.

Theoharis, Athan. *Seeds of Repression: Harry S. Truman and Origins of McCarthyism.* New York: Quadrangle, 1971.

Thompson, Ernest Trice. *Presbyterians in the South: Volume Three: 1890–1972.* Richmond, Virginia: John Knox Press, 1973.

Thompson, John. *Closing the Frontier: Radical Response in Oklahoma, 1889–1923.* Norman: Univ. of Oklahoma Press, 1986.

Underwood, Kenneth. *The Church, the University, and Social Policy: The Danforth Study of Campus Ministries.* Vol. 1. Middletown, Connecticut: Wesleyan Univ. Press, 1969.

Warren, Frank A. III. *Liberals and Communism: The "Red Decade" Revisted.* Westport, Connecticut: Greenwood Press, 1976.

White, Ronald C. Jr. and C. Howard Hopkins. *The Social Gospel: Religion and Reform in Changing America.* Philadelphia: Temple Univ. Press, 1976.

Wittner, Lawrence S. *Rebels Against War; The American Peace Movement, 1941–1960.* New York: Columbia Univ. Press, 1969.

Worster, Donald. *Dust Bowl: The Southern Plains in the 1930s.* New York: Oxford Univ. Press, 1979.

Zeitzer, Glenn. "The American Peace Movement During the Second World War." Ph.D. diss., Bryn Mawr College, 1978.

Selected
Bibliography

INDEX

329

Index

330

331

Index